NURTURING AN
ENDANGERED GENERATION

NURTURING AN ENDANGERED GENERATION

Empowering Youth with Critical Social, Emotional, and Cognitive Skills

Rosemary Thompson, Ed.D., N.C.C., L.P.C.

ACCELERATED DEVELOPMENT
A member of the Taylor & Francis Group

USA	Publishing Office:	ACCELERATED DEVELOPMENT
		A member of the Taylor & Francis Group
		1101 Vermont Avenue, N.W., Suite 200
		Washington, DC 20005-3521
		Tel: (202) 289-2174
		Fax: (202) 289-3665
	Distribution Center:	ACCELERATED DEVELOPMENT
		A member of the Taylor & Francis Group
		1900 Frost Road, Suite 101
		Bristol, PA 19007-1598
		Tel: (215) 785-5800
		Fax: (215) 785-5515
UK		Taylor & Francis Ltd.
		1 Gunpowder Square
		London EC4A 3DE
		Tel: 0171 583 0490
		Fax: 0171 583 0581

NURTURING AN ENDANGERED GENERATION: Empowering Youth with Critical Social, Emotional, and Cognitive Skills

1 2 3 4 5 6 7 8 9 0   E B E B   0 9 8 7

This book was set in Times Roman. Editing by Sharon L. Emmons. Technical development by Cynthia Long and Candise M. B. Heinlein. Cover design by Michelle Fleitz.

A CIP catalog record for this book is available from the British Library.
∞ The paper in this publication meets the requirements of the ANSI Standard Z39.48-1984 (Permanence of Paper)

Library of Congress Cataloging-in-Publication Data

Thompson, Rosemary, 1950–
  Nurturing an endangered generation: empowering youth with critical social, emotional, and cognitive skills / by Rosemary Thompson.
     p.   cm.
  Includes bibliograpical references and index.

  1. Problem youth—Counseling of. 2. Adolescent psychotherapy.
3. Solution-focused therapy. 4. Multimodal psychotherapy. 5. Life skills—Study and teaching. I. Title.
RJ506.P63T48   1997
618.92'89—dc21   97-30458
                                                                                      CIP
ISBN 1-56032-668-9 (cloth)
ISBN 1-56032-669-7 (paper)

To Ryan and Jessica—an investment in their future.

CONTENTS

PART III
CREATING POSITIVE RELATIONSHIPS
THROUGH EMPOWERMENT OF OTHERS

PREFACE

ONE YEAR IN THE LIVES
OF AMERICAN YOUTH

Every year in the United States:

- 208 children under 10 are killed by firearms
- 506 children ages 10 to 14 are killed by firearms
- 2,243 children and youth under 20 commit suicide
- 4,173 children ages 15 to 19 are killed by firearms
- 73,886 children under 18 are arrested for drug abuse
- 112,230 children under 18 are arrested for violent crimes
- 124,238 children under 18 are arrested for drinking or for drunken driving
- 232,093 babies are born to women who received late or no prenatal care
- 531,591 babies are born to teenage mothers
- 928,205 babies are born to mothers without high school degrees
- 1,047,000 babies are born into poverty
- 1,200,000 latchkey children come home to houses where there is a gun
- 1,939,456 children under 18 are arrested
- 2,695,010 children are reported abused or neglected (Children's Defense Fund, 1994)

When you look for truth through a prism, you see only a fraction of it; the rest is colored over, hidden, obscured. So is the state of American youth, among whom hope and self-worth are refracted by anger and alienation; self-sufficiency and pride are replaced by self-deficiency and despair. The threats to the physical, social, and emotional well-being of our young people are unparalleled in human history. This pervasive condition will have long-range implications for schools and communities, business and industry, children and families.

The statistics on child and adolescent health and well-being are not new. They extend across a decade. Our response as advocates for children, however, has been slow. Kevin Bushweller (1994), project manager for *Educational Vital Signs* and assistant editor of the *American School Board Journal*, listed some of the long-range economic and social implications for schools and communities. The changes reflect family breakdown, poverty, violence, abuse, and all the factors that underlie the state of childhood in America today:

Abuse. The number of abused and neglected children has almost tripled, to 3 million a year, since 1980. The United States lags far behind other industrialized nations in providing child-care services and other benefits designed to promote the well-being families and their children, such as extended maternity leave, paternity leave, flex-time, job-sharing arrangements, and personal leaves for parents when their children are ill (Bronfenbrenner, 1986). Each year, at least 3.3 million children witness parental abuse, ranging from hitting to fatal assaults with knives or guns. As they mature in an atmosphere of violent relationships between men and women—husbands battering wives, women assaulted by boyfriends, mothers maltreated and then abandoned by a succession of men— these children come to adopt the same attitudes and practices in dealing with peers and eventually with their own families (*Carnegie Quarterly,* 1994).

Poverty. More than 1 in 5 children in the United States (22.7%) is living in poverty. Poverty is associated with multiple risk factors, such as lack of immunizations and health care, poor nutrition, inadequate housing, homelessness, Acquired Immunodeficiency Syndrome (AIDS), substance abuse, violence, and underachievement. The United States is the only industrialized society in which nearly one-fourth of all infants and preschool children live in families whose incomes fall below the poverty line. These children lack such basics as adequate health care (Kamerman & Kahn, 1980).

Alcohol and other drug abuse. Fourteen percent of 8th graders, 23% of 10th graders, and 28% of 12th graders report that they consume five or more drinks in one sitting at least once every two weeks. The crack-cocaine epidemic is manifesting itself in babies exposed prenatally to drugs, and gang violence has neighborhoods from all economic strata under siege. The United States also has the highest incidence of alcohol and drug abuse among adolescents of any country in the world. Smoking among 13- and 14-year-olds rose 30% between 1991 and 1994. Marijuana use among 8th graders more than doubled between 1991 and 1994. The rate of suicide among young adolescents increased 120%, and increased most dramatically among young black males (300%) and young white females (233%) from 1980 to 1992 (Carnegie Council on Adolescent Development, 1995).

Violence. America has the highest homicide rate in the world (*Carnegie Quarterly*, 1994). Since 1988, the adolescent homicide rate has more than doubled to become the second leading cause of death among Americans ages 15 to 24. *It is the leading cause of death among African Americans in that range.* In 1990, almost 3,000 youth under the age of 19 were murdered by guns alone (*Carnegie Quarterly*, 1994). The firearm homicide rate for 10- to 14-year-olds more than doubled between 1985 and 1992 (*Carnegie Quarterly*, 1994).

Families. Since 1981, the percentage of children not living with both biological parents increased from 33% to 43%. Households with children under 18 years of age now commonly include foster parents, extended families, children living with other relatives, adoptive parents, skip-generation parents (parents who are raising their children's children), extended families, or reconstituted and blended families. The U.S. divorce rate is the highest in the world—nearly double that of its nearest competitor, Sweden (Kamerman & Kahn, 1980). Today, slightly more than half of all American children will spend at least part of their childhood or adolescence in a single-parent family—a much higher proportion than a few decades ago (Carnegie Council on Adolescent Development, 1995).

The growing concern over adolescent suicide rates, alcohol abuse, sexual irresponsibility, gang behavior, HIV/AIDS, dropout rates, and increasing violence demonstrates the *critical need for responsible adults to establish close, helping relationships with our young people.* The growing list of responsibilities American schools have undertaken—violence prevention, AIDS/HIV education, substance abuse prevention, crisis intervention, divorce counseling, and safe schools initiatives—reflects the changing demographics that strain economic resources in order to provide services. Policy makers are concerned that endangered youth not only must struggle to reach their potential, but may become so dysfunctional that they are incapable of self-support or establishing rewarding relationships within various systems (i.e., home, school, workplace, and community). Helping professionals have come to view the final decade of the 20th century as the *Age of Dysfunction.*

Furthermore, all too many young people do not receive consistent, positive, and realistic validation of themselves from the adults on whom they depend. It becomes critical that young people know adults care about them not only intellectually but emotionally and socially, as well. This means placing as much importance on *social literacy*—including skills such as assertiveness, decision making, conflict resolution, impulse control, and anger management—as on *cognitive literacy*—preparing students academically to meet the challenges of the cyber-revolution and the first computational millennium of the 21st century. Social literacy also includes *emotional literacy,* which focuses on cultivating emotional skills such as empathy, sensitivity, and tolerance of differences.

Social, emotional, and cognitive skill deficits seem to permeate all dysfunctional manifestations of child and adolescent behavior. For example, *conflicted* youth often have skill deficits in anger management and conflict resolution skills; the teenager facing an unintended pregnancy often lacks assertiveness skills and abstract reasoning (i.e., the ability to see the long-range consequences of high-risk behaviors); and the high school dropout often lacks the cognitive skills of problem solving, decision making, and time management.

At-risk youth include those from divorced, abused, neglected, or dysfunctional families; those from poverty; and those who have experienced a significant loss of a loved one. Risk factors include a disruptive home environment, low self-esteem, learning disabilities, emotional difficulties, developmental delays, interpersonal problems, and few social supports.

This book goes beyond the stilted rhetoric on the problems of youth and the dilemma for society by outlining specific treatment intervention and prevention strategies that address the full spectrum of dysfunctional behavior, including these:

1. **Structured intervention strategies** for school/community collaboration, with an emphasis on remediation and treatment.
2. **Counseling strategies and psychoeducational techniques** for educators and helping professionals that focus on primary prevention.
3. **Critical social, emotional, and cognitive skills to support primary prevention strategies**.

Primary prevention initiatives seek to reduce risk factors and to increase protective factors of both healthy people and those at risk for dysfunction (Albee & Ryan-Finn, 1993). Prevention strategies address behaviors such as locus of control, self-concept, conflict resolution, problem solving, interpersonal relations, social support, group dynamics, depression, and wellness. Essentially, educational and psychological principles can be converted into teachable skills and disseminated by means of systematic strategies and intervention programs. Youth-helping professionals can provide a pivotal role in assisting youth and families with the appropriate intervention and prevention skills.

Chapters 1 through 3 introduce the text, providing both a rationale and a theoretical framework for the intervention strategies that follow. Chapter 1 focuses on social, emotional, and cognitive deficits that emerge in children's and adolescents' self-defeating behavior. Chapter 2 outlines the benefits of *solution-focused counseling* and *multimodal interventions*. Both approaches are models that are appropriate in institutional settings when opportunities for counseling are limited by time constraints and accessibility. Chapter 3 details the efficacy of small-group counseling. Through the mutual sharing of anxieties and problem-solving strategies in a secure environment, children and adolescents discover a commonality of fears, stressors, ambitions, goals, and aspirations and learn successful ways to prevent and solve problems. Problems are no longer unique but, rather, are universal and shared by others.

Chapters 4 through 9 focus on specific categories of child and adolescent self-defeating behavior that require *structured intervention* (i.e., alcohol and other drug abuse, unintended teenage pregnancy, depression and suicide, delinquency and violence, underachievement and dropouts, and victimization and abuse) and *primary prevention initiatives.* Each chapter introduces the latest demographic data, factors that make children and adolescents vulnerable to self-defeating or self-destructive behaviors, and structured intervention and primary prevention initiatives.

Therapeutic initiatives concentrate on counseling session plans that focus on specific techniques and multimodal treatment plans. These are followed by *collective initiatives,* which focus on the developmental needs of children and adolescents and critical social, emotional, and cognitive skills, following the format of the *Life Skills Paradigm.*

Chapter 10 focuses on empowering youth, families, institutions, and agencies from the perspective that it takes a whole community to nurture a healthy child. The book's intent is to identify critical social, emotional, and cognitive skills that can enhance the well-being of children and adolescents. Multiple strategies and multidisciplinary teams of helping professionals can organize to reduce risk factors and enhance protective factors for this imperiled generation of young people.

ACKNOWLEDGMENTS

There are a number of individuals who have influenced the development of this book. First and foremost are the children—the children whom I have taught, counseled, or nurtured through the years as they struggled to overcome preconceived notions that they just weren't smart enough, that they just couldn't behave well enough, or that they really didn't have feelings that were worth considering. This book acknowledges the children who don't have someone to tuck them in at night, those who have never eaten a full breakfast, and those at the young age of 14 who sleep in a bed with their own children. We are reminded every day that our children are struggling with serious social, emotional, or cognitive deficits.

Others I would like to acknowledge for their helpful suggestions and encouragement are Nina Brown and Leslie Kaplan, the graduate students at Old Dominion University, Norfolk, Virginia, and the New England School Counselors Institute, Lyndonville, Vermont. A special acknowledgment is extended to Cindy Long for her steadfast support by following up on the details to bring this book to fruition. Finally, a very sincere appreciation also is extended to Joe Hollis, whose vision for the profession of counseling has nurtured the contributions of more than 106 authors and 140 publications. He truly has accelerated our development as a viable and thriving profession. His energy and commitment are unprecedented.

PART I
RATIONALE
AND THEORETICAL
FRAMEWORK

SOCIAL, EMOTIONAL, AND COGNITIVE SKILLS DEFICITS: ESSENTIAL LIFE SKILLS FROM A DEVELOPMENTAL PERSPECTIVE

> It appears we have lost sight of some of the fundamental goals of our educational system: namely, to foster the development of human relationships (National Education Association, Educational Policies Commission, 1938) and to teach respect for other persons, develop insights into ethical values and principles, and strengthen our children's ability to live and to work cooperatively with others. (National Education Association, Educational Policies Commission, 1952)

In 1990, the Carnegie Foundation released a report entitled *Turning Point: Preparing American Youth for the 21st Century*, which concluded that half of America's youth were "extremely vulnerable to multiple high-risk behaviors and school failures" or were "at moderate risk, but remain . . . a cause for serious concern" (p. 36). Growing evidence of predictors for high-risk behaviors can be found in many sources.

For example, the Heritage Foundation's *Index of Leading Cultural Indicators* gives a statistical portrait of seven cultural indicators that critically affect schools, communities, businesses, and industry at large illustrated in Table 1.1. Since 1960, there has been a 560% increase in violent crime in the United States; a 419% increase in illegitimate births; a quadrupling of divorce rates; a tripling of the percentage of children living in single-parent homes; a more than 200% increase in the teenage suicide rate; and a drop of almost 80 points in Scholastic Aptitude Test scores (Bennett, 1993).

Further, Growald (1994) maintained:

> [O]ur children are getting lost in a sea of uncensored images. They see X-rated pictures of love, and lose their childhood before the age of 10. Along with the images go the disappearance of confidence in self that can only develop with adequate nurturance and parenting, but are no longer available where we formally found them. . . . I believe that one of the roots for the rise in crime throughout our nation is the screaming plea to be seen, heard, and loved. If children can't get positive attention, they seek the negative. Without love the soul shrivels and the body atrophies. (p. 3)

The United States has the highest murder rate for 12- to 24-year-olds of any industrialized nation (Viadero, 1993). Marian Wright Edelman, president of the Children's Defense Fund, recently gave a graphic illustration of the reality of violence that directly confronts our children: "Our worst nightmares are coming true, after years of family disintegration, the crisis of children having children has been eclipsed by the greater crisis of children killing children" (Edelman, 1994, p. 7). Between 1979 and 1991, nearly 50,000 children under the age of 19 were killed by guns.

Not coincidentally, the number of juvenile arrests for weapons possession and murder also has increased. The number of juveniles arrested for murder and manslaughter climbed 93% from 1982 to 1991, while the number of adults arrested for the same crimes rose only 11 percent. Columnist William Raspberry (1994) perhaps summarized our nation's mission most succinctly:

> A top priority should be a movement to rescue our children. An astounding number of children are being lost: to drugs, to hopelessness, to violence, to death. They fail at school, become parents before they are grown-ups, and reach adulthood without acquiring the education or skills to earn a living. Our young women suffer debilitating effects of low self-esteem, and our young men, who ought to

Table 1.1
Seven Cultural Indicators

Average daily TV viewing		S.A.T. scores		% of illegitimate births		Children with single mothers		Children on welfare		Teen-suicide rate (per 100,000)		Violent crime rate (per 100,000)	
1960	5:06 hours	1960	975	1960	5.3%	1960	8%	1960	3.5%	1960	3.6	1960	16.1
1965	5:29 hours	1965	969	1970	10.7%	1970	11%	1960	4.5%	1965	4.0	1965	20.0
1970	5:56 hours	1970	948	1980	18.4%	1980	18%	1970	8.5%	1970	5.9	1970	36.4
1975	6:07 hours	1975	910	1990	26.2%	1990	22%	1975	11.8%	1975	7.6	1975	48.8
1980	6:36 hours	1980	890	*Source:*		*Sources:*		1980	11.5%	1980	8.5	1980	59.7
1985	7:07 hours	1985	906	National Center		Bureau of		1985	11.2%	1985	10.0	1985	53.3
1990	6:55 hours	1990	900	for Health		the Census;		1990	11.9%	1990	11.3	1990	73.2
1992	7:04 hours	1992	899	Statistics		Donald		*Source:*		*Source:*		1991	75.8
Source: Neilsen		*Source:* The				Hermandez,		Bureau of		National		*Source:* F.B.I.	
Media Research		College Board				The American		the Census;		Center for			
						Child;		U.S. House of		Health			
						Resources		Representatives		Statistics			
						from Family,							
						Government							
						and the							
						Economy							

5

be the strength of their communities, are more likely to terrorize them. (p. C24)

The long-range implications of such behavior are just beginning to emerge. For example, 66% of college freshmen admit to having cheated in high school. One in four college women has been the victim of rape or attempted rape, most often by an acquaintance (Viadero, 1993). In addition, a disquieting number of young adults do not bother to vote, are unprepared to join in public policy debates, or are unwilling to take part in community-building activities that are the central components of civic participation and responsibility (O'Neil, 1991).

The litany of statistics on violent crime, racial and ethnic discrimination, gang violence, school dropouts, post-high school unemployment, teenage pregnancy, teenage suicide, drug and alcohol abuse, and general social maladaption has contributed to a sense of national emergency of unprecedented proportions (Gates, 1988; Orr, 1987; Soderberg, 1988; Thompson, 1992; U.S. Department of Education, 1995). Social, emotional, and cognitive skills are commonly viewed as being in critically short supply, which leads to the dysfunctional behavior of contemporary youth.

DANGEROUS DEFICITS

A Social Skill Deficit

Basic social skills essential for constructive interpersonal interactions— which, in turn, are linked to community, social, family, and career adjustment— are significantly lacking for many of today's youth (Gresham & Elliot, 1984; LeCroy, 1983). In response, many educators, researchers, helping professionals, and advocates for youth are proclaiming the need to develop social literacy skills in today's children and adolescents. Nurturing social literacy in children and adolescents gives them advantages in their cognitive abilities, in their interpersonal adjustment, and in their resiliency skills during stressful life events.

The concept of social literacy is not new. It first evolved in the 1970s under the cloak of deliberate psychological education, affective education, or values clarification, then reemerged in the theoretical framework of Howard Gardner's model of multiple intelligences.

In his book *Frames of Mind*, Gardner (1983) revealed seven major domains of intellectual performance and academic competence. Traditional education addresses only two domains: mathematical and linguistic (both left-brain dominated). Two other intelligences are intrapersonal—the ability to know one's own feelings and inner experiences and manage them well—and interpersonal—the capacity for handling relationships skillfully. Key abilities in these areas include being able to monitor and manage one's own feelings, being able to empathize and handle personal relationships, and being able to harness emotions for positive motivation in doing cognitive tasks, including problem solving and creative thinking. The other three intelligences (Gardner, 1983) include (a) visual/spacial intelligence, which relies on the sense of sight and the ability to visualize an object such as creating internal mental images/pictures, (b) body/kinesthetic intelligence, which relates to physical movement, motion, and awareness; and (c) music/ rhythmic intelligence, which recognizes tonal patterns, sensitivity to rhythm and beats, and environmental surroundings.

Cawelti (1989) maintained that, "to be successful socially and professionally, people need to complement their cognitive knowledge with good interpersonal skills, a strong value base, and a positive view of self." These skills are not systematically taught in schools or in the community, or adequately nurtured in many homes (Greenberger & Steinberg, 1987).

David Hamburg, president of the Carnegie Corporation (1990), also stressed the importance of teaching basic skills such as "sharing, taking turns, learning to cooperate, and helping others." It used to be assumed that children received such training outside of school. This was never a sound assumption, and it is less so now than it ever was.

The need for social literacy has been further documented by recent studies showing a correlation between delinquent behaviors and certain experiences of adolescents in their development, including these: poor performance in school, negative labeling, poor peer relations, multiple health problems (e.g., speech, vision, motor, hearing, or neurological impairment), attention deficits, learning disabilities, alcohol and other drug abuse, violence, and increased involvement with law enforcement and juvenile and domestic courts. Concurrently, Stellas (1992) found that violent adolescents (as well as adult offenders) often were missing one or more of the following six social skills or characteristics.

- **Assertiveness**: the ability to speak up appropriately for oneself. (Offenders often swing between passivity and aggression.)
- **Decision-making skills**: the ability to anticipate consequences.
- **Social support/contacts**: the ability to use community systems.
- **Empathy**: the ability to identify with the felt experiences of someone else.

- **Impulse control/problem-solving skills:** self-control and the ability to find and use solutions.
- **Anger management:** the ability to deal with frustration without violating the rights of others.

Further, many criminologists are now finding a common psychological fault line in rapists, child molesters, and perpetrators of family violence: They are incapable of empathy, one of the fundamentals of emotional intelligence (Goleman, 1994). This inability to feel a victim's pain provokes a proclivity toward violent or aggressive acts. For example, an adolescent gang member may show little remorse for killing someone in a dispute over drug turf, or an elementary student may be insensitive to another child's possession as he destroys it.

Armstrong and McPherson (1991) maintained that social skills promote successful interactions with peers and adults. According to social validity definition (Gresham, 1981), social skills are those behaviors that, within a given situation, predict important social outcomes such as (1) peer acceptance or popularity, (2) significant others' judgments of behavior, and (3) other behaviors known to correlate consistently with peer acceptance or significant others' judgments.

Kain, Downs, and Black (1988) described social skills as "life tools needed to successfully survive in society." When these skills are absent, there is an increase in the likelihood that a child's behavior will be labeled disabling, deviant, or antisocial. According to many researchers (Armstrong & McPherson, 1991; Goldstein, Sprafkin, Gershaw, & Klein, 1982; L'Abate & Milan, 1985; Larson, 1984), social skills fall into several categories, including these:

1. being kind, cooperative, and compliant to reduce defiance, aggression, and antisocial behavior;
2. showing interest in people and socializing successfully to reduce behavior problems associated with withdrawal, depression, and fearfulness;
3. possessing the language skills to increase expressive vocabulary to allow for interesting conversation with peers and adults;
4. critical thinking skills and peer-pressure refusal skills to cope with peer and media pressure to take dangerous risks; and
5. establishing and maintaining realistic goals for health, wellness education, leisure pursuits, and career development.

Other researchers have demonstrated the value of integrating social skills across community and institutional settings. Thompson, Bundy, and Boncheau

(1995) found that adolescents could learn and retain cognitive information basic to assertion skills. Social skills training for adolescents has been associated with positive outcomes such as improved self-esteem, increased problem-solving skills, refusal of alcohol and other drugs, and refusal of premarital sex.

A Cognitive Skills Deficit

A number of researchers have identified several cognitive skills that today's youth lack, with implications for educators and helping professionals. Here are some of their findings:

- Many delinquents are *externally oriented.* They believe what happens to them depends on fate, chance, or luck. They believe that they are powerless and are controlled by people and circumstances (Ross & Ross, 1989, p. 126).
- External locus of control also is prevalent in the behavior of underachievers and teenage mothers (Thompson, 1986).
- Many delinquents are quite concrete in their thinking, and their lack of *abstract reasoning* makes it difficult for them to understand their world and the reason for rules and laws (Ross & Ross, 1989, p. 126).
- Many antisocial individuals have *deficits in interpersonal functioning, problem-solving,* and *cognitive skills,* which are required for *decision making and interacting with people.* A delinquent's *lack of awareness of or sensitivity to* other people's thoughts or feelings severely impairs his or her ability to form acceptable relationships with people.

A lack of cognitive skills places individuals at a distinct disadvantage academically, vocationally, and socially, making them more vulnerable to criminal influences and to self-destructive and self-defeating behavior. This trend can be reversed, however, by converting strategies into teachable psychoeducational skills that are systematically integrated into a cognitive skills curriculum.

Cognitive skills fall into categories such as *knowing how to problem solve, describe, associate, conceptualize, classify, evaluate, and think critically.* Cognitive psychologists advocate teaching at-risk youth a repertoire of cognitive and metacognitive strategies using *graphic organizers, organizational patterns, monitoring, self-questioning, verbal self-instruction, self-regulation,* and *study skills.* Inherently, social, emotional, and cognitive skills can be taught and cultivated giving youth advantages in their interpersonal adjustment and their academic/vocational success, as well as enhancing their resiliency through life's ultimate challenges.

An Emotional Skills Deficit

> America's children are desperately in need of lessons in how to handle their emotions and settle disagreements, in caring, and just plain getting along. (Goleman, 1994a, p. 4)

> Institutions and communities across the United States are experiencing a new kind of deficit in youth behavior, one that is, in many ways, more alarming than a cognitive skills deficit: Today's youth demonstrate an *emotional skills deficit.* The results of this deficiency are seen in the increase in incidents of violence and the sharp rises in the numbers of teenage suicides, homicides, and abusive and violent acts in the last decade. (Goleman, 1994b, p. 2)

Goleman (1994b) poignantly revealed that we pay the price for emotional illiteracy

> in failed marriages and troubled families; in stunted social and work lives; in deteriorating physical health and mental anguish; and in tragedies such as random acts of violence. Our social nets for the emotionally illiterate are prisons, safe houses for abused wives and families, shelters for the homeless, mental hospitals, and the psychotherapist's office (p. 2).

Goleman (1994b) also maintained that a single intervention will not cover the full range of emotional skills that a proactive mental health program should provide. He proposed the following emotional literacy curriculum:

Self-awareness. Building a vocabulary for feelings; knowing the relationship between thoughts, feelings, and reactions; knowing if thought or feeling is ruling an action.

Decision making. Examining actions and knowing their consequences; a self-reflective view of what goes into decisions; applying this to issues such as sex, alcohol, and drugs.

Managing feelings. Monitoring "self-talk" to catch negative messages such as internal put-downs; realizing what is behind a feeling (e.g., the hurt that underlies anger).

Self-concept. Establishing a firm sense of identity and feeling esteem and acceptance of oneself.

Handling stress. Learning the value of exercise, guided imagery, and relaxation methods.

Communications. Sending "I" messages instead of blame; being a good listener.

Group dynamics. Learning the value of teamwork, collaboration, and cooperation; knowing when and how to lead, and when to follow.

Conflict resolution. Learning to resolve conflicts with other peers, with parents, and with teachers; learning the win-win model for negotiating compromise (pp. 7-8).

Many schools and institutions and business and community initiatives assume that social, emotional, and cognitive skills will develop as a natural consequence of maturation and development. It has become increasingly apparent that this is an erroneous assumption. Goleman (1995) aptly stated in his treatise on emotional IQ, that "IQ will get you hired, but emotional EQ will get you promoted" (p. 35).

The foundation of emotional literacy includes being able to monitor and manage one's own feelings, empathize and handle personal relationships, and manage emotions for positive motivation (Goleman, 1994b). And there is a definite link between emotional skills and cognitive skills. Young people who are experiencing emotional discord and who harbor hurt feelings, anger, depression, or anxiety have difficulty attending, processing, and remembering new information. Emotional literacy actually promotes cognitive well-being and can act as a crucial inoculation against obstacles that impede development. And emotional and social skills can be cultivated, giving young people advantages in their cognitive abilities, their interpersonal adjustment, and their resiliency through life's challenges.

IMPORTANCE OF SELF-ESTEEM

The universal solution researchers offer to the crisis of our youth is *enhanced self-esteem*, especially for high-risk adolescents. Studies have identified two factors that seem to foster positive self-esteem: unconditional love and acceptance from a primary caregiver (which provides an internal sense of value and worth) and social competence—the successful management of one's social milieu. Marton, Golombek, Stein, and Korenblum (1988) found that self-esteem is related to adaptive skills and the ability to reflect a sense of self and a sense of significant attachment to another adult. Further, when stressful events do not overwhelm an individual's ability to cope, the triumph over adversity fosters a sense of self-competence.

"When people are socially competent, their worth is not dependent on someone else's opinion of them but rather on their skills to affect their environment in the way they choose" (Stellas, 1992, p. 25). Children learn through physical and emotional rewards and punishments, which can be negative or positive. A negative self-concept generates an ongoing cycle of academic failure, lower self-esteem, and a diminished willingness to risk failure—in other words, an unmotivated and distracted learner—all of which perpetuates failure.

People achieve social competence by learning and utilizing the skills listed earlier: assertiveness, decision-making skills, social support contacts, empathy, impulse control/problem-solving skills, and anger management. These skills should be taught to all children. That means, as a nation, placing as much importance on social literacy as we do on academic literacy. The result could well be an environment in which the norm is cooperation, respect, and nonviolence instead of alienation, aggression, and exploitation.

To build self-esteem in children and adolescents it is important to help them develop a sense of security by defining expectations and boundaries. It also is important to help them see themselves as having potential and success in a specific area, as well as a sense of belonging and of purpose.

Fortunately, self-concept has the capacity to continually change and develop. Through psychoeducational groups, we can perhaps begin to address our young people's emotional and cognitive skills deficits and reduce self-destructive and self-defeating behavior. Table 1.2 shows a partial spectrum of the critical deficits affecting our young people today.

Table 1.2
Selected Social, Cognitive, and Emotional Skill Deficits

Social skills deficits	Cognitive skill deficits	Emotional skill deficits
Assertiveness	External locus of control	Self-awareness
Decision making	Concrete thinking	Managing feelings
Social support contacts	Critical thinking	Stress management
Impulse control	Academic organization skills	Sensitivity to others
Problem solving	Probable consequences	Coping skills
Anger management	Comparing, contrasting, predicting	Giving feedback
Conflict resolution	Evaluating actions	Giving empathy
Cooperating	Creative problem solving	Confronting
Self-acceptance	Brainstorming	Relating to others
Communicating	Attention deficits	Self-esteem

Educators, researchers, and helping professionals often feel compelled to create a comprehensive initiative to remediate the broad spectrum of threats to the physical, intellectual, emotional, and social well-being of contemporary youth. The growing concern over adolescent subpopulations who are at risk demonstrates the critical need for responsible adults to establish close, helping relationships with young people. What is needed is a comprehensive, integrated curriculum to help young people master daily problem-solving skills such as self-competency, enhancement of interpersonal relationships, communications, values, and the awareness of rules, attitudes, and motivation (Worrell & Stilwell, 1981).

Interpersonal and personal development should become an integral part of systematic intervention and prevention programs. The effect of such programs is to make counseling and learning available on a larger scale to the many people who need help but are not currently receiving it. Life skills training could provide children and adolescents with support services to help with social, emotional, and cognitive problems. Students with any of the following difficulties would benefit from such a systematic delivery of skills.

School-Behavior Difficulties. Students experiencing school-behavior difficulties might exhibit the following behaviors:

- Recent behaviors "unlike" the student's typical behavior
- Disruptive behavior in the class or in the building
- Fear of attending school; unusual phobic or anxiety reactions
- Beginning truancy, tardiness, or cutting classes
- An unusual negative attitude toward school
- A resistance to school rules
- Frequent suspensions

Personality Difficulties. Students with personality difficulties might display the following behaviors:

- Recent depression
- Age-inappropriate behavior
- Recent isolation and withdrawal
- Negative change in self-perception or self-esteem
- Psychosomatic complaints

Social Difficulties. Students with social difficulties might display the following behaviors:

- Increase in peer conflict or poor peer relations
- Conflicts with authority
- Increase in physical aggression
- Increase in verbal aggression

Educational Difficulties. Students with educational difficulties might display the following behaviors:

- Evidence of knowledge gaps
- Lack of interest in work
- Inconsistent and erratic performance
- A drop in grades
- Inability to concentrate
- Unwillingness to finish work
- Alienation from the classroom

Education and counseling in life skills can be delivered as a comprehensive system to facilitate effective functioning throughout the life span. Woody, Hanson, and Rossberg (1989) explained that counseling focuses on a cooperative relationship that encourages self-exploration and self-understanding and provides the opportunity for people to practice appropriate behaviors. Successful counseling produces a working alliance and creates opportunities for the client to restructure emotional experiences, develop self-confidence, and internalize the therapeutic relationship. The following life skills reflect the full spectrum of program components. When integrated into prevention and intervention programs, such social, emotional, and cognitive skills will have long-term implications for future well-being.

> **Interpersonal communication/human relations:** skills necessary for effective verbal and nonverbal communication (e.g., attitudes of empathy, genuineness, clearly expressing ideas and opinions); giving and receiving feedback; assertiveness and peer-pressure refusal skills
> **Problem solving and decision making:** skills of seeking, assessing, and analyzing information; problem solving; responsible decision making; assessment of goal attainment
> **Identity development/purpose in life:** skills that contribute to the ongoing development of personal identity, enhance self-esteem, and ease life transitions
> **Physical fitness/health maintenance:** skills necessary for nutrition, stress management, and wellness; skills in reducing high-risk sexual activity
> **Career awareness:** skills in obtaining and maintaining desired career goals; opportunities to practice these skills

Conflict resolution and conflict mediation: skills in effective problem-solving techniques; skills to build more effective interpersonal skills

Study skills: skills to improve academic work by developing greater academic mastery and enhancing cognitive skills

Family concerns: skills to improve communication with parents, step-parents, and siblings to bring about a more harmonious family life (Stellas, 1992, p. 53)

Anxiety coping skills: skills to promote emotional well-being and relaxation and stress inoculation

Today, young people suffer from deficits in more than one life skill. Helping them develop life skills requires a psychoeducational intervention. Developmentally appropriate instruction is critical in such areas as interpersonal communication, making thoughtful choices, setting manageable goals, and refusing peer pressure. Social and emotional skill development is critical in building character, enhancing emotional intelligence, promoting social competence, and preventing high-risk behaviors.

McWhirter, McWhirter, McWhirter, and McWhirter (1994) isolated five basic skill strengths or skill deficits that mark a critical difference between low-risk and high-risk youth. The researchers called these characteristics the *Five Cs of Competency.* They are (1) critical school competencies, (2) concept of self and self-esteem, (3) communication skills, (4) coping ability, and (5) control. Enhancing children's and adolescents' strengths in these areas enhances their well-being during the storms and stresses of emerging adulthood.

LIFE SKILLS TRAINING MODEL

Essentially, life skills are those that involve behaviors and attitudes necessary for coping with academic challenges, communicating with others, improving relationships, and developing strategies for social, emotional, and cognitive well-being.

When teaching a life skill session, it helps to follow a five-step model: instruction (teach), modeling (show), role-play (practice), feedback (reinforce), and homework (apply). These steps, when used with situational logs and homework assignments, reinforce desired behaviors.

The instructional techniques for skills training have evolved from social learning and typically consist of verbal instructions, modeling the desired behavior, role-playing, and performance feedback. Skill training can cover one skill in one or two sessions, with the goal of learning and transfer (McWhirter, McWhirter, & McWhirter, 1993). Helping professionals in school and community settings can reinforce coping skills and teach or model behaviors that enhance self-management skills. Rak and Patterson (1996) proposed that helping professionals focus on building transferable skills with the following selected techniques:

- Role-playing to help youth improve their self-expression
- Conflict resolution techniques that help youth work through their interpersonal struggles at home, in school, and in the community
- A nurturing stance that conveys unconditional positive regard, encouragement, positive reinforcement, and genuine hope
- Modeling the principles of a healthy self-concept
- Establishing peer support models, such as peer-counseling programs
- Empowering self-awareness through journaling, positive imagery, and bibliotherapy.

A more in-depth explanation of this intervention strategy is included in Chapter 3.

CONCLUSION

Children and adolescents universally need the critical skills of communication, cooperation, conflict resolution, self-confidence, clear thinking, and managing distressing or self-destructive feelings. The challenge for helping professionals is integrating these skills into prevention and intervention programs. Life skills programs that focus on social, emotional, and cognitive deficits can enhance the efforts of schools across the nation.

Today's youth show serious deficits in cognitive, social, and emotional skills—deficits that impair their chances for social, emotional, and intellectual success. In addition, there is a critical need in this country to create just and caring educational communities and to ensure that *all* youth are valued, have a safe and secure learning environment, and receive opportunities to experience a sense of belonging, respect for their rights, and freedom from violence and abuse.

Chapter 2

EMPOWERING YOUTH: SOLUTION-FOCUSED COUNSELING AND MULTIMODAL INTERVENTIONS

> The reason persons are not solving their life problems is not because they aren't smart enough, but rather because they are working with the wrong data. (Carnevale, 1989, p. 16)

In today's society, children and adolescents experience a tremendous amount of stress, much of which is not within their control. In an extensive study, Sandler and Ramsay (1980) found that loss events (e.g., death of a parent, sibling, or friend; divorce; and separation) were the primary promoters of crisis reactions in children and adolescents, followed by family troubles (e.g., abuse, neglect, loss of job). Lower on the scale were environmental changes (e.g., moving or attending a new school), sibling difficulties, physical harm (e.g., illness, accidents, and violence), and disasters (e.g., fire, floods, hurricanes, or earthquakes). Kashani and Simonds (1979) maintained, "the life stresses for children are probably different from those for adults and center mainly around the behavior of significant adults" (p. 149).

Children and adolescents can respond to these stresses with adaptive or maladaptive behaviors, both of which can have critical implications for long-term functioning. Children in crisis or under constant and extreme stress manifest pervasive feelings of anxiety, confusion, failure, and entrapment. They frequently are sick, isolated, unable to concentrate, and noncommunicative. They can be uncooperative, negative, defensive, easily angered, and unable to see the resources in others. Further, acute stressors (such as failing a final exam, losing a close friend, or breaking up with a boyfriend or girlfriend) may precipitate depression or an impulsive suicide attempt. More recently, Zitzow (1992) provided an overview of the multiplicity, intensity, and commonality of the stress experienced by today's adolescents. His study revealed the stress indicators listed in Table 2.1.

Zitzow (1992) claimed that the data support marshaling resources within systems such as schools, communities, agencies, churches, synagogues, and youth organizations, and maintained that priorities should be established to respond to issues such as child and adolescent grief (e.g., family death, separation, and

Table 2.1
Assessing Stress in Youth

Rank	Stress item
1	Death of a brother or sister
2	Death of a parent
3	Being responsible for an unwanted pregnancy
4	Being suspended from school or on probation
5	Having parents who are separated or divorced
6	Receiving a "D" or "F" on a test
7	Being physically hurt by others while in school
8	Giving a speech in class
9	Feeling that much of my life is worthless
10	Being teased or made fun of
11	Feeling guilty about things I've done in the past
12	Pressure to get an "A" or "B" in a course
13	Pressure from friends to use alcohol or other drugs
14	Fear of pregnancy
15	Failure to live up to family expectations
16	Feelings of anxiousness or general tension
17	Pressure to have sex
18	Feeling like I don't fit in
19	Fear of being physically hurt by other students
20	Past/present sexual contact with a family member

Source: Reprinted from Zitzow, D. (1992). Assessing student stress: School adjustment rating by self-report. *The School Counselor, 40*(1), 20-24. © ACA. Reprinted with permission. No further reproduction authorized without written permission of the American Counseling Association.

divorce); sexual dilemmas (e.g., unintended pregnancies, fear of pregnancies and sexually transmitted diseases, pressure to have sex, and abuse and incest); academic pressures (e.g., underachievement, lack of study skills, performance anxiety, and cognitive skill deficits); and psychosocial stressors (e.g., anxiety and guilt, alcohol and other drug abuse, feelings of worthlessness, low self-esteem, and dealing with failure). Conversely, protective factors—such as positive, open relationships with parents or significant adults and perceived competence due to scholastic, athletic, or public service achievements—may help youth cope more effectively with stressful events.

PSYCHOSOCIAL STRESSORS
AND COPING SKILL DEFICITS

Psychosocial stressors interact with personal dispositions and support factors in one's social environment. Stress management, stress reduction, and stress relief are key intervention strategies for both children and adolescents, as well as for the adults who care for them. Debilitating stress and vulnerability intensify an individual's risk. Risk is diminished if an individual has reliable coping skills, a positive sense of self, and feels social support in his or her immediate environment. To assess risk factors, Albee (1982) provided the following equation for the *individual*:

$$\text{Incidence of behavioral and emotional disorder} = \frac{\text{stressors} + \text{physical vulnerability}}{\text{coping skill} + \text{social support} + \text{self-esteem}}$$

There is an environmental-centered analogue to this equation that focuses on risk of psychopathology for a *population*:

$$\text{Likelihood of disorder in a population} = \frac{\text{stressors} + \text{risk factors in the environment}}{\text{socialization practices} + \text{social support resources} + \text{opportunities for connectedness}}$$

Psychosocial stressors are less likely to occur in a population if there are socialization practices that teach and promote social competence, create supportive resources, and provide opportunities for people to form positive social bonds and identities connected with the mainstream of society. Both equations are interdependent and reflect the paramount need for stress-related interventions that are multidimensional (Elias, 1989).

QUEST FOR RESILIENT YOUTH

Some children grow up with a number of risk factors, yet don't evidence developmental or adjustment problems. Many children and adolescents who fit the profile of risk—the lower achiever, potential dropout, drug abuser, or teen parent—defy the prophecy that they won't succeed. They demonstrate the personal quality of *resilience*. Resilience refers to individual variation in response to stress, risk, and adversity. (Some risk and resiliency factors are included in Table 2.2.)

Werner(1982, 1986, 1992) and colleagues (Werner & Smith, 1977, 1982, 1992; Werner, Bierman, & French, 1971) undertook an ambitious longitudinal study that followed a cohort of high-risk children (n = @700) born in 1955 to study "resilient" children—those able to overcome risks in family and environment and go on to lead healthy lives. Participants in Werner's studies experienced four or more of the following risk factors: poverty, perinatal stress, family discord, divorce, parental alcoholism, and parental mental illness. The children studied faced many of the same pressures confronting today's youth, such as erosion of the family, abuse, neglect, and alcohol dependency.

Werner (1982) identified three key qualities of resilient children: a personal temperament that elicits positive responses from family members; a close

Table 2.2
Risk and Resiliency Factors

Risk factors	Resiliency factors
rebelliousness	self-control
low self-esteem	high self-esteem
shyness	good communication skills
antisocial behavior	good team member skills
susceptible to negative peer pressure	good decision-making skills, responsible
feelings of helplessness	sense of contributing to something greater than oneself
poor academic performance	good academic performance
lack of connection to school or neighborhood	active and contributing participant in positive school and neighborhood activities
lack of positive role models	availability of positive role models
lack of goal-setting abilities and future goals	ability to set goals and plan for education and vocational opportunities

bond with a caregiver during the first year of life; and an active engagement in acts of required helpfulness in middle school and adolescence (e.g., community service learning projects). Marton, Golombek, Stein, and Korenblum (1988) found that self-esteem, sense of self, and attachment to adult figures enhance adaptive skills. Bolig and Weddle (1988) and Jens and Gordon (1991) noted that the experience of stressful events made resilient youth stronger.

Brendtro, Brokenleg, and Bockern (1990) described autonomous, independent, and resilient children as coping successfully in the face of seemingly overwhelming difficult environments. These children seemed invulnerable to family problems, disadvantaged neighborhoods, and inadequate schools. Hawkins, Lishner, and Catalano (1985) and Hawkins, Lishner, Catalano, and Howard (1986) found that resilient children share a number of characteristics (or sets of conditions) that provide immunity to risk factors, including these:

1. Resilient children think for themselves and can solve problems creatively.
2. They tolerate frustration and manage emotions.
3. They avoid making other people's problems their own.
4. They show optimism and persistence in the face of failure.
5. The resist being put down and shed negative labels.
6. They have a sense of humor and can "forgive and forget."
7. They build friendships based on care and mutual support (p. 46).

Other factors that promote these critical resiliency skills in children are *a sense of autonomy, an internal locus of control, and an ability to manage their lives and influence their environment* (Werner, 1982). Schools, institutions, and community groups can foster these qualities by helping young people establish relationships with caring adult role models and by providing environments that recognize achievements, provide healthy expectations, nurture self-esteem, and encourage problem solving and critical thinking skills. Resilient children and adolescents overcome their vulnerability because of protective factors within themselves, in their families, or in critical support systems.

Individual factors that provide a buffer to stressful events include these: efforts toward self-improvement, good communication skills, good problem-solving skills, an internal locus of control, a personal orientation toward achievement, and good coping and self-help skills. Other longitudinal studies (Garmezy, 1981; Garmezy, Master, & Tellegen, 1984; Rak & Patterson, 1996; Rutter, 1983, 1985; Werner & Smith, 1992) identified critical personality factors that distinguish resilient children from those who become overwhelmed by risk factors:

- An active, evocative approach toward problem solving
- An ability to negotiate an array of emotionally debilitating experiences
- An ability from infancy to gain positive attention from others
- An optimistic view of experiences even in the midst of suffering
- An ability to maintain a positive vision for a meaningful life
- An ability to be alert and autonomous
- A tendency to seek novel experiences
- A proactive experience (Rak & Patterson, 1996, p. 369)

Family factors that buffer children from stressful events include these: ample attention by a primary caretaker during the first five years, adequate rule structure during adolescence, stable behavior on the part of parents during chaotic times, a self-confident mother, and a support network of caregivers. Rak and Patterson, (1996) identified family conditions that buffer youth from risk:

- A younger opposite-sex parent (younger mothers for resilient boys; older fathers for resilient girls)
- Four or fewer children in the family, spaced more than two years apart
- Focused nurturing during the first year of life and little prolonged separation from the primary caregiver
- An array of alternative caregivers—grandparents, siblings, neighbors—who supervise children when parents are not consistently present
- A network of kin of all ages who share similar values and beliefs, and to whom the child can turn for counsel and support
- The availability of sibling caretakers in childhood or another young person to serve as a confidant
- Structure and rules in the household during adolescence despite poverty and stress

Environmental or external social support factors that buffer a person from stressful events include these: a close adult with whom to share experiences; a supportive figure who can serve as a model for a child; positive recognition for activities; and informal sources of support from peers, relatives, teachers, and clergy.

Beardslee and Podorefsky (1988), Bolig and Weddle (1988), Dugan and Coles (1989), and Werner (1986) identified a number of role models outside the family as potential buffers for vulnerable youth. Resilient youth often have mentors outside their family network, including teachers, school counselors, caregivers at before- and-after school programs, coaches, social workers, mental health workers, clergy, and neighbors.

Rak and Patterson (1996) developed an informal, 25-item resiliency questionnaire for children (ages 6 to 12 years) and adolescents (Table 2.3). The questionnaire was designed to identify risk factors and protective or buffering factors in the life stories of youth. It highlights temperament; family environment; interactions and support outside the family; self-understanding; self-esteem; previous history of stress response; influences on the child that promote optimism; and a positive attitude about service to others and to the community (Rak & Patterson, 1996, p. 370).

By evaluating both at-risk and resiliency factors, helping professionals can plan interventions that either protect the at-risk youth or activate his or her resiliency factors to respond to the stress or crisis. This questionnaire facilitates a thorough evaluation of the client's life space, support system, and capacity to endure and overcome stressful factors.

Finally, intervention efforts are shifting toward enhancing resiliency with gender-specific adolescent programs (Turner, Norman, & Zunz, 1995). Some researchers have discovered that boys and girls may require different protective mechanisms, since they go through different developmental stages at different times and are subject to different social, cultural, and psychological mores at each developmental stage. Resiliency factors for girls include having been perceived as affectionate infants and toddlers, having a mother who is successful in a career and a highly educated father, experiencing few behaviors problems prior to middle school, and having a caring network of significant adults. Protective factors for girls that can be nurtured include responsibility, assertiveness, problem-solving skills, and an environment that encourages positive risks and independence (Turner, Norman, & Zunz, 1995).

Protective factors for boys are difficult to influence during early development. They include being viewed as active in infancy, with few distressing habits; having an educated mother and a father present; being the first-born son; and being a high-achieving adolescent with realistic educational and career goals. Turner, Norman, and Zunz (1995) suggested that, because of developmental differences, gender-specific strategies for enhancing self-esteem, self-efficacy, and problem-solving would have more significant outcomes in same-sex groups. They also proposed social skills training in preschool to encourage the emotional responsiveness of males.

NURTURING HOPE

Hope is defined as the process of thinking about one's goals, in tandem with the motivation to move toward (agency) and the ways to achieve

Table 2.3
A Resiliency Questionnaire

1. What is your position in the family? Oldest? Youngest? Middle? Oldest girl? Oldest boy?
2. Do your have any memories or recollections about what your mother or father said about you as a young baby? Or anyone else?
3. Did anyone ever tell you about how well you ate and slept as a baby?
4. Do members of your family and friends usually seem happy to see you and to spend time with you?
5. Do you feel like you are a helpful person to others? Does anyone in your family expect you to be helpful?
6. Do you consider yourself a happy and hopeful (optimistic) person even when life becomes difficult?
7. Tell me about some times when you overcame problems or stresses in your life. How do you feel about them now?
8. Do you think of yourself as awake and alert most of the time? Do others see you that way also?
9. Do you like to try new life experiences?
10. Tell me about some plans and goals you have for yourself over the next year. Three years. Five years.
11. When you are in a stressful, pressure-filled situation, do you feel confident that you'll work it out, or do you feel depressed and hopeless?
12. What was the age of your mother when you were born? Your father?
13. How many children are in your family? How many years are there between children in your family?
14. What do you remember, if anything, about how you were cared for when you were little by mom and others?
15. When you were growing up, were there rules and expectations in your home? What were some of them?
16. Did any of your brothers or sisters help raise you? What do you remember about this?
17. When you felt upset or in trouble, to whom in your family did you turn for help? Whom outside your family?
18. From whom did you learn about the values and beliefs of your family?
19. Do you feel it is your responsibility to help others? Help your community?
20. Do you feel that you understand yourself?
21. Do you like yourself? Today? Yesterday? Last year?
22. What skills do you rely on to cope when you are under stress?
23. Tell me about a time when you were helpful to others.
24. Do you see yourself as a confident person? Even when stressed?
25. What are your feelings about this interview with me?

Source: Reprinted from C. F. Rak & L. E. Patterson (1996). Promoting resilience in at-risk children. *Journal of Counseling and Development, 74*(4), 368-373. © ACA. Reprinted with permission. No further reproduction authorized without written permission of the American Counseling Association.

(pathways) those goals. Goal-directed thoughts are the impetus for human learning and coping. Snyder (1995) delineated two necessary components to goal-directed cognitions: (1) the cognitive will power or energy to move toward one's goal (the agency component) and (2) the perceived ability to generate routes to get somewhere (the pathways component). To think about goals, individuals inherently perform a cognitive analysis of their agency and pathways (i.e., both the "will and the way").

The dichotomy of low and high hope can be further delineated. Higher hope reflects an elevated sense of mental energy and pathways for goals. Snyder (1995, p. 355) defined hope as "a cognitive set that is based on a reciprocally derived sense of successful (a) agency (goal-directed determination) and (b) pathways (planning of ways to meet goals)."

Hope is dependent on the cognitive appraisal of one's goal-related capabilities. Low-hope individuals approach goals with negative expectations, a sense of ambivalence, and a focus on failure rather than success. In contrast, high-hope individuals approach their goals with the expectation of succeeding rather than failing, the perception that they will reach their goals, and a positive emotional state.

Scoring and Norms for the Hope Scale

The Hope Scale, shown in Table 2.4, was developed by Snyder (1995) to measure aspects of hope. The agency subscale score is derived by adding items, 2, 9, 10, and 12; the pathways subscale score is derived by adding items 1, 4, 6, and 8. The total score is derived by adding the 4 agency and the 4 pathways items. (Items 3, 5, 7, and 11 were added as distracters, to make the content of the scale less obvious.)

The highest possible *Hope Scale* score is 32, and the lowest is 8. The average score for college and noncollege samples of people was 24, with significantly lower scores for people who are seeking psychological help and inpatients at psychiatric hospitals (Snyder, 1995, p. 356).

Synder (1995) revealed that hope can be nurtured. Agency- and pathway-enhancing lessons include the following strategies:

- Learning self-talk about succeeding
- Reframing difficulties as the result of using the wrong strategy rather than of a lack of talent or skill

Table 2.4
The Hope Scale

Directions: Read each item carefully. Using the scale shown below, please select the number that best describes you and put that number in the blank provided.

1 = Definitely false	3 = Mostly true
2 = Mostly false	4 = Definitely true

_____ 1. I can think of many ways to get out of jam.
_____ 2. I energetically pursue my goals.
_____ 3. I feel tired most of the time.
_____ 4. There are lots of ways around any problem.
_____ 5. I am easily downed in an argument.
_____ 6. I can think of many ways to get the things in life that are most important to me.
_____ 7. I worry about my health.
_____ 8. Even when others get discouraged, I know I can find a way to solve the problem.
_____ 9. My past experiences have prepared me well for my future.
_____ 10. I've been pretty successful in life.
_____ 11. I usually find myself worrying about something.
_____ 12. I meet the goals that I set for myself

When administering the scale, it is labeled the Future Scale.

Source: Reprinted from C. R. Snyder (1995). Conceptualizing, measuring, and nurturing hope. *Journal of Counseling and Development, 73*(30), 355-360. © ACA. Reprinted with permission. No further reproduction authorized without written permission of the American Counseling Association.

- Thinking of setbacks as challenges, not failures
- Recalling past successes
- Identifying role models
- Cultivating goal-directed friends
- Adjusting and modifying goals, and rewarding subgoals

Hope theory proponents suggest that counselors and therapists can understand emotions by looking at how effective people are in the pursuit of their goals. Enhancing agency and pathways has the potential to produce more positive interactions between parents and children, psychotherapists and clients, managers and employees, coaches and athletes, teachers and students, and partners in relationships (Synder, 1989, 1994, 1995).

> From the perspective of emotional intelligence, having hope means that one will not give in to overwhelming anxiety, a defeatist atti-

tude, or depression in the face of difficult challenges and setbacks. Indeed, people who are hopeful evidence less depression than others as they maneuver through life in pursuit of their goals, are less anxious in general, and have fewer emotional distresses. (Goleman, 1995, p. 87)

EMPOWERING YOUTH

Empowerment—defined as "nurturing belief in capability or competence, or assisting others in gaining a sense of personal power or control over their lives" (Ashcroft, 1987)—is central to helping children and adolescents. The paramount goal of empowerment is to help people live in a way that maximizes their potential for developing a positive and satisfying lifestyle. One of the major assumptions underlying the empowerment process is the need to recognize and foster strengths and competencies.

Empowerment promotes autonomy rather than dependency, and an internal rather than an external locus of control. Empowerment is helping people develop the resources to cope constructively with the forces that undermine or hinder coping and achieve some reasonable control over their destiny. Empowerment is rooted in attitude and behavior, and is defined as the ability to promote one's own abilities, interests, rights, and needs in both interpersonal relationships and within the broader realm of school/community/work settings. If young people perceive their role in the empowerment process as active and important, they are more likely to assume ownership of positive outcomes and continue the intervention on their own.

For youth, empowerment means critical life skills development. For example, life skills training in decision making, problem solving, assertiveness, and conflict resolution contribute to increased control over themselves and their environment. These skills enable students to make realistic self-appraisals, to network within the school and community, to brainstorm alternatives, and to reframe problem situations. Empowerment focuses on self-responsibility, on the need to be assertive in creating one's own lifestyle, rather than passively reacting to circumstances.

For educators and helping professional, empowerment is universal in all institutional and community intervention strategies. Casas (1990) stressed that problem analysis within the school and community is empowering when responsibility for the problem is shared between youth and helping professionals.

SOLUTION-FOCUSED COUNSELING

Counselors and therapists have a growing interest in becoming more efficient in their practice through the development and use of various forms of short-term counseling (Gentner, 1991). Solution-focused counseling is rapidly becoming one component of proactive counseling programs. Solution-focused counseling is active, focusing on the answers to problems rather than on the pathology of problems. This counseling intervention identifies what individuals are already doing well and enhances those strengths. Key components of the model include these:

1. A competency-based orientation in which people are viewed as resourceful and capable of improving their lives
2. A focus on the present and future
3. The systemic notion that small changes in any aspect of the situation can instigate eventual resolution of a complaint
4. The assumption that people will work for change only if they perceive a need to do so (Murphy, 1994, p. 59)

The assumption is that problems are temporary and that clients have the resources to solve their own problems. Solution-focused counseling builds on clients' identified strengths, thus empowering them with self-sufficiency and positive change. Bergin (1991, p. 11) maintained, "It is simpler for clients to repeat already successful behavior patterns than it is to try to stop or change existing symptomatic or problematic behavior."

The de Shazer group developed a set of correlates that guide the solution-based approach (Bergin, 1991; de Shazer, 1991, 1988, 1982; Zimstrad, 1989). The major task of counseling is to help the client do something different than current self-defeating behaviors. The solution-focused approach shifts the emphasis from the self-defeating behavior to the exceptions, the times when the problem *does not* occur (O'Hanlon & Weiner-Davis (1989). The counselor redirects the focus away from the problem and toward solutions already existing within the client's coping repertoire. Goals are framed in positive terms, with an expectancy for change (no matter how small) to create the context for further change.

The model consists of seven stages, which may take place all in one session or over the course of 6 to 10 sessions. Some time between counseling sessions provides the client and his or her support network time to alter the system and integrate new behaviors. The approach is pragmatic, specific, and focused on the here-and-now, avoiding in-depth exploration of problems in the there-and-then. This contemporary approach emphasizes the client's perception of the presenting problem, discovers the client's goal for solving it, reveals solution-focused behavior used by the client in the past, and provides a venue for the client to practice solution behaviors.

Stage I: Defining the Problem

The counselor's task in this stage is to reconstruct the problem through careful analysis of various frames of reference presented by the client. The initial question asked is, "What is it you would like to change?" The counselor also uses language to achieve the following steps:

1. Communicate an expectancy for change
2. Reframe the problem situation as normal and modifiable
3. Change labels and diagnoses of the problem situation into action descriptions

These steps are accomplished using transactional and systemic questions (Bergman, 1985) to search for *exceptions to the rule*—exceptions to the problem episodes, times when the problem *could* occur but *does not*. For example, if the therapist is meeting with a client who is experiencing test anxiety, he or she would ask questions like these:

- What is different about the times when you are not having test anxiety?
- How does it make your day go differently when you are having test anxiety?
- Who else notices when you are having test anxiety (teacher, classmate, boyfriend or girlfriend)?
- How is your test anxiety different from the way you handled it a year ago?
- How do you respond when you have test anxiety during an important examination?

Murphy (1994) proposed using the *5-E method* of using exceptions:

Task 1: Elicit. The counselor or therapist should ask specific questions to elicit information on exceptions, such as these: *When is the problem absent or less noticeable during the day? What is happening (at school or work) that you want to see continue happening?*

Task 2: Elaborate. Once exceptions have been identified, the counselor or therapist should ask about related features and circumstances: *Who* *is around when things seem to be less stressful at home? What do you do or say differently when you and your spouse are getting along better?*

Task 3: Expand. Next, the counselor or therapist asks questions to help the client expand the exceptions to other contexts or to a greater frequency: *What situations or circumstances are positive, and how can you increase them?*

Task 4: Evaluate. Solution-focused counseling focuses on attaining small, concrete changes (de Shazer, 1991). To assess goal attainment, the counselor or therapist should use a rating scale of 1 to 10: *On a scale of 1 to 10, 1 being the worst and 10 the best, how would you rate the presenting problem right now?*

Task 5: Empower. Finally, clients must assume rightful ownership for the desired changes and feel empowered to continue implementing the intervention on their own. To facilitate that process, the counselor or therapist should ask questions such as these: *What will it take for you to be able to continue doing this? What did you do differently this time that proved successful?* (Murphy, 1994, pp. 60-61).

The counselor should gather additional information on the frequency, intensity, and duration (FID) of the problem. The goal is to have the client be more specific about the presenting problem. This approach acknowledges that "any change in an individual's attempted solutions will change their beliefs about their difficulties and will alter the manner in which they attempt to resolve them" (Huber & Backlund, 1991, p. 29).

Stage II: Establishing Treatment Goals

Setting therapeutic goals facilitates evaluation of progress and establishes a point of termination. Goals should be concrete, specific, and observable. If the client resists being specific about goals, it may be germane to address his or her paradoxical role of requesting change within the context of resistance. The process of setting goals initiates the intervention. However, the goals should be constantly monitored with a mechanism for revision, adaptation, and reassessment.

Critical questions to ask would include these:

- What will be the very first sign that things are moving in the right direction?
- Who will be the first to notice?

- Are there small pieces of this that are already happening?
- What do you need to do to make it happen more?
- What else will you be doing differently when you no longer have test anxiety?

Stage III: Designing the Intervention

Solution-focused counseling is designed to prevent repetitive, dysfunctional behavior patterns by introducing alternative ways of experiencing interactions associated with problem behavior (Madanes, 1981). The foundation of this counseling model is the perspective of introducing change, however small. Gentner (1991) outlined three integral steps in the delivery of the intervention design: reframing, utilization, and strategic tasks.

> **Reframing** means providing a positive new meaning, perception, or understanding of the problem that allows the client to perceive his or her behavior as constructive and useful (Boscolo, Cecchin, Hoffman, & Penn 1987) Reframing a problem in a more positive light provides the mechanism that encourages change.
>
> **Utilization** means using whatever the client presents—including rigid belief systems, behaviors, demands, and characteristics—to motivate him or her to act differently. From this perspective, solutions are seen as contained within the presenting problem. The counselor should use the same structures expressed by the client to introduce some alternative that can precipitate a different way of experiencing the problem. This process allows the client to generate solutions from the altered structure (Gentner, 1991).
>
> **Strategic tasks** are carried out between sessions. The primary goal is to help the client do something different to fulfill the goals that were outlined in the first stage. Strategic tasks are designed to build upon and interface with the treatment components of reframing and utilization. They serve as a conceptual map to guide the client through familiar boundaries and new behavior alternatives (Gentner, 1991, p. 234).

Stage IV: Assigning Strategic Tasks

Strategic tasks should be assigned at the end of the session and should be clearly outlined (de Shazer, 1982; Weeks & L'Abate, 1982). The counselor should make sure the client understands the task and encourage the client to write down any instructions that are critical to completion of the task, such as monitoring the frequency of a desired behavior (e.g., how many times during the week a shy client manages to engage others in a conversation).

Stage V: Emphasizing Positive New Behaviors

In this stage, the counselor asks questions that are future-oriented, encouraging positive change and solutions. These questions should help the client see him- or herself responding in new ways that are consistent with treatment goals and task assignments. Critical questions would include these:

- What is happening that you would like to continue?
- How did it make things go differently?
- Who else will notice your progress?
- Is there anything that might happen in the next week or so which might keep these positive things from happening?

The most engaging intervention developed by de Shazer and his associates has been termed the *miracle question* (de Shazer, 1991). One account of the miracle question follows: "Imagine tonight while you sleep, a miracle happens and your problem is solved. What will be happening the next day, and how will you know that your problem has been resolved?" Often, clients are able to give specific and concrete answers to the question because the focus is on what will be present in their lives when the problem is absent. The primary tasks are these: to elicit news of a difference, to amplify the difference, and to help changes continue.

Stage VI: Stabilization

Restraint is integrated into the counseling process to promote and maintain change (Fisch, Weakland, & Segal 1983). The catalyst for change is to move slowly. This approach to intervention serves to anchor the client to a framework for change that allows for gradual adjustment, and to integrate the assimilation of the new behavior. Restraint is necessary. Grandiose goals are difficult to accomplish and can sabotage intervention efforts.

Stage VII: Termination

Typically in solution-focused counseling, the client recognizes problem resolution and then initiates termination. This empowers the client to control behavior change and promotes a smooth transition, necessary closure, and a sense of security in the change that has occurred.

SOLUTION-FOCUSED COUNSELING IN SCHOOLS, COMMUNITIES, AND INSTITUTIONAL SETTINGS

Solution-focused counseling is most appropriate in community or institutional settings when opportunities for counseling are limited by time constraints and accessibility. It is emerging in the literature because of its effectiveness, efficiency, and optimism. Bonnington (1993), Downing and Harrison (1992), LaFountain, Garner, and Eliason (1996), and Morrison, Olivos, Dominguez, Gomez, and Lena (1993) maintained that, as a form of brief therapy, solution-focused counseling is "working with what works" and is appropriate for counselors and other helping professionals working with youth because of the following attributes:

1. The student determines the issue or problem to be addressed (i.e., what is wrong in his or her life).
2. Emphasis is placed on the student identifying the change or coping goals related to the specific problem.
3. The student is encouraged to actively search for exceptions to the problem (i.e., exceptions to the rule). It is important to be alert to verbal cues of exceptions (Murphy, 1994). For example, if a client says he is "failing everything except science," the counselor should focus on what makes science better than most subjects.
4. The client is encouraged to identify strengths in his or her coping repertoire.
5. The emphasis is on helping the client develop and carry out a plan to have more success with this specific problem.

What follows is an illustration of a specific problem. First, the client is asked to determine *how he would like things to be* in regard to his concern. Second, he discusses *what would have to be different* in order to realize this goal:

> *Ryan complained that his parents' punishment for his not making the honor role was too strict. When asked to state how he would like things to be different, he said he would like an opportunity for input to the rules that affect him. Ryan decided that he and his parents would need someone (such as the counselor) to help them negotiate the terms. Ryan is beginning to establish a goal for counseling. He is also beginning to define what would need to change in order to obtain this goal.*

Third, using a solution-focused approach, the client is asked to identify the exceptions to the rule. Counselors should assume that an *"exception to the rule always exists,"* and their goal is to promote the client's own identification of that exception. Once an exception to the rule is discovered, the goal is to help the client "do more of what is already working." Setting goals is a crucial aspect of solution-focused counseling (de Shazer, 1991).

Fourth, the counselor can use "when" questions, such as, *"When have your parents been more understanding?"*

> *"When" questions helped Ryan find an exception to the rule. He recalled that his parents were adamant that he would not get off restriction until the semester grades came out. Ryan talked with his parents, however, and helped them understand his needs, which resulted in their allowing him to modify the restrictions occasionally. By focusing on what Ryan did in his talk and how his behavior affected change, the counselor helped Ryan appreciate his own power in bringing about the change.*

Solution-focused counseling is active, focusing on solutions rather than on problems. Rak and Patterson (1996, p. 371) maintained that a solution-focused strategy allows counselors to "operationalize a salutogenesis [solution-focused] perspective with clients." The solution-focused model is competency-based and views individuals as resourceful and capable of improving their own lives. It is goal-centered and focuses on the present and the future. Incremental changes in behavior are acknowledged as progress as individuals build on existing competencies. Solution-focused counseling uses people's identified strengths, empowering to effect their own behavior changes.

Youth empowered to change and to see their role as active are more likely to assume ownership and maintain the new behavior on their own. Gaining control over behavior and circumstances is empowering to children and adolescents. Solution-focused counseling can benefit children and adolescents with conduct disorders; alcohol and other drug problems; poor coping skills; and cognitive, emotional, and social deficits. It also can be applied to counseling issues surrounding grief, loss, separation, and divorce.

COMPREHENSIVE INTERVENTIONS
WITH MULTIMODAL COUNSELING

Another trend in counseling and psychotherapy is the move toward a multidimensional, multidisciplinary, and multifaceted approach that does not attempt to fit clients into a preconceived treatment plan (Lazarus, 1977, 1981, 1992,

1993). In multimodal therapy, the therapist/client interaction focuses on seven modalities of human interaction: Behavior, Affect, Sensation, Imagery, Cognition, Interpersonal relationships, and Diet/physiology (BASIC ID). These modalities are interactive as well as interdependent as they relate to behavior change.

Multimodal intervention uses techniques from behavior modification and incorporates elements of social learning theory, general systems theory, and group communications theory. It emphasizes growth and actualization rather than pathology (Lazarus, 1981; Seligman, 1981; Thompson, 1986). Its major thrust is educational; it views counseling as a broad-based learning process, aimed at helping clients function more effectively with concrete and measurable improvement. It offers a comprehensive structure for assessing client needs and developing treatment plans. This structure also allows counselors to maximize the use of referral sources and adjunctive modes of treatment.

Several researchers and practitioners have reported distinct advantages of the multimodal approach with youth (Breunlin, 1980; Edwards, 1978; Green, 1978; Keat, 1976a, 1976b, 1979; O'Keefe & Castaldo, 1980). Gerler (1977, 1978a, 1978b, 1979, 1980, 1982, 1984), Gerler and Herndon (1993), and Gerler and Keat (1977) applied multimodal theory to educational settings such as career education programs, school counseling offices, reading programs, and elementary classrooms. Smith and Southern (1980) applied multimodal techniques to the fields of vocational development and career counseling. Edwards and Klein (1986) outlined a multimodal consultation model for the development of gifted adolescents.

Research and case studies have demonstrated the positive effects of multimodal interventions on social and emotional development (Keat, 1985), on self-concept (Durbin, 1982), and on performance of various school-related tasks (Starr & Raykovitz, 1982). Multimodal counseling groups improved school attendance (Anderson, Kinney, & Gerler, 1984; Keat, Metzger, Raykovitz, & McDonald, 1985) and achievement in mathematics and language arts (Gerler, Kinney, & Anderson, 1985), and reduced procrastination (Morse, 1987) and psychoemotional difficulties such as oppositional defiant disorder, conduct disorder, and attention deficit disorder (Martin-Causey & Hinkle, 1995). Finally, Judah (1978) found that multimodal parent training provided a framework for achieving significant changes in parental levels of acceptance and for decreasing authoritarian attitudes, with benefits to elementary school children.

Multimodal therapy assumes that one effective way to understand clients is to assess their problems across the seven modalities of functioning. It provides a systematic and comprehensive assessment and treatment approach. Debilitating behaviors among children and adolescents are represented within these s even domains in a variety of ways. Lazarus (1992) provided a brief description of the BASIC ID as follows:

1. Behavior refers mainly to the overt responses, actions, habits, gestures, and motor reactions that are observable and manageable. Adolescent feelings or their need to conform to others' expectations of them may be one of the most powerful factors in determining their behavior. Behavior can be erratic and out of control or withdrawn and self-absorbed. What remains to be true is that every behavior is a communication.

2. Affect refers to emotions, moods, and feelings. Adolescence is often characterized by emotional highs and lows. Anxiety is a common malady. Self-medication with drugs and alcohol often begins to emerge in adolescence in on effort to cope with their interpersonal pain. They often feel shut off from family and friends with delusions that no one else has had such a similar experience.

3. Sensation covers inputs from each of the five senses. Physical sensations of adolescence differentiate them from childhood. Issues of sensuality are rarely addressed by adults while the media bombards adolescents relentlessly having a tremendous impact on high risk behavior such as the use of alcohol, drugs, and high risk sexual behavior.

4. Imagery includes dreams, fantasies, and vivid memories; mental pictures, and the way people view themselves (self-image). Auditory images recurring tunes or sounds also fall into this category. Dreams of future potential are often filled with feelings of anxiety regarding failure.

5. Cognition refers to attitudes, values, opinions, ideas, and self-talk. (Clinically, in this modality, the main task is to identify and modify dysfunctional beliefs and replace them with views that enhance adaptive functioning). Adolescents often have irrational beliefs about themselves in relation to others with unrealistic expectations such as "I must be liked by everyone." "I must be the perfect student." Thinking is often black or white; such rigidity perpetuates anxiety.

6. Interpersonal relationships include all significant interactions with other people (relatives, lovers, friends, colleagues, coworkers, acquaintances, etc.). The peer group and a growing circle of interpersonal relationships are an integral part of adolescence. Negative self-perceptions often lead them to regard themselves as uniquely unacceptable to others. Such feelings can be very debilitating leading self-destructive behaviors such as suicide.

7. Diet/physiology includes drugs (self-medication or physician prescribed)

in addition to nutrition, hygiene, exercise, and all basic physiological and pathological inputs. It involves the panoply of neurophysiological-biochemical factors that influence temperament and personality. Adolescents are often preoccupied with the way they look. Extreme behavioral manifestations are recognized as anorexia nervosa and bulimia. Substance abuse often emerges as an attempt to fit in with peers or to deal with stress or for the purposes of self medication for anxiety. Physical health and well-being is often neglected, with many health advocates claiming that we are creating a generation of "couch potatoes" with serum cholesterol levels that exceed recommended doses.

Essentially, the multimodal treatment intervention embraces four principles:

1. Clients act and interact across the seven modalities of the BASIC ID.
2. These modalities are connected by complex chains of behavior and other psychophysiological events, and exit in a state of reciprocal transaction.
3. Accurate evaluation (diagnosis) is served by the systematic assessment of each modality and its interaction with every other.
4. Comprehensive therapy calls for the specific correction of significant problems across the BASIC ID. (Lazarus, 1992, p. 50)

A multimodal orientation is considerably more systematic and comprehensive than most cognitive and cognitive-behavioral approaches (Lazarus, 1992). Treatment and intervention has demonstrated positive outcomes (Brunell, 1990; Gumaer, 1990; Martin-Causey & Hinkle, 1995; Weed & Hernandez, 1990; Weikel, 1989, 1990). It is pragmatic and didactic in approach, reflecting a "technical eclecticism" in constructing a modality profile for the client. The multimodal therapy model has been successful in treating such maladies as depression, alcoholism, agoraphobia, obesity, anorexia, procrastination, teen pregnancy, and assertiveness deficits. Some of the most frequently used group techniques or strategies are listed in the following section. The multimodal approach assumes a holistic intervention with the intent to create long-term behavioral, cognitive, and emotional changes.

Multimodal Techniques

Bibliotherapy. This technique uses recommended readings or literature to facilitate therapeutic change. Goals of bibliotherapy might include teaching positive thinking, making self-improvements, encouraging free expression concerning problems, helping others to analyze their attitudes and behaviors, or looking for alternative solutions to problems. Bibliotherapy provides the opportunity to discuss story outcomes, behavioral consequences, and alternative behaviors. Martin, Martin, and Porter (1983) and Timmerman, Martin, and Martin (1990) cited the merits of using bibliotherapy with children and adolescence.

Contingency Contracting. A contract is a verbal or written agreement between counselor and client that facilitates the achievement of a therapeutic goal. It provides structure, motivation, incentives for commitment, and assigned tasks for the client to carry out between counseling sessions. It also can be viewed as a consulting and teaching technique for reaching agreed upon goals and activities.

Meditation. This technique encompasses mental and sometimes physical exercises for relaxation, improved thought processes, and insight into self and the world. It includes transcendental meditation, Zen meditation, positive affirmations, and various yoga methods.

Communication Training. This technique teaches sending and receiving skills. To improve sending skills, the client learns the importance of eye contact, voice projection, and body posture. The client also learns to use simple, concrete terms, to avoid blaming, and to make statements of empathy. Good receiving skills require active listening, verification, acknowledgment, and rewarding the sender for communicating. Role-playing and behavioral rehearsal reinforce the development of communication skills (Lazarus, 1993).

Feeling Identification. This technique centers on exploring the client's affective domain in order to identify significant feelings that might be obscured or misdirected.

Friendship Training. Friendship is dependent on sharing, caring, empathy, concern, self-disclosure, give-and-take, and positive reinforcement. Power plays, competitiveness, and self-aggrandizement undermine friendship. In friendship training, prosocial interactions are explored and put into practice.

Social Skills and Assertiveness Training. Often, clients need to learn how to stand up for their personal rights and how to express their thoughts, feelings, and beliefs in direct, honest, and appropriate ways without violating the rights of others. Assertive behavior can be reduced to four specific response patterns: the ability to say no; the ability to ask for favors or to make requests; the ability to express positive and negative feelings; and the ability to initiate, continue, and terminate conversations. Behavioral rehearsal and modeling assertive behavior are two techniques used to train clients to develop social skills and assertive responses (Lazarus, 1993).

Stimulus Control. The presence of certain stimuli tend to increase the frequency of certain behaviors. Stimulus control can increase desired behaviors by arranging environmental cues to trigger them. For example, a student who wants to study more might arrange her desk so that no distracting stimuli are present, and will sit at her desk only while studying and not while listening to CDs or talking to friends. Thus, sitting at the desk sets the stimulus conditions for studying.

Journal Writing. Clients may use journals to record their innermost feelings and thoughts about events. Children and adolescents often respond well to a homework assignment of keeping a diary; this technique also provides a feeling of closeness to the counselor between sessions. The journal also provides the counselor and client with a record of feelings, thoughts, and events to be explored. In addition, it is helpful to have group members write comments at the end of every group session. An index card entitled *group reflections* provides a useful format. The cards can be signed so that the leader can keep in closer touch with each member. The index cards never should be read aloud to the group or referred to in the group by the leader.

Assertiveness Training. In assertiveness training, the client learns to stand up for his or her rights *without infringing on the rights of others.* Assertive behaviors include saying no without feeling guilty and learning to ask for what one wants more directly. Activities include instruction, modeling behavior, role-playing, and homework assignments.

Brainstorming. Brainstorming is a group problem-solving technique that collects everyone's ideas without evaluation or censure to gain all possible input before a decision is reached.

Cognitive Restructuring. At-risk children and adolescents exhibit an inordinate number of self-defeating beliefs (Bradshaw, 1988; Elkind, 1988; McMullin, 1986; Whitfield, 1987). It is crucial that they be taught to correct faulty belief systems, to "unlearn" irrational beliefs (for example, "I must be liked by everyone" or "I must be perfect in everything"), and to replace them with new ones that are more rational.

Relaxation and Imagery Training (RIT). In this technique, the client is asked to simply relax and envision the desired behavior as if it were occurring at that moment (Carey, 1986).

Systematic Desensitization. This is a behavioral technique used to reduce anxiety about a situation or event. The client is taught complete muscle relaxation techniques. An *anxiety hierarchy* is constructed, from least anxiety-provoking experience to most anxiety-provoking experience. (Using test anxiety as an example: the least anxiety-provoking time is a month before the exam; the most anxiety-provoking is the day of the test.) An anxiety-causing stimulus is then paired with positive mental images and the process of relaxation. The pairing continues up the hierarchy (from least to most), until the entire hierarchy can be imagined without anxiety.

Cognitive Aids. Cognitive aids are short inventories, exercises, strategies, or experiential activities designed to facilitate awareness, knowledge, and greater understanding of experiences, thoughts, feelings, or behaviors.

Behavioral Rehearsal. This technique uses repetition or practice to help the client learn effective interpersonal skills; decrease social, cognitive, or emotional skill deficits; and increase appropriate behaviors.

Guided Fantasy. Using this technique, the counselor leads a client through a guided fantasy, in which the client resolves on paper some unresolved event of the past. Reliving past events and fantasizing different outcomes can relieve feelings of guilt or unfinished business. It also can be used to test out newly learned behaviors and to construct a future scenarios on paper before actually trying the new behavior. An event can be rewritten to include more positive outcomes.

Role-Playing. In this technique the client assumes a role or character and acts out a scene for the purpose of better understanding his- or herself and significant relationships.

Role Reversal. This is a role-playing technique in which the client is asked to play a role opposite to his or her own natural behavior (for example, an assertive role versus a submissive role). The client also may play the role of another person he or she knows, or switch roles with another person in a dyadic role-playing situation within a group setting.

The ABCs of Stopping Unhappy Thoughts. Clients are directed to respond in their journals when they notice they are upset following a situation or an event (Maultsby, 1975):

A. **Facts and events:** Record the facts about the unhappy event.
B. **Self-talk:** Record the things you told yourself about the event.
C. **How you felt:** Record how you felt.

D. **Debate:** Debate or dispute any statement in "A" that is not logical or objective.

E. **Examine the future:** This is how I want to feel in the future in this kind of situation.

Self-Management. The major difference between self-management and other procedures is that clients assume major responsibility for carrying out their programs, including arranging their own contingencies or reinforcements. To benefit from self-management strategies, clients must use the strategies regularly and consistently. Clients should be given the following instructions:

1. Select and define a behavior you want to increase or decrease.
2. Self-record the frequency of the behavior for a week to establish a baseline measure before you start your self-management procedures. Record the setting in which the behavior occurs, the events leading to the behavior, and the consequences resulting from the behavior.
3. Using self-monitoring, either increase or decrease the targeted behavior, depending on your goal. Do this self-monitoring for two weeks. (A contract with the client will reinforce this process.)
4. Evaluate the use of self-management on the targeted behavior at the end of the contractual period. Arrange a plan to maintain the new, more desirable behavior.

Goal Rehearsal or Coping Imagery. Goal rehearsal implies the deliberate and thorough visualization of each step in the process of assimilating a new behavior. The deliberate picturing of a new situation enhances transfer to the actual event. Clients should be encouraged to be realistic in reaching their goal, and not to expect perfection. For example, a client may still experience a severe panic attack when called on to speak in public. If he or she can reduce three out of five anxiety symptoms, that should be viewed as a success.

Reframing. This is a technique that relabels behavior in a more positive framework (e.g., "When you fight, you are demonstrating that you care about the issue.") This changes the perspective of individuals involved and allows them to explore new options.

Play. Cognitive and emotional development can be enhanced through constructive play (Eheart & Leavitt, 1985; Hartley & Goldenson, 1963). Play provides the venue for children to master fundamental physical, social, emotional, and cognitive skills and to learn new skills and receive feedback in a setting that is less threatening.

Modeling. Through the process of modeling (Bandura, 1976) appropriate skills and behavior can be demonstrated. Videotaping the behavior that is practiced also provides an opportunity for the transfer of learning.

The Step-Up Technique. Some clients are paralyzed by anxiety or panic about upcoming events, such as a public speech, a job interview, or a blind date. The step-up technique consists of picturing the worst thing that could possibly happen, then imagining oneself coping with the situation—surviving even the most negative outcome. Once the client successfully pictures him- or herself coping with the most unlikely catastrophes imaginable, anticipatory anxiety tends to recede. When the real situation occurs, the individual may feel less anxious. Difficult cases may require self-instruction training (Lazurus, 1977, p. 240).

Self-Instruction Training. This technique is used to break a chain of negative feelings, such as fear, anger, pain, and guilt. Michenbaum (1974) and Ellis (1962) showed empirically that negative self-talk contributes to people's failures and anxiety. On the other end of the spectrum, the deliberate use of positive, self-creative statements can facilitate successful coping.

Lazurus (1977) cited the following sequence of self-instruction to use with a client experiencing anxiety over an upcoming event:

> I will develop a plan for what I have to do instead of worrying. I will handle the situation one step at a time. If I become anxious I will pause and take in a few deep breaths. I do not have to eliminate all fear; I can keep it manageable. I will focus on what I need to do. When I control my ideas, I control my fear. It will get easier each time I do it. (p. 238)

Theoretically, the number of techniques in the counselor's repertoire is limitless. Those listed above are only a few of the many possibilities. Most

Table 2.5
Evaluation Scale for Multimodal Interventions

Behavior	Client managed anxiety during stressful event	1 2 3 4 5
Affect	Client managed anxiety more appropriately	1 2 3 4 5
Sensation	Anxiety experienced by client during stressful event	1 2 3 4 5
Imagery	Client mastered imagery technique to control anxiety	1 2 3 4 5
Cognition	Client's rumination about anxiety-provoking situations	1 2 3 4 5
Interpersonal relationships	Client's relationships increased/decreased	1 2 3 4 5
Drugs/Diet	Client has eliminated stimulants from diet (e.g., caffeine)	1 2 3 4 5

practitioners are constantly on the lookout for new methods, strategies, or techniques to serve their diverse client populations.

CONCLUSION

The advantages of using solution-focused counseling—and of finding and using exceptions to the rule—are apparent: Solution-focused counseling is pragmatic and competency-based and focuses on existing strengths and resources available to youth. It also fosters helping relationships between youth and the adults on whom they depend. The present-future focus of both solution-focused and multimodal interventions provides an opportunity for altering difficult problems in a limited time period.

The solution-focused goal of small, concrete changes in any aspect of a problem situation empowers youth to change with specific, achievable goals (e.g., managing time, managing stress, improving communication skills, decreasing self-defeating behaviors). Multimodal interventions provide a more comprehensive, holistic approach when intervention depends on resolving multiple difficulties (e.g., a teen facing an unintended pregnancy, with health and wellness concerns, facing emotional discord and the threat of dropping out of school). Both counseling approaches present opportunities within school and community settings.

Accessible helping professionals and other support staff who encourage and reinforce a child's coping efforts may promote more adaptive development in the presence of risk factors. Ideally, children and adolescents need coping strategies and behaviors to help tolerate stressors. Solution-focused counseling and multimodal interventions are models that promote collaboration. They are pragmatic, accountable, and competency-based. And by actively involving youth in their own behavior changes, they foster self-reliance and self-sufficiency.

Chapter **3**

PSYCHOEDUCATIONAL GROUPS IN INSTITUTIONAL AND COMMUNITY SETTINGS

> Self-understanding promotes change by encouraging individuals to recognize, to integrate, and to give free expression of previously dissociated parts of themselves. When we deny or stifle parts of ourselves, we pay a heavy price: we feel a deep amorphous sense of restriction; we are "on guard"; we are often troubled and puzzled by inner, yet alien, impulses demanding expression. When we can reclaim these split-off parts, we experience a wholeness and a deep sense of liberation. (Yalom, 1985, p. 86)

Any school, community, or institutional setting is a microcosm of group work. Formal and informal groups already exist for the purpose of furthering the educational process and promoting community involvement.

These communities include task-oriented groups to complete projects, cooperative learning groups, groups to organize and plan social events, groups to learn new athletic skills, groups to socialize, assessment groups to scrutinize curricula, and community projects groups.

Psychoeducational groups should be an integral component of prevention and intervention efforts in these communities. Psychoeducational groups help members learn new, effective ways of dealing with problematic issues and behavior, and teach and encourage them to practice and use these new behaviors

45

with current and future problems (Association for Specialists in Group Work [ASGW], 1990). The efficacy of psychoeducational groups in helping people change attitudes, perspectives, values, and behavior has been well-documented (Dyer & Vriend, 1977; Egan, 1982; Ohlsen, 1977; Yalom, 1975).

Young people, however, need to gain a sense of trust, confidence, and ownership in the group in order to feel secure and to remain loyal.

The following components are necessary for the group process to work with young people:

A sense of belonging. Young people need to feel that they are sincerely welcome, that no one objects to their presence, and that they are valued for who they are rather than for what they have or where they have been.

Planning. Young people need to be involved in planning the ground rules and goals of the group, suggesting group guidelines and testing boundaries.

Realistic expectations. Young people need to know in some detail what is expected of them. Their role in the group, their level of involvement, and issues of confidentiality are important. This information should also be made available to parents, teachers, and administrators so that they can support the program.

Reachable goal. Young people need to feel that their goals are within reach.

Responsibility. Young people need to have responsibilities that are challenging and within the range of their abilities. They need to stretch for improvement and growth.

Progress. Young people need to experience some successes and see some progress for what they want to achieve. Milestones should be celebrated and shared with family and peers.

GROUP-FOCUSED FACILITATION SKILLS

Many helping professionals want to be able to identify group helping behaviors to provide for structure and accountability of service delivery. Gill and Barry (1982) provided one of the most comprehensive classifications of counseling skills for the group process. Such a classification system can assist helping professionals by delineating an organized, operational definition of group-focused facilitation skills. A classification of specific group-focused facilitation skills has a number of significant benefits, including clear objectives, visible procedures, competency-based accountability, and measurable outcomes. This information is an important component of the group process that needs to be shared with all those involved in prevention and intervention efforts.

Gill and Barry (1982) suggested the following selection criteria for building a system of group-focused counseling skills to change behavior:

Appropriate. The behavior can be reasonably attributed to the role and function of a group counselor.

Definable. The behavior can be described in terms of human performances and outcomes.

Observable. Experienced as well as inexperienced observers can identify the behavior when it occurs. The behavior can be repeated by different people in different settings.

Measurable. Objective recording of both the frequency and quality of the behavior can occur with a high degree of agreement among observers.

Developmental. The behavior can be placed within the context of a progressive relationship with other skills, all contributing to movement of the group toward its goals. The effectiveness of the behaviors at one stage in the counseling process is dependent on the effectiveness of the skills used at earlier stages.

Group-focused. The target of the behavior is the group, or more than one participant. The behavior is often related to an interaction between two or more participants. The purpose of the group is to facilitate multiple interactions among participants, to encourage shared responsibility for promoting participation, or to invite cooperative problem solving and decision making (Gill & Barry, 1982, pp. 304-305).

Further, the group setting is a pragmatic approach for adjustment concerns of children and adolescents, allowing them to share anxieties in a secure environment and to enhance their self-sufficiency.

TYPES OF PSYCHOEDUCATIONAL GROUPS

Primary Prevention and Structured Intervention Groups

Counseling groups can be categorized into two types: (1) developmental/primary prevention groups and (2) problem-centered/structured intervention groups. Developmental groups are designed for *primary prevention counseling.* Problem-centered groups are designed for *structured intervention counseling.*

Developmental/primary prevention counseling is a proactive approach to avert dysfunctional or debilitating behavior by providing critical social, emotional, and cognitive skills to promote healthy functioning. Primary prevention refers to early programmatic strategies designed to promote cognitive, emotional, and social well-being by preventing debilitating behavior before it occurs. It focuses on strengthening and supporting existing skills. Preventive counseling exists along a continuum with remedial and developmental counseling (Albee & Ryan-Finn, 1993). Multiple strategies can be used to reduce risk factors and to promote protective factors. Some researchers contend that prevention strategies can be used to address behaviors such as self-sufficiency, social support, conflict resolution, problem solving, decision making, communication, peer-pressure resistance training, mental and emotional disorders, and disease prevention to reduce social pathogens such as those identified in Chapters 4 through 9 and to enhance competencies (Albee, 1986; Albee & Joffe, 1977; Albee, Bond, & Monsey, 1992; Albee, Gordon, & Leitenberg, 1983; Bond & Compas, 1989; Botvin, 1985, 1986; Botvin & Tortu, 1988; Comer, 1989; Garland & Zigler, 1993; Pedro-Carroll, 1991).

Acquiring the desired competencies will help prevent potential problems. For example, for date rape a prevention might be, "To be able to negotiate clearly one's wants and needs with a date." For substance abuse, a prevention might be, "How to say no without loosing your friends."

> Primary prevention is defined as being proactive and is aimed predominately at high-risk groups not yet affected by the condition to be prevented. Its success is measured in a decline in the incidence of the condition. . . . Only through prevention can we reduce its incidence, and it seems that it is the only feasible way to deal with the unbridgeable gap between the enormous number of individuals at risk for emotional disturbance and the limited availability of treatment resources. (Albee & Ryan-Finn, 1993, p. 115)

The purposes of developmental/primary prevention groups are to provide information and skills for more accurate decision making and to prevent critical developmental issues from becoming intervention concerns. Descriptions of developmental/primary prevention groups gleaned from the literature include, but are not limited to, the following:

- *Listening skills* (Merritt & Walley, 1977; Rogers, 1980)
- *Dealing with feelings* (Papagno, 1983; Vernon, 1989, 1990)
- *Social skills and interpersonal relationships* (Barrow & Hayaski, 1980; Brown & Brown, 1982; Cantor & Wilkinson, 1982; Johnson, 1990;

Keat, Metzger, Raykovitz, & McDonald, 1985; Morganett, 1990; Rose, 1987; Vernon, 1989)

- *Academic achievement, motivation, and school success* (Ames & Archer, 1988; Blum & Jones, 1993; Campbell & Myrick, 1990; Chilcoat, 1988; Gage, 1990; Gerler, Kinney, & Anderson, 1985; Malett,1983; Morganett, 1990; Thompson, 1987)
- *Self-concept/personal identity/self-esteem* (Canfield & Wells, 1976; Morganett, 1990; Omizo & Omizo, 1987, 1988; Tesser, 1982; Vernon, 1989)
- *Career awareness, exploration, and planning* (McKinlay & Bloch, 1989; Rogala, Lambert, & Verhage, 1991; Super, 1980)
- *Problem solving/decision making* (Bergin, 1991; Vernon, 1989)
- *Communication and assertiveness* (Alberti & Emmons, 1974; Donald, Carlisle, & Woods, 1979; Huey, 1983; Morganett, 1990; Myrick, 1987)

Primary prevention programs promote a nurturing and caring environment for high-risk youth, reducing such maladies as the debilitating consequences of poverty by providing transition skills and employment, and identifying and encouraging the development of social support groups.

Further, the developmental task of youth is to achieve a sense of identity, autonomy, and differentiation from family of origin. For youth to accomplish this life transition, they need to acquire skills, knowledge, and attitudes that may be classified into two broad categories: those involving self-development and those involving other people. Table 3.1 provides a framework of basic needs and basic skills inherent for all children, regardless of race, sex, or ethnic origin. It focuses on the continuum from deficiency to fulfillment, and serves as a graphic organizer for prevention and intervention efforts. Inherent are the critical need to belong, the need to communicate and be understood, the need to be respected, the need to be held in high esteem, the need to be assertive, the need to communicate effectively, and the need to resolve conflicts.

Maslow's needs hierarchy and levels of personality function (Table 3.1) illustrates the conditions of efficiency and conditions of fulfillment, providing a more detailed dimension of developmental tasks and behavior. Preventive counseling with primary prevention/developmental groups helps youth actualize their full potential.

The developmental task may serve as a catalyst or bridge between an individual's needs, environmental demands, and the total framework of such tasks, providing a comprehensive network of important psychosocial learning essential for living and well-being. Further, according to Burrett and Rusnak (1993), personal growth is seen as a function of knowledge, emotion, and environment and occurs in the following developmental stages:

Table 3.1
Hierarchy of Developmental Needs:
Conditions of Deficiency and Fulfillment

Need hierarchy	Condition of deficiency	Conditions of fulfillment	Illustration
Self-actualization	Alienation Defenses Absence of meaning in life Boredom Routine living Limited activities	Healthy curiosity Understanding Realization of potentials Work which is pleasurable and embodies values Creative living	Realizing what friendship really is or feeling awe at the wonder of nature
Esteem	Feeling incompetence Negativism Feeling of inferiority	Confidence Sense of mastery Positive self-regard Self-respect Self-extension	Receiving an award for an outstanding performance on some subject
Love	Self-consciousness Feeling of being unwanted Feeling of worthlessness Emptiness Loneliness Isolation Incompleteness	Free expression of emotions Sense of wholeness Sense of warmth Renewed sense of life and strength Sense of growing together	Experiencing total acceptance in a love relationship
Safety	Insecurity Yearning Sense of loss Fear Worry Rigidity	Security Comfort Balance Poise Calm Tranquillity	Being secure in a full-time job
Physiological	Hunger, thirst Tension Fatigue Illness Lack of proper shelter	Relaxation Release from tension Experiences of pleasure from senses Physical well-being Comfort	Feeling satisfied after a good meal

Ages 1 to 7: development of a sense of hope (openness and trust), autonomy, and imagination

Ages 7 to adolescence: development of competence (beyond simple skill and technique) in the expression of self and of harmony with one's physical and social environment

Adolescence: development of consistency and fidelity predicated on a combined sense of ability and commitment

Adulthood: development of a sense of justice, love, care and wisdom (Burrett & Rusnak, 1993, p. 8)

Problem-Centered Intervention Groups

Problem-centered intervention groups are initiated to meet the needs of clients who are have dysfunctional or self-defeating behaviors. The stressors from their particular circumstance may interfere with or hinder normal functioning. The group experience allows clients to handle more serious concerns rather than resolve typical developmental problems. Group members share anxieties in a secure environment and attempt to empower themselves to take action on their decisions by providing support, feedback, and unconditional acceptance. With the assistance of the group, members try out new behaviors and develop and implement strategies to resolve their problems. These groups build on young people's inherent tendencies to turn to their peers for needed support, understanding, and advice.

A problem-centered intervention group provides young people with experiences that enhance their self-awareness and increase their problem-solving and decision-making skills so that they can better cope with real-life situations. Themes for problem-centered intervention groups range from dealing with physical or sexual abuse to coping with loss or adjustments such as parental death, separation, or divorce. Topics for problem-centered intervention groups include, but are not limited to, the following:

- *Obesity, bulimia, or anorexia nervosa* (Frey, 1984; Lokken, 1981)
- *Physical or sexual abuse* (Baker, 1990; Powell & Faherty, 1990)
- *Grief and loss* (McCormack, Burgess, & Hartman, 1988; Peterson & Straub, 1992; Thompson, 1993)
- *Aggressive behavior* (Amerikaner & Summerlin, 1982; Huey, 1987; Lane & McWhirter, 1992; Lawton, 1994; Prothrow-Stith, 1993; Reiss & Roth, 1992)
- *Divorce, loss, and separation* (Bonkowski, Bequette, & Boonhower, 1984; Bradford, 1992; Burke & Van de Streek, 1989; Cantrell, 1986; Gwynn & Brantley, 1987; Hammond, 1981; Omizo & Omizo, 1987)
- *Drug abuse prevention* (Berkowitz & Persins, 1988; Daroff, Marks, & Friedman, 1986; Sarvela, Newcomb, & Littlefield, 1988; Tweed & Ruff, 1991)
- *Teen pregnancy* (Blythe, Gilchrist, & Schinke, 1981; Thompson, 1987)

Group membership is targeted at youth who are currently having difficulty with a specific problem or are considered at-risk. Problem-focused groups frequently use media and structured activities to stimulate discussion of issues and to present relevant information (Bergin, 1993). Role-playing, homework, contracts, and journal writing enhance problem-solving and coping skills.

The group setting provides a secure arena to share anxieties, express feelings, and identify coping strategies. Members learn that their feelings are normal and that their peers share similar experiences. Bergin (1993, p. 2) stressed the concept of involvement, maintaining that the interactive process of the group affects members in a number of positive ways:

1. The group offers acceptance and support for each member and encourages mutual trust and the sharing of individual concerns.
2. The group's orientation to reality and emphasis on conscious thoughts leads members to examine their current thoughts, feelings, and actions and to express them in a genuine manner.
3. The group's overt attempt to convey understanding to each member encourages tolerance and acceptance of individual differences in personal values and goals.
4. The group's focus on personal concerns and behavior encourages members to consider alternative ways of behaving and to practice them within the context of a supportive environment.

CURATIVE AND THERAPEUTIC FACTORS

Hansen, Warner, and Smith (1980), Yalom (1985), and others have stressed the "curative" and "therapeutic factors" responsible for producing change in productive groups. The 11 primary factors that are highly visible in groups with children and adolescents are listed below:

Instillation of hope. Group members develop the belief that their problems can be overcome or managed. By learning new skills, such as listening, paraphrasing, and expressing empathy, the child or adolescent develops a stronger sense of self as well as a belief in the efficacy of the helping process, (i.e., that they have meaning and relatedness to their school, their community, and their families).

Universality. Group members overcome the debilitating notion that their problem is unique to them. Through mutual sharing of problems in a secure environment, the members discover a commonality of fears, fantasies, hopes, needs, and similar problems. Problems are no longer unique to them; they are universal and shared with others.

Imparting information. Group members receive new information as well as advice, suggestions, or direct guidance about developmental concerns. Advice-giving and advice-seeking behavior is central to the school counselor's role. When they receive specific information, children and adolescents feel more self-sufficient and in control of their own behavior. Vicarious learning also occurs in the group setting as children and adolescents observe the coping strategies of others.

Altruism. Group members offer support, reassurance, and assistance to one another. Adolescents become other-centered rather than self-centered, often rediscovering their self-importance by learning that they are of value to others. They feel a sense of purpose, and that others value their expertise. Altruism can extend from the group to the community to more global concerns, such as service learning projects to protect the environment, help the homeless, or assist the elderly.

The corrective recapitulation of the primary family group. The group environment promotes a mirror of experiences typical of one's primary family group. During the group experience, the focus is on the vitality of work in the here and now. Outside of the group experience, the adolescent may internalize behavior change and enhance more interpersonal skills.

Development of social skills. The development and rehearsal of basic social skills is a therapeutic factor that is universal to all counseling groups. Adolescents learn such skills as establishing relationships, refraining from critical judgment, listening attentively, communicating with empathy, and expressing warmth and genuineness. Once assimilated, these skills create opportunities for personal growth and more rewarding interpersonal interactions that are transferred to daily functioning at home, in school, or on the job.

Imitative behavior. Group members learn new behaviors by observing the behavior of the leader and other members. In training, the process of modeling serves to create positive behavior that the adolescent can assimilate (e.g., body language, tone of voice, eye contact, and other important communication skills). The learner not only sees the behavior in action but also experiences the effects of it.

Interpersonal learning. Within the social microcosm of the group, members develop relationships typical of their life outside the group. Group training facilitates self-awareness and interpersonal growth. Adolescents often come to a training program with distorted self-perceptions. These distortions can be the impetus of self-defeating behaviors, such as procrastination, unrealistic expectations, self-pity, anxiety, guilt, rigid thinking, ethnocentricity, psychological dependence, or an external locus of control. The nature and scope of the training process encourage self-assessment, risk taking, confrontation, feedback, goal setting, and decision making.

Group cohesiveness. Group membership offers participants an arena to receive unconditional positive regard, acceptance, and belonging, which enables them to fully accept themselves and be congruent in their relationships with others. The group community creates a cohesiveness, a "we-ness," or a common vision. Once a group attains cohesiveness with established norms, members are more receptive to feedback, self-disclosure, confrontation, and appreciation, making themselves more open to one another. An effective training process facilitates this component.

Emotional expression. Learning how to express emotions reduces the need for debilitating defense mechanisms. Sharing emotions and feelings diminishes destructive fantasy building and repressed anger and sets the stage for exploring alternatives to self-defeating behaviors.

Responsibility. As group members face the fundamental issues of their lives, they learn that they are ultimately responsible for the way they live, no matter how much support they receive from others. Contributions of the adolescent are validated, issues of personal responsibility and consequences are stressed, choice and the development of their potential are encouraged.

When observing the group process with children and adolescents, many of these therapeutic factors appear. The curative factors that emerge more consistently in child and adolescent groups are universality, instillation of hope, and interpersonal learning. For example, adolescents often feel that no one else has a problem as devastating as theirs. They are relieved when they realize that others share similar pain, such as feelings of abandonment or guilt regarding a parent's divorce or post-traumatic stress disorders from a recent traumatic loss. From that realization, adolescents gain a more hopeful perspective, believing that they, like their peers, can effect change, improve their conditions, or build their coping skills. This fosters personal empowerment. Rather than relying on the collective adolescent angst of blaming others or blaming the system, children and adolescents are provided with skills to enhance relationships and effect changes in themselves and others.

THERAPEUTIC INTENTIONS

Within the therapeutic relationship, counselors and therapists want to provide assistance effectively and efficiently. For the most part, counselors find themselves gathering information, exploring feelings, generating alternatives, or merely providing support in a secure environment.

Hill (1989) and Hill and O'Grady (1985) delineated between counselor intentions and response mode when developing interventions. *Intentions* are the plans and goals the counselor develops after analyzing input data from the client (i.e., presenting problem, diagnosis, behavioral observations, personal reactions, and clinical hypotheses). Intentions guide therapeutic interventions, or response modes. Thus, *response modes* refer to what counselors do, and intentions refer to why they do it (Hamer, 1995, p. 261).

Research by Kivlighan (1989, 1990), Kivlighan and Angelone (1991), and Hill, Helms, Spiegel, and Tichenor (1988) suggested five distinct intention clusters:

Set limits (*intention*: to assess, get information, focus, and clarify intentions)
Explore (*intention*: to assess cognitions, feeling, and behavioral domains)
Restructure (*intention*: to assess resistance, challenge, and insight)
Educate (*intention*: to give information)
Change and support (*intention*: to support and reinforce change)

Counselor intention in the therapeutic process recognizes that actions, motivation, and intention are interdependent and can affect the course of counseling and outcomes.

One means that counselors and therapists might use to clarify their intended purpose and to provide a focus for interventions could revolve around Hill and O'Grady's (1985) 18 therapeutic intentions:

- **Set limits.** To structure, make arrangements, establish goals and objectives of treatment, and outline methods.
- **Get information.** To elicit specific facts about history, client functioning, future plans, and present issues.
- **Give information.** To educate, give facts, correct misperceptions or misinformation, and give reasons for procedures or client behavior.
- **Support.** To provide a warm, supportive, empathetic environment; to increase trust and rapport so as to build a positive relationship; and to help the client feel accepted and understood.
- **Focus.** To help client get back on track, change subject, and channel or structure the discussion if he or she is unable to begin or has been confused.
- **Clarify.** To provide or solicit more elaboration; to emphasize or specify when client or counselor has been vague, incomplete, confusing, contradictory, or inaudible.
- **Hope.** To convey the expectations that change is possible and likely to

occur; to convey that the therapist will be able to help the client; to restore morale and build the client's confidence to make changes.

- **Catharsis.** To promote a relief from tension or unhappy feelings; to allow the client a chance to talk through feelings and problems.
- **Cognitions.** To identify maladaptive, illogical, or irrational thoughts or attitudes (e.g., "I must perform perfectly").
- **Behaviors.** To identify and give feedback on the client's inappropriate or maladaptive behaviors and the consequences of such; to do a behavioral analysis and point out discrepancies.
- **Self-control.** To encourage the client to own or gain a sense of mastery or control over his or her own thoughts, feelings, behaviors, or actions; to help the client become more appropriately internal in taking responsibility.
- **Feelings.** To identify, intensify, or enable acceptance of feelings; to encourage or provoke the client to become aware of deeper underlying feelings.
- **Insight.** To encourage understanding of the underlying reasons, dynamics, assumptions, or unconscious motivations for cognitions, behaviors, attitudes, or feelings.
- **Change.** To develop new and more adaptive skills, behaviors, or cognitions in dealing with self and others.
- **Reinforce change.** To give positive reinforcement about behavioral, cognitive, or affective attempts to enhance the probability of change; to provide an opinion or assessment of client functions.
- **Resistance.** To overcome obstacles to change or progress.
- **Challenge.** To jolt the client out of a present state; to shake up current beliefs, patterns, or feelings; to test for validity, adequacy, reality, or appropriateness.
- **Relationship.** To resolve problems; to build or maintain a smooth working alliance; to heal ruptures; to deal with dependency issues; and to uncover and resolve distortions.

STRUCTURED INTERVENTION: COLLECTIVE INITIATIVES

Waldo (1985) differentiated the curative factor framework when planning activities in structured groups.

In a 6-session structured group, activities can be arranged in relation to the group's development so that group dynamics can foster curative factors. The group can be structured as follows:

Session 1: Establish goals and ground rules (installation of hope) and share perceptions about relationships (universality).

Session 2: Identify feelings about the past, present, and future relationships (catharsis, family reenactment).

Session 3: Demonstrate understanding of other group members' feelings (cohesion).

Session 4: Allow feedback between group members (altruism).

Session 5: Allow confrontation and conflict resolution between group members (interpersonal learning).

Session 6: Plan ways group members can continue to improve relations with others; closure (existential factors).

Each session involves lectures and reading materials (imparting information), demonstrations by the leader (interpersonal learning), and within- and between-meeting exercises (social skills and techniques; Waldo, 1985, p. 56). This model provides a conceptual map that can be used in structured intervention groups on conflict resolution, decision making, interpersonal relations, or any intervention that teaches important life skills.

Once children and adolescents recognize that their problems are not unique but universal, they begin to feel obligations to other people. The "I" becomes strongly submerged in the "we." When youth reach this stage of interpersonal identity, they are able to enhance their own problem solving. By observing how a member discusses his or her needs or reliance on others, the counselor can help that person realize that it is possible to change behavior and to ask for support.

Psychoeducational groups can effectively meet the needs of young people if they are conducted with these parameters in mind:

1. Six to eight children or adolescents should meet for a maximum of 45 minutes at a time.
2. The chronological age difference in the group should not exceed 2 years.
3. The intellectual age should be controlled to prevent extremes (e.g., a gifted student and a special education student with severe handicapping conditions may not benefit from the same group experience).

The therapeutic intention is to build a caring program to support and assist youths who are experiencing problems. The group serves to provide a secure environment to share experiences, to express and experience conflicting feelings, and to share personal struggles and develop support systems.

Techniques and Strategies

In the remaining chapters are a compilation of counseling techniques and strategies that can be used during the life of the group. They are often experiential, to help children and adolescents process feelings and thoughts. They are not intended to be games or gimmicks but, rather, are structured activities for experiential learning. *Selected techniques* are useful for multimodal interventions. *Selected strategies* are useful for facilitating the group process. The techniques are ones that I have found to work well with children and adolescents. They provide structure for further exploration for members within the group setting.

Beginnings and Universal Concerns. Group members anonymously write on an index card a self-defeating behavior they would like to change. The leader collects the completed cards and redistributes them, instructing members to take any card but their own. Members read their new cards aloud and the group assigns a ranking of the presenting problem on a scale of 1 to 10 (1 = low/10 = high). The leader tallies the scores and ranks the problems. The highest rated problem is identified. The individual who wrote it is identified, and group work begins, focusing on the identified person's concern. One caveat is important here: The leader should assure group members that everyone's self-defeating behaviors are of equal importance. This exercise merely provides a gentle structure to begin the work of changing self-defeating behaviors that may inhibit personal growth.

Unfinished Statements. Completing unfinished statements about likes and dislikes, families and friends, or goals and wishes can help the counselor understand the group members, identify problem areas, and establish rapport. Selected unfinished statements follow:

My greatest fear is
The thing that creates the most difficulty for me is
The person in my family who helps me the most is
I used to bebut now I'm
The thing I would like people to admire me for is
The one thing I most want to accomplish is

Empty Chair. Empty chair is a role-playing technique involving the client and an individual who not present but with whom the client has a conflict. The client sits opposite an empty chair and begins a dialogue with the individual not present. Unresolved conflicts, unfinished business, or personal regrets are frequent themes.

Group Debriefing After Role-Playing. Debriefing after role-playing is an essential component of the process that often is overlooked. After role-playing, the group should join in a circle and each member, one at a time, should say, "I am not a, I am *your own name*." "I am not an expert know-it-all, I am Jessica Thompson." The counselor can follow this exercise by having group members perform a few mathematics drills or say their addresses three times fast to make the transition from role-playing to reality.

The Three Most Important People in Your Life. Have members identify "who were three important people in your life at age 5, 12, 16?" Then have them project into the future: "Who will be the most important people in your life?" This technique helps the counselor gain valuable insights into the members' worlds at various life stages, particularly in the dimension of psychological dependency, support networks, and resources available.

Writing a Letter Aloud. The leader asks a group member to write an oral letter right in the group. The recipient of the letter is an individual who is significant in the group member's life, someone with whom he or she has trouble relating or has an unresolved conflict, or someone who is deceased. The letter should contain whatever the group member would like to say that has not been previously said, the reasons for any existing bitterness, and how the relationship should change. When the letter has been completed, everyone in the group is invited to react and say what thoughts and feelings the letter elicited.

This technique is most appropriate when an individual has expressed a concern about a significant other that is troublesome, agonizing, bitter, or frustrating or has given considerable data about relationship difficulties and has expressed obvious frustration about the attitudes and abusive actions of another person (Dyer & Vriend, 1977).

Rewriting the letter is very important to demonstrate what the group member can say in a more positive and effective manner. The contrast in letters will actively demonstrate differences in effective and self-defeating thinking patterns. This is a very powerful tool (Dyer & Vriend, 1977).

I Take Responsibility for . . . . The purpose of this exercise is to help clients accept personal responsibility for their own feelings. Have a client make a statement out loud describing his or her own feelings, and then add "and I take responsibility for it." For example, if the client often feels helpless, he or she might say "I feel helpless, and I take responsibility for it." Other feelings that can be objects of this exercise are boredom, isolation, rejection, stupidity, feeling unloved, and so on.

I Have a Secret. This exercise can be used to explore fears, guilt, and catastrophic expectations. Group members are asked to think of some personal secret. They do not actually share the secret with others, but imagine themselves revealing the secret. They are to explore what fears they have about other people knowing their secret and how they imagine others might respond.

Playing the Projection. The purpose of this exercise is to demonstrate how often we see clearly in others qualities or traits that we do not want to see or accept within ourselves. Group members are to make a direct statement to each person in the group, and then apply that statement to themselves. For example, one member might say to another, "I think you are very manipulative." The same member would then say, "*I* am manipulative." "I don't think you really care about me" becomes, "*I* don't care about me." This technique serves to create a deeper awareness of one's own projections.

Reversal Technique. This exercise is useful when a group member has attempted to deny or disown a side of his or her personality. For example, a client who often plays the role of the tough guy might be covering up a gentle side. Or someone who is always excessively nice might be trying to deny or disown negative feelings toward others. Have members select one of their traits, then assume the opposite characteristic as fully as possible. Have clients process what the experience was like for them.

Here-and-Now Face. The here-and-now face is used to help group members disclose and discuss their feelings and emotions. The counselor should instruct members to draw a face that represents the feelings they are experiencing at the present. Below the face have them write a verbal description of those feelings and the reasons for them. The discussion should include both what the feelings are and why they exist. For example, "I am feeling . . . because . . . ." This exercise generates a discussion of the importance of feelings in their lives and brings the group into personal contact.

Life-Picture Map. Ask group members to draw an illustrated road map that represents their past, present, and future. The map should pictorially depict experiences the members have had, obstacles they have overcome, their present lives, their goals for the future, and the barriers that stand in the way of accomplishing those goals. Upon completion of the drawings, members share their maps with the group, explaining the various illustrations; finally, the experience is processed.

Paint a Group Picture. Divide the group into groups of four to eight, and supply these smaller groups with paper and markers. Ask them to paint a picture as a team that reflects the personality of the subgroup. The picture should be creative and integrate individual efforts. Members could also decide on a group name and sign the picture with it. (This also can be used in the classroom when building cooperative learning teams; see Chapter 8 for details.)

Break In. In this exercise, members are asked to stand in a tight circle, and one person is left outside the circle. The "outsider" attempts to penetrate the group in any way that he or she can. *Break in* can be used as a springboard for members to explore their feelings of being rejected, isolated, or "out of the group," either with the current group or in their own lives at the present. The use of "territoriality" to define ingroup-outgroup expectations also can be processed.

Meeting Someone Halfway. Divide the group into two sections at opposite sides of the room, facing each other. Members are instructed that, when they choose (or if they choose), they may walk out to the center of the room and wait for someone on the other side to join them. When the two meet, whatever communication they desire can take place—but all communication is to be nonverbal. Members should process their reactions to the experience and explore their relationship with the person who met them and those who did not.

Competitive Thumb Wrestling. This exercise is useful when the leader perceives that two members may be experiencing hidden aggression or hostility toward one another. Those involved should select their preferred hand and interlace their fingers, hooking their thumbs. One person then attempts to force the thumb of the other person down for a count of three. The leader assists in processing the feelings of hostility between members.

Territoriality and Group Interaction. After the group has been in session for a time, ask them to change seats. Process the issues of territoriality: Did they tend to arrange themselves in the same seating order? How did they feel when they saw someone else sitting in their territory? Ask members to diagram with arrows the interactions of a given period of group discussion. Discuss crosscurrents in the group. Who are isolates? Who are stars? Is there ease of communication, direct eye contact, and equal air-time?

Strength Bombardment. One group member volunteers to tell his or her personal strengths; the group responds by telling the strengths they see in that person. The member then asks, "What do you see that is preventing me from using my strengths?" The group responds again. Finally, group members construct a group fantasy in which they imagine what the focus member can be doing in five or more years if he or she uses his or her strengths to their full potential. The focus member reflects on this experience in the group.

I Am Becoming a Person Who . . . . Group members are given paper and pencils and are instructed to write their first names in large block letters on the top of the sheets. Then they are asked to complete the following sentence in as many ways as they can: "I am becoming a person who . . . " They silently mill around the room reading each other's sheets, then process the group session.

Map of Life. On sheets of newsprint, members draw maps of their lives, illustrating significant events. In an insert, they draw a map of the current week, up to the here and now. Each member explains his or her map to the group.

Think-Feel. Members are instructed to write on one side of an index card a sentence beginning with the phrase "Now I am thinking . . . " and on the other side a sentence beginning with "Now I am feeling . . . " Members are asked to process their thoughts and feelings from both sides of their cards.

Making the Rounds. In this exercise a person goes around the group and says something that is difficult to say. For example, a member might have mentioned that she doesn't trust the other group members enough to risk any self-disclosure. She may be given the opportunity to go around the group and say to each member: "I don't trust you, because . . . " or "If I were to trust you then . . . " The person making the rounds completes the sentence with a different ending for each group member. The purpose of the exercise is to give participants the experience of confronting a given fear and concretely stating that fear.

The Here-and-Now Wheel. This can be used as a closure activity to enable people to get in touch with the emotions they are feeling, to put a label on them, and to try to determine why they are feeling them. Have group members draw a circle on a piece of paper and divide the circle into four parts (four quadrants). In each part, they are to write a word that describes a feeling they have at the moment. The leader can ask for five volunteers to share their wheels with the entire group.

Unfinished Story. This is a counseling technique in which in an unfinished story is completed through role-playing or discussion or in writing to stimulate identification, personal information, or a group member's concerns.

The What-If Technique. This technique is used to get the client to project, imagine, or explore what it would be like if he or she could attain desired wishes, feelings, or behaviors.

Strength Test. An index card for each group member is passed around the group. The leader asks each member to write a positive strength for every group member on his or her card.

Group Reentry Questions. Group reentry questions help to establish the level of group rapport that has been developed, as well as positively enhance the self-concepts of group members. Here are some examples of group re-entry questions:

- What was the most exciting thing that happened to you in the last week? Over the weekend? Yesterday? What was the most exciting thing you did?
- Share with the group an experience in which you made someone happy.
- If you could be talented in something you are not talented in now, what would it be? Why? Is it something that would please you? Would it please others?

LIFE SKILLS TRAINING PARADIGM

Teaching a life skill session follows a five-step social learning model: instruction (teaching); modeling (showing); role-play (practicing); feedback (reinforcing); and homework (applying). Modeling, feedback, role-playing, instruction, situational logs, and homework assignments are used to reinforce desired behaviors.

Goldstein (1988) developed a training paradigm to help clients integrate life skills into their behavioral repertoire. The five-step model is outlined below. Steps are outlined according to what the trainer-as-facilitator should say and do.

1. **The trainer-as-group-facilitator presents an overview of the social, emotional, or cognitive skill.**

   - The trainer asks questions to help the members define the skill in their own language, such as *"Who can define _____ ?" "What does _____ mean to you?"*
   - The trainer then makes a statement about what will follow the modeling of the skill. *"After we see the examples, we will talk about times you have used the skill and about how you will use it in the future."*
   - The trainer distributes skill cards and asks a member to read the behavioral steps aloud.
   - The trainer asks members to follow each step as the skill is modeled

2. **The trainer-as-facilitator models the behavior following the steps listed on a flipchart or chalkboard.**

3. **The trainer-as-facilitator invites discussion of the skill that is being modeled.**

   - *"Did any of the situations you observed remind you of times that you had to use the skill?"*
   - He or she encourages a dialogue about skill usage and barriers to implementation.

4. **The trainer-as-facilitator organizes a role-play between main actor and co-actor.**

   - He or she designates one member as *main actor* (the individual who will be working on integrating a specific cognitive, emotional, or social skill such as assertiveness, impulse control, or problem solving).
   - He or she asks the main actor to choose a *co-actor* (someone who reminds the main actor of the person with whom would most likely use the skill). For example, *"Who in the group reminds you of _____ in some way?"*
   - He or she sets the stage for the role-play, providing props and furniture if necessary.
   - He or she asks questions such as, *"Where will you be talking?" "What will be the time of day?"*
   - He or she rehearses with the *main actor* what should be said and done during the role-play: *"What will be the first step of the skill." "What will you do if the co-actor does _____?"*
   - He or she provides final instructions to the main actor, *"Try to follow the steps as best you can,"* and to the co-actor, *"Try to play the part of _____ as best as you can by concentrating on what you think _____ would do when the main actor follows the steps."*
   - He or she designates the remaining members of the group as observers. Their role is to provide feedback to the main actor and the co-actor after the exercise.
   - He or she designates one group member to stand at the chalkboard or flip chart and point out each step.

5. **The trainer-as-facilitator coaches and prompts role-players when needed.**

6. **The trainer-as-facilitator elicits feedback from group members and processes after the exercise is completed.**

   - He or she instructs the main actor to wait until everyone's comments have been heard.
   - He or she allows the co-actor to processes his or her role, feelings, and reactions to the main actor.
   - He or she asks observers to report on how well the behavioral steps were followed; about specific likes and dislikes; and for comments on the roles of the main actor and co-actor.
   - He or she processes group comments with the main actor and asks the main actor to estimate how well he or she did in following the behavioral steps of the skill. For example, *"On a scale from 1 to 10, how satisfied were you about following the steps?"*

7. **The trainer-as-facilitator encourages follow-through and transfer of training. The main actor is assigned homework to practice and apply the skill in real life. Group members are assigned to look for situations relevant to the skill they might role-play during the next group meeting.**

   - He or asks the main actor how, when, and with whom might he or she attempt the behavioral steps prior to the next class meeting.
   - He or she assigns a "homework report" to get a written commitment from the main actor to try out the new skill and report back to the group at the next group meeting.
   - He or she directs members of the group to look for situations relevant to the skill that they might role-play during the next group meeting.

CONCLUSION

Before children and adolescents can change self-defeating behaviors, they need a secure environment to share their anxieties and developmental concerns. Small-group counseling provides this opportunity. Psychoeducational and problem-centered intervention groups provide the safety, security, and confidentiality that youth need. Group process fosters positive peer pressure that encourages youth to learn from each other, a process that has proven quite effective. Support groups bring a manageable solution to the dilemma of overwhelming numbers and devastating problems.

Finally, educators, counselors, therapists, helping professionals, and community volunteers from a variety of backgrounds can be excellent group leaders. With the appropriate training in skills such as problem solving, decision making, and conflict resolution, all those who interact within the school and community can be involved in delivering effective services in a genuinely caring and empathetic environment. It takes an entire community to raise a healthy child. Only collective involvement can provide enduring interventions in the well-being of our youth.

PART II
MANIFESTATIONS
OF BEHAVIORS
AND RELATED SKILLS

Chapter 4

ALCOHOL
AND OTHER DRUG ABUSE

> Tell the people to hear this. If they want to get rid of drugs, they
> better focus on the problem. Drugs just ain't the problem, man. Drugs
> is the crutch. Loneliness is the problem. Drugs is a way of getting
> away from the problem. (Baucom, 1989, p. 34)

The truth about drug use by contemporary youth is elusive. Self-reported data are sometimes of dubious validity, but they are an important source of information on substance use and abuse. *Monitoring the Future* (1993) addressed a broad array of research objectives, including measuring and explaining changes in drug use among American young people. At present, 50,000 8th-, 10th-, and 12th-graders in more than 400 schools are surveyed annually by the University of Michigan's Institute for Social Research.

Substance abuse among children and adolescents increased explosively in the 1960s and 1970s. Alcohol and drug use remain prevalent in this population group. Today, the United States has the highest incidence of alcohol and other drug abuse among adolescents of any country in the world (Anderson, Kinney, & Gerler, 1984). The research data reflect a number of concerns:

- In 1991, 88% of high school seniors had used alcohol, 37% had tried marijuana, and 8% had tried cocaine at least once (Brookman, 1993).
- In 1991, 4% of seniors reported daily use of alcohol, and 2% reported daily use of marijuana; more than 30% reported having five or more

drinks in one sitting at least once in the previous two weeks (Brookman, 1993).

- Substance abuse begins prior to 9th grade for one-third of those students who use alcohol, one-fourth who get drunk, one-third who smoke daily, and one-fourth who have tried marijuana (Brookman, 1993).
- Teenage drinkers account for nearly 50% of all fatal automobile accidents in the United States (Sherouse, 1985). Alcohol is a factor in nearly half of all accidental deaths, suicides, and homicides, and in 42% of all deaths from motor vehicle accidents.
- Children are beginning to use alcohol at an earlier age: The average beginning age today is 12.5 years, and children as young as 9 years old are being treated for alcoholism (Brookman, 1993).
- Sexually active teenagers are three to four times more likely to use substances than those who have not become sexually active (Brookman, 1993).

Chasnoff, Landress, and Barrett (1990) reported that about 14% of pregnant women who use drugs or alcohol cause permanent physical damage to a child during pregnancy; 400,000 children are born annually to mothers who used crack or cocaine; 5,000 children are born with fetal alcohol syndrome (Burgess & Streissguth, 1992; Hawks, 1993).

Research continues to show that drug use among children is 10 times more prevalent than parents suspect. In addition, many youth know that their parents do not recognize the extent of drug use, which leads them to believe they can use drugs with impunity.

Alcohol and substance abuse correlate significantly with school vandalism, absenteeism, tardiness, truancy, discipline problems, classroom disruptions, violence, declining academic achievement, dropout rates, and automobile-related deaths. Marijuana, the most frequently used illegal drug, can result in impaired psychomotor performance and impaired immediate recall. Passivity and loss of motivation also have been reported (Cohen, 1981). In addition, decreased pulmonary function, bronchitis, and sinusitis have been reported for frequent users (Millman & Botvin, 1983).

Alcohol continues to be the drug most frequently associated with violent crime. America's schools have assumed responsibility for primary prevention and intervention activities. Ironically, schools are perceived by both those who sell drugs and those who would prevent their sale as the single most important point of access to young people. Today, the activities of both groups intrude on instruction, discipline, and school safety.

PREDICTORS OF ALCOHOL AND DRUG USE

Family Factors

It is estimated that 28 million Americans have at least one addicted parent. Parental drug use is correlated with initiation of use of many substances, as is parental use of alcohol and other legal drugs. Children of alcoholics are four times more likely to become chemically dependent than the rest of the population. Research on family dynamics reveals that children of alcoholics suffer emotional damage, which may create a predisposition to alcoholism. In addition, children of chemically dependent parents have a high probability of marrying chemically dependent spouses (Berkowitz & Persins, 1988; Brook, Whiteman, & Gordon, 1983; Gravitz & Bowden, 1985).

Further, the self-esteem of children who grow up with alcoholism often is severely damaged. Children from alcoholic homes often have self-defeating expectations. For example, many criticize their accomplishments when they succeed. The enabling atmosphere in the alcoholic home can cause children to feel they must be perfect or their parents will not love them, or that what they do is never good enough. Years later, the grown child as employee experiences greater anxiety, stress, and dissatisfaction with self and performance that comes from feeling "not good enough" (Martin, 1988).

When there is a standard or a performance level to be met, children of alcoholics worry about their ability to meet that standard(as do children from any dysfunctional home environment). They reexperience their anxiety, their all-or-nothing thinking, their sense of inadequacy, their guilt, and their lack of self-esteem (Gravitz & Bowden, 1985). These are the children who have mastered the art of "looking good"—of concealing the reality of their lives by overachieving, striving for perfection—so that no one will suspect what they are really living with or without (Black, 1984).

Among the problems children of alcoholics seem to carry into adulthood are issues of control, difficulty expressing feelings and trusting others, issues related to guilt, compulsive behaviors, and an overdeveloped sense of responsibility (Gravitz & Bowden, 1985; Wilson & Blocher, 1990).

From another perspective, Goodman (1987) maintained that, although there can be little argument that some people growing up in alcoholic families are negatively affected by the experience, it is unwise to assume (1) that all people are affected in the same way; (2) that their experiences were necessarily negative; or (3) that these people, as adults, are psychologically maladjusted or in need of counseling or a recovery program. And one does well to remember that parental inconsistencies, double-bind messages, hidden feelings, incomplete information, shame, uncertainty, mistrust, and roles that stifle development and identity can be found in nonalcoholic families, too.

Family risk factors include parental absence, inconsistent discipline, poor communication, parental conflicts, and family breakup. Factors that place youth at risk include being latchkey children or coming from an abusive family, a single-parent family, a blended family, or a family with inconsistent rules for behavior (Black, 1984; Daroff, Marks, & Friedman, 1986; Harbach & Jones, 1995). However, Newcomb and Bentler (1990) found that family disruption per se does not lead directly to drug use; rather, family problems may lead to disenchantment with traditional values and to the development of deviant attitudes, which in turn lays the foundation for substance use or other high-risk behavior.

School Factors

A range of school problems—academic failure, poor performance, truancy, placement in a special education class, early dropping out, and a lack of commitment to education—are common antecedents to initiation, use, and abuse of alcohol and other drugs (Bahr, Marcos, & Maughan, 1995; Jessor & Jessor, 1978). Early antisocial behavior also has direct implications for substance abuse. Boys who are aggressive in kindergarten through 3rd grade are at higher risk for substance abuse. Beginning in the 4th, 5th, and 6th grades, academic failure increases the risk for both drug abuse and delinquent behavior. For the early elementary grades, it seems that social adjustment is more important than academic performance as a predictor of later delinquency and drug use.

Alcohol and other drug abuse is more likely to occur in students who do not care about their education or about going to college. As drug involvement increases, academic performance decreases. However, school problems themselves may not lead to drug use; rather, social factors that lead to poor school performance may be linked to drug involvement.

Peer Factors

Association with drug-using peers is perhaps the most strongly supported predictor of adolescent substance use (Bahr et al., 1995; Hawkins, Lishner, Catalano, & Howard, 1986). Youth who associate with peers who use drugs are much more likely to use drugs themselves. This is one of the most consistent predictors researchers have identified regarding experimentation and use. Even for children from well-managed families, simply being with friends who use drugs greatly increases the risk of drug use. Newcomb and Bentler (1989) suggested that modeling drug use, providing substances, and encouraging use are the most salient components of peer influence.

Influence of the Media

The average young adolescent in this country watches television 22 hours a week; some watch as many as 60 hours. By the time they reach 18, adolescents as a group will have logged more hours in front of the television than in the classroom. During this viewing time, the average adolescent will see about 1,000 murders, rapes, or aggravated assaults each year.

The young people who have the poorest chances in life watch more television than any adolescent group (Carnegie Foundation, 1990). Passive consumption of commercial television can lead to attention deficits, nonreflective thinking, irrational decision making, and confusion between external reality and packaged representation (Carnegie Foundation, 1990). Further, on television, perpetrators of violent acts go unpunished 73% of the time.

Alcohol and drug abusers have cited the media most frequently as their source of information (Aas, Klepp, Labert, & Aaro, 1995; Peters & Peters, 1984). Previous studies suggested that drug users learned about drugs from their friends and their own experiences (Sarvela, Newcomb, & Littlefield, 1988). Yet behaviors presented in the media can be interpreted as "the norm" by many viewers. Many movies, for example, imply that people use substances to better enable them to cope with stress or for recreation. The implications foster the belief that it is all right to use drugs (Redican, Redican, & Baffi, 1988).

Attitudes, Beliefs, and Personality Traits

Attitudes, beliefs, and personality traits closely linked with substance use include lack of attachment to parents, lack of commitment to education, and alienation from dominant societal norms and values (Bahr et al., 1995; Hawkins, Lishner, & Catalano, 1985; Hawkins, Lishner, Catalano, & Howard, 1986; Hussong & Chassin, 1994). Fields (1992) synthesized and correlated research descriptions of the personality traits and characteristics of alcohol and other drug abusers. These traits and characteristics included the following:

- High emotional arousal, anxiety, and panic attacks
- Low frustration tolerance

- Inability to express anger
- Difficulty with authority
- Low self-esteem
- Obsessiveness and compulsiveness
- Feelings of loneliness and isolation
- Dependence and possessiveness in interpersonal relationships
- Anger and hostility
- Rigidity and inability to adapt to change
- Simplistic, black-and-white thinking
- Depression

Psychosocial factors include external locus of control, low self-esteem, high need for social approval, low self-confidence, high anxiety, lack of assertiveness, and impulsivity (Forman & Neal, 1987).

Pulkinnen and Pikanen (1994) found different protective factors (variables that buffer against substance abuse) between males and females. Their research confirmed that school success and prosociality were protective factors against problem drinking for both males and females. Yet they found one factor that lead to widely different results in males and females: anxiety. For females it was a risk factor for problem drinking, while for males anxiety protected against problem drinking (Pulkinnen & Pikanen, 1994).

A high incidence of phobic and anxiety disorders also is found in substance abusers. A large number of chemically dependent persons experience panic attacks and high levels of psychopathology and report significant levels of distress and avoidance as a result of the panic. There is evidence that these individuals may be using alcohol primarily for self-medication (Cox, Norton, Dorward, & Fergusson, 1989).

Newcomb and Bentler (1990) studied substance abuse in adolescents as a response to perceived loss of control, a sense of meaninglessness, and a lack of direction in life. Teenagers may use drugs as a means of temporarily alleviating discomfort connected to life events that they perceive as being out of their control.

Finally, certain negative or perfectionist personality traits are associated with alcohol use among adolescents. Negative personality traits can be predictive of increased alcohol use (Newcomb, Bentler, & Collins, 1986). Alcohol and other drug use appears to be associated with pessimism, unhappiness, boredom, aggressiveness, frustration, impulsiveness, distrust, cynicism, rigidity, and dissatisfaction (Kozicki, 1986). In addition, **various studies** have pointed out that the rates for both suicide and suicide attempts are between 5 and 20 times greater for drug abusers than for the general population (Allen, 1985; Cox, Norton, Dorward, & Fergusson, 1989; Cruley, 1990; Hussong & Chassin, 1994).

Substance abusers usually have long histories of abuse, extremely strong defenses against change, and relatively little ability to follow through on commitments (Schneider & Googins, 1989).

Defense Mechanisms

Defense mechanisms are cognitive processes that individuals use to distance themselves from situations that are unpleasant, threatening, or anxiety-provoking. Defense mechanisms are generated automatically and unconsciously. For the chemically dependent, defense mechanisms become embedded in the illness and are used to block reality.

For example, denial becomes a defense mechanism when drug users become unable to recognize the unpleasant situations that result from their drug use. Even when adolescents face unhappy consequences of their chemical abuse, they often decide that the good feelings outweigh the consequences. They see the pain they are receiving from the drug use, feel bad momentarily, then regroup by using defense mechanisms such as making excuses, making promises, and rationalizing to continue their use (Brook, Whiteman, & Gordon, 1983). This dysfunctional cognitive process affects both them and their relationships.

Adolescents continually struggle with boundary and identity issues. The transition from adolescence to young adulthood is fraught with difficult decisions and important changes that set the direction for one's life. The stress of this life transition may contribute to the use of alcohol to relieve discomfort and anxiety (Newcomb, Bentler, & Collins, 1986).

Research on risk and resiliency factors indicates that substance use by youth is associated with multiple factors. Programs must be comprehensive and all-inclusive. Schools and communities must identify ways to integrate the prevention message into multiple service areas—including community agencies, health services, the courts, clergy, businesses, and education—to provide comprehensive services for youth and their families. Until the alcohol and drug problem is controlled, we cannot expect other adolescent problems—teen pregnancy, suicide, violence, poor academic performance, and juvenile crime—to diminish significantly.

Concurrently, providing awareness, information, and motivation to "just say no" is not enough. The goals of early intervention with children and adolescents should include these:

- Establish a warm and caring environment.
- Help children understand and express their feelings.
- Help children understand the effects of alcoholism on their families and on themselves.
- Promote friendships and reduce isolation.
- Generate openness to formal and informal help.
- Improve coping skills and reinforce new ways of expressing emotions (adapted from National Institute on Alcohol Abuse and Alcoholism, 1990, p. 86).

Substance abuse prevention programs that help youth develop social and emotional coping skills have received empirical support. The social and emotional approach views alcohol and other drug use as a socially learned behavior—having both purpose and function—that is the result of social and emotional factors.

Information, education, and skill-based training—such as training in assertiveness and decision-making skills—can help the adolescent make informed decisions about high-risk behavior such as substance abuse (McWhirter, McWhirter, & McWhirter, 1993). Dryfoss (1990) maintained that incorporating behavioral, cognitive, and affective strategies is important in prevention efforts. Drug-specific assertiveness training and peer-pressure refusal skills also seem to have a positive effect in reducing experimental drug use. Social skills training for adolescents has been associated with positive outcomes such as improved self-esteem, increased problem-solving and assertiveness skills, refusal of drugs, and refusal of sex (Thompson, Bundy, & Broncheau, 1995).

Botvin's (1983) *Life Skills Training (LST)* program encompassed affective, cognitive, and behavioral components, including short- and long-range consequences of use, critical thinking skills, decision-making skills, anxiety-coping skills, and social skills to resist peer pressure. The social inoculation model assumes that resistance to social pressures for substance abuse will be greater if the individual has been given experience in a controlled setting with social pressures.

The LTS program (Botvin 1983) teaches general life skills as well as skills specifically related to substance abuse and other self-defeating behaviors. The 10-week training sessions consist of five major components:

1. **Cognitive:** presenting information concerning short- and long-term consequences of substance abuse, prevalence rates, social acceptability, and the process of becoming dependent on tobacco, alcohol, and marijuana.
2. **Decision-making:** addressing the process of critical thinking and decision making.
3. **Anxiety management:** providing youth with cognitive and behavioral techniques such as imagery and physical relaxation to cope with anxiety.
4. **Social skills training:** including general social and communication skills and assertiveness training, which can be used to resist peer pressure.
5. **Self-improvement:** providing youth with the principles of behavioral self-management and improving self-esteem.

LST can be conducted by counselors, peer leaders, teachers, administrators, or community agencies.

Figure 4.1 provides a developmental perspective on adolescent alcohol and drug abuse.

STRUCTURED INTERVENTIONS
FOR HIGH-RISK BEHAVIORS

Therapeutic Initiatives

Therapeutic intervention can be informational, educational, or more comprehensive, depending on the climate and resources within the school, the home, and the community. Often, intervention focuses on the concept of *enabling.* Enablers are those who allow drug problems to continue or worsen by preventing the drug user from experiencing the consequences of his or her actions in order to enhance, maintain, or promote the enablers' sense of well-being (Anderson, 1987).

> Enabling is camouflaging addiction by telling family, friends, employers, or neighbors that the addicted person has some malady (e.g., the flu, a migraine, a cold) to explain why that person was absent from school, work, or a social occasion; taking upon themselves the major responsibilities of running a household or a business or an office; becoming acutely responsive to the addictive person's mood swings; rescuing the addicted person by driving when that person is incapable; cleaning up after they have become sick from drinking; bailing that person out of jail, then minimizing the situation, telling oneself "Things could be worse." (Storti, 1988, p. 13)

Developmental Task: Physical Maturation

Prominent developmental issues: Physical development is erratic and some-times traumatic. Adolescents often feel insecure, ugly, or gawky

AODA effects on adolescent health: Vitamin depletion, AIDS, hepatitis, lung problems, overstressed physical system, impaired hormone secretion (cocaine), loss of muscle tone due to lethargy and lack of exercise.

Developmental Task: Cognitive Growth

Prominent developmental issues: Abstract thinking and reasoning begin to emerge. Adolescents begin to generate ideas of their own; more thoughts about the future; flexible thinking, systematic problem solving strategies, and process information from a variety of outside sources.

AODA effects on adolescent cognitive development: Delayed, impaired, distorted.

Developmental Task: Membership in Peer Group

Prominent developmental issues: Adolescents often turn to friends for acceptance and reassurance. The peer group provides security, gives support to challenge authority, follows group code and standards.

AODA effects on the peer group: Peer pressure, diminished judgment; conflicts in interpersonal interactions with families and friends; increased risk-taking behavior; proclivity to act without considering consequences.

Developmental Task: Sexual Relationships

Prominent developmental issues: Increased dating becomes the focus of social life. Adolescents experience such emotions of anxiety, curiosity, confusion, pride, embarrassment, and stress; values may conflict or need to be clarified; peer interactions often revolve around flirting, teasing, approach and avoidance issues.

AODA effects on sexual relationships: Reduces impulse control; promiscuity increases; AIDS, sexually transmitted diseases, pregnancy, and suicide (because of love loss) increase under the influence of alcohol and other drugs.

Developmental Task: Autonomy and Differentiation from Family

Prominent developmental issues: Conflict may emerge as a result of discrepancies among the adolescent's need to be assertive and independent, his or her skills and resources available to achieve independence, and parental perceptions and expectations. Control issues revolve around money, curfew, rules, decisions, and consequences. Defiance, anger, frustration, criticism, and self-doubt emerge from the tension of autonomy.

AODA effects on autonomy. Diminishes potential; clouds thinking; generates stress around trust issues; impedes this developmental task.

Developmental Task: Internalized Belief and Value System

Prominent developmental issues: Adolescents begin to select standards, values, and beliefs from among many systems in their environment to internalized for themselves.

AODA effects on internalized belief and value system: Adolescent feels guilty, becomes defensive, rationalizes use, drops out, or creates distorted systems to struggle against or succumb to.

Developmental Task: Academic Achievement and Career Choice

Prominent developmental issues: Social and family pressures revolve around being part of the "in" group, pressure for scholastic achievement, pressure to stay in school, and pressure to make decisions about one's future.

AODA effects on academic achievement and career choice: Interferes with academic progress; reduces motivation; preoccupation with alcohol and other drugs may distort values and alter priorities; damages reputation and alters self-image.

Figure 4.1. Effects of Alcohol and Other Drug Abuse (AODA) on Adolescent Social, Emotional, and Cognitive Development

The solution to the disease involves education, intervention, and follow-up support. It is important to *carefront* the person--sharing concerns without lecturing, threatening, or berating the individual. Intervention often involves a team of people close to the individual who share the same concerns; who want the individual to regain control of his/her life. After treatment, it is critical that a support group becomes available to prevent alcohol or drug relapse.

Interventions can involve collaborative partnerships between community agencies such as the local community services board, office of youth services, and the health department, and public/private partnerships with organizations that foster the well-being children and adolescents. The current climate in most cities across the nation is one of collaboration. It is important to share the responsibility when nurturing young people. What follows are counseling treatment and session plans for structured interventions for high-risk behaviors, including a multimodal treatment plan. The chapter concludes with a section outlining primary prevention initiatives.

Treatment Plan: Stress Management.
Counseling Intention: To manage the situation causing the stress (problem-focused coping) and relieve or regulate the emotional responses associated with the stress (emotion-focused coping).

Session 1: Introductions and overview of the manifestations of stress and coping skills

Session 2: Deep breathing, muscle relaxation, and positive imagery exercises

Session 3: Exercise and physical fitness; deep breathing and simple yoga exercises for muscle relaxation

Session 4: Time management and systematic organization; role-play assertiveness and how to say "no"

Session 5: Identifying situations that enable self-defeating behavior; setting boundaries in relationships; discussing the difference between assertiveness and aggression

Session 6: Handling anger through patience; life skill practice; role-playing appropriate and inappropriate anger responses to various experiences

Session 7: Dealing with feelings and expressing emotions

Session 8: Getting social support from friends and family

Session 9: Problem solving and decision making; brainstorming creative strategies for coping with stressful situations

Treatment Plan: Education Group.
Counseling Intention: To provide a follow-up for violations of drug policies; to determine the student's involvement with drugs; to contract with the

student and parents for "no use" of drugs; to offer a structured curriculum that will provide the following:

- Information about the health risks and legal, social, and emotional effects of drug use
- Decision-making skills
- Communication skills
- Support for becoming drug free
- Peer pressure refusal skills

The group was structured into seven sessions, covering the following:

Session 1: Introductions and getting acquainted; establishing group rules

Session 2: History of alcohol or other drug use; stages of adolescent alcohol and drug use

Session 3: Reasons for using chemicals; identifying relationship between feelings and chemical use

Session 4: Defense mechanisms; identifying defenses related to alcohol and other drug

Session 5: Learning about the family illness of alcohol or other drug dependency; identifying consequences of use; identifying youth affected by family chemical dependence; understanding effects of chemical dependence on the family

Session 6: Working with feelings; dealing with anger

Session 7: Evaluation and closure; final personal assessment; developing plans and goals

Treatment Plan: Aftercare Group.
Counseling Intention: To provide care to children or adolescents who have finished a recovery program, to support their drug-free lifestyle, and to prevent relapse.

One of the most difficult transitions for adolescents is leaving their drug-using friends and establishing new relationships. Essentially, recovering abusers must change their "playmates and their playground" and forge new, healthy relationships.

Session 1: Introductions and getting acquainted; establishing group goals

Session 2: Problem solving regarding recovery issues (i.e., staying sober and staying clean)

Session 3: Exploring a sober lifestyle; peer-pressure refusal skills

Session 4: Identifying symptoms of sobriety; planning relapse prevention; establishing a buddy system for support and understanding; warning signs of relapse (HALT = Hungry, Angry, Lonely, Tired)

Session 5: Covering the 12 steps of Alcoholics Anonymous; feedback and self-disclosure

Session 6: Exploring family illness, codependency, and enabling behaviors

Session 7: Learning stress management and relaxation techniques; establishing an exercise regimen

Session 8: Planning for wellness; developing action plans and support networks; integrating new behaviors

Session 9: Closure; opportunities for support group meetings

Treatment Plan: Multimodal Profile for Substance Abuse.

Counseling Intention: To provide a more comprehensive intervention for substance abuse prevention.

Lazarus (1981) provided the following profile:

Modality	Problem	Proposed Treatment
Behavior	Excessive drinking	Aversive imagery and other self-control procedures
	Avoids confronting most people	Assertiveness training
	Negative self-statements	Positive self-talk
	Always drinks to excess when alone at home at night	Change stimulus conditions by developing social outlets
Affect	Holds back anger (except with her siblings)	Assertiveness training
	Anxiety feelings	Self-hypnosis with positive imagery
	Depression	Increase range of positive reinforcement
Sensation	Butterflies in stomach	Abdominal breathing exercises
	Pressure at back of head	Relaxation of neck muscles
Imagery	Vivid pictures of parents fighting	Desensitization
	Beatings from father	Retaliation images
	Being locked in bedroom as a child	Images of escape and/or release of anger
Cognition	Irrational self-talk about low self-worth	Disputing irrational ideas
	Numerous regrets	Elimination of categorical imperatives (remove "shoulds," "musts," "oughts")
Interpersonal relationships	Ambivalent responses to parents and siblings	Possible family therapy and specific training in the use of positive reinforcement
	Secretive and suspicious	Discussion and training in greater self-disclosure
Drugs/ biological	Self-medicating; using alcohol as anti-depressant and as a tranquilizer	If necessary ask M.D. about anti-depressants

Collective Community Initiatives

Positive relationships that emerge in one's life are dependent on the critical life skills that children and adolescents learn during the developmental process. For example, helping professionals need to stress communication skills and effective cooperation as critical educational goals. Group dynamics, techniques, and strategies can facilitate relationship skills among members of a group. The following activities are useful for support groups for youth. With some basic training in communication skills, process skills, and the developmental needs of children and adolescents, other adults can be on the *team for youth empowerment*.

CONCLUSION

Today, children and adolescents are endangered primarily by their own behavior. As children grow into adolescence, they become increasingly at risk for ever-more-complex problems. Among adolescents, the three major causes of death (accidents, homicide, and suicide) and the major causes of serious illness or disability (sexually transmitted disease, unintended pregnancy, depression, and nonfatal accidents) often are caused by a cluster of risk-taking behaviors, particularly the use of alcohol and other drugs. Studies demonstrate that alcohol and other drug abuse correlates significantly with school vandalism, truancy, absenteeism, tardiness, delinquency, violence, irresponsible sexual activity, teen pregnancy, running away, poor academic performance, and automobile-related deaths. This high-risk behavior emanates from such illusive variables as low self-esteem, poor family support, poor relationship skills, immaturity, low frustration tolerance, problems with communication, and problems with authority.

Both prevention and intervention programs need to be directed at enhancing social, emotional, and cognitive deficits of youth. It is important to recognize that no single strategy or technique has demonstrated long-range implications (Wallack & Corbett, 1990). Broadly based school- and community-level prevention and intervention programs must involve a wide variety of agencies and institutions, target multiple subpopulations, and provide multiple interventions aimed at reducing risk factors and enhancing resiliency factors. Comprehensive programs must be of long duration in order to realize significant change. The importance of prevention and early intervention cannot be overemphasized.

SOCIAL, EMOTIONAL, AND COGNITIVE SKILLS

If we are to help today's youth develop the social, emotional, and cognitive skills they need, we must focus on significant developmental issues such as the need to belong, the need to clarify values, the need to make good decisions, and the need to resolve conflicts. What follows is a series of exercises helping professionals can use with young people to help them develop the skills they need to prevent high-risk behaviors.

Social Literacy Skills

Social literacy skills, which are essential for constructive interpersonal interaction, are significantly lacking for many of today's youth. Social skills are interpersonal skills such as the ability to know one's feelings and inner experiences and the capacity for handling relationships skillfully. Social skills are those behaviors that, within a given situation, predict important social outcomes such as peer acceptance, popularity, self-efficacy, competence, and high self-esteem. Social skills fall into categories such as being kind, cooperative, and compliant to reduce defiance, aggression, and antisocial behavior; showing interest in people and socializing successfully to reduce behavior problems associated with withdrawal, depression, and fearfulness. Social skills include problem solving, assertiveness, thinking critically, resolving conflict, managing anger, and utilizing peer pressure refusal skills.

(*Note*: **Permission is granted to reproduce skills boxes for individual client use.**)

How to Say "No" and Still Keep Your Friends

Reverse the peer pressure with statements such as these:

"Drugs are boring. I can't believe you want to do that stuff."

Excuse yourself. Let personal obligations excuse your presence: *"I can't drink; I'm in training for football."* Or, *"I can't go with you, I have a concert and I have to rehearse."*

Give the person the cold shoulder; act preoccupied or ignore him or her.

Avoid places where drugs or alcohol are being used. Hang out with nonusers.

If pressure seems too threatening, walk away.

Learn to say "no" repeatedly: *"Want a drink?"* *"No, thanks."* *"C'mon!"* *"No thanks."* *"Not even a sip?"* *"Nope."*

Allude to the unhealthy effects: *"No. Drugs are illegal and unsafe."*

Change the subject: *"No thanks. By the way, are you going to Janice's party Saturday night?"*

Return the challenge: *"What's wrong? Scared to do it by yourself?"*

Put the blame on someone else: *"No thanks. I don't want to get into trouble with my parents, coach, stepmother, etc."*

Blame yourself: *"No thanks, I usually end up getting stupid."* *"No thanks, drinking makes me tired."* *"No thanks. I want to keep a clear head."* *"No thanks, it's just not me."* *"No thanks, I just don't drink."* *"No thanks."*

Peer-Pressure Refusal Skills

Children and adolescents need skills in refusing peer pressure. High-risk behaviors can include drinking, drugs, or premature sexual activity. A list of responses follows:

Invent a routine excuse: *"I have to be at work at . . . "*

Use delay tactics: *"I'm not ready."*

Walk away and avoid the situation.

Shift the blame and try to make the pressure group feel guilty.

Act ignorant about how to do something.

Identify other things that are more important to do at the moment.

Get away from the situation as soon as possible.

Take control of the situation: *"I don't want to get high. I want to meet my girlfriend at the movies."*

Ask them to justify why you should do what they want you to do. *"What is in it for me?"*

Resisting Peer Pressure

This program involves five steps and can be used for high-risk situations that involve alcohol, drugs, or sex.

Step 1. Ask questions regarding the proposed activity to avoid potential trouble.

> Risk Proposer: *"Let's go over to my brother's apartment after school."*
> Risk Resister: *"What are we going to do over there?"*
> Risk Proposer: *"Well, my brother and his roommate are away."*
> Risk Resister: *"So?"*
> Risk Proposer: *"I thought we'd raid his fridge for beer and wine coolers."*

Step 2. Name the crime and identify the consequences.

> Risk Resister: *"That's illegal; we could lose our licenses just having the stuff in our possession, even if we aren't driving in a car."*

Step 3. Suggest an alternative activity.

> Risk Resister: *"Lets go over to rent some movies instead."*
> A response such as this says that the friendship is important but the high-risk activity is not.

Step 4. Walk away, but leave the door open for the risk proposer.

> Risk Proposer: *"No, I don't think so, that sounds pretty lame."*
> Risk Resister: *"If you change your mind, I'll be home around four. I'm going to rent . . ."*

This response suggests an alternative that is positive, and saves face on the part of the risk resister.

Defusing Anger

1. Let the person vent, uninterrupted.

2. Relax and go with the flow. Above all, don't become defensive.

3. Paraphrase. In your own words, repeat back to the person what you understood him or her to say.

4. Try to solve it together; compromise.

5. Keep listening.

6. Keep talking.

7. Keep seeking a solution.

Formula for Attentive Listening

C - H - O - I - C- E - S

C is concentrating: focus completely on the individual's concerns; listen attentively; maintain eye contact.

H is hearing totally and completely: ask for feedback to check for understanding.

O is being open: listen for the "unspoken" words; listen for the feelings behind the words.

I is insisting on listening critically: think about the content.

C is comparing: read gestures and body language; check for accuracy; ask direct, open questions.

E is emphasizing: learn to provide feedback with an emphasis on *feeling* and on *content.*

S is sensing: ask questions to listen actively; check for understanding; use silence diplomatically; become an expert in paraphrasing and summarizing what others say.

Sending an Effective Message

If an individual's needs are known, problems or conflicts can be confronted without making others feel defensive. Confirming expectations and feelings involves three parts:

1. owning feelings
2. sending feelings
3. describing behavior

Ownership of feelings focuses on *behaviors and expectations.* The communication formula for sending feeling messages looks like this:

Ownership + Feeling Word + Description of Behavior = Feeling Message

For example: *"I (*ownership) *am nervous* (feeling word) *about fulfilling the requirements of this course* (description of behavior)."* Such feeling messages promote open communication.

Behavioral descriptions provide feedback about the other person's behavior without evaluating it.

"I" messages honestly express feelings and place the responsibility on the sender. They reduce the other person's defensiveness and resistance to further communication. Behavioral descriptions also provide feedback about the other person's behavior without evaluating it.

When you want to modify another person's behavior, "I" messages let the other person know (1) how his or her behavior makes you feel and (2) that you trust him or her to respect your needs by modifying the behavior appropriately. "You" messages tell people they are not responsible for changing their behavior, while "I" messages make it clear that such responsibility rests with the persons who receive the message rather than with the sender.

Using an "I" Message to Change Behavior

Identify the unacceptable behavior. Without blaming, describe what the other person says or does that you find unacceptable. (Do not make inferences about the person's motives, character, or personality.)

Explain the effects. Describe in factual, observable ways how the person's behavior is affecting you adversely.

Describe congruent feelings. Describe your feelings about the effects of the other's behavior on you. *"I want to continue car pooling, but when you are late, I am late, and that gets me into trouble with my boss. He's a stickler about being on time."*

Responding Assertively Using the "I" Message

The use of "I" messages is especially beneficial for responding assertively and for resolving interpersonal conflicts. Alberti and Emmons (1986) developed the following three-step empathetic/assertive response model:

1. Let the person know you understand his or her position: *"I know it's not your fault."*

2. Let the person know your position (what the conflict is): *"But, I ordered my steak well-done not medium-rare."*

3. Tell the person what you want or what you plan to do: *"I would like you to take it back and have it cooked some more."*

The communication formula for an assertive response is this:

"I know (their position) *but* (your position) *and* (what you want)."

Emotional Literacy Skills

The model of emotional literacy was first proposed by Salovey and Mayer (1990). Emotional literacy skills are intrapersonal abilities such as knowing one's emotions by recognizing a feeling as it happens and monitoring it; managing emotions (i.e., shaking off anxiety, gloom, irritability, and the consequences of failure); motivating oneself to attain goals, delay gratification, stifle impulsiveness, and maintain self-control; recognizing emotions in others with empathy and perspective taking; and handling interpersonal relationships effectively. Emotional skills fall into categories such as knowing the relationship between thoughts, feelings, and actions; establishing a sense of identity and acceptance of self; learning to value teamwork, collaboration, and cooperation; regulating one's mood; empathizing; and maintaining hope.

Indications of troubled youth are all too familiar: school dropouts, drug abuse, unintended pregnancy, crime, violence, and suicide. Contemporary youth are confronted indiscriminately with a number of critical issues and decisions without the practice of critical social, emotional, and cognitive skills. Solutions lie within the combined efforts of the entire community—children and families, schools and institutions, and business and industry. Collective efforts are an investment with multiple returns.

(*Note*: **Permission is granted to reproduce skills boxes for individual client use.**)

Handling Stress Effectively

1. **Work it off.** Hard physical activity—sports, running, working out, karate—is a good outlet.

2. **Talk it out.** Share your feeling of being overwhelmed and stressed with others. Sometimes another person can help you get a new perspective on your problem and suggest coping strategies.

3. **Learn to accept what you cannot change.** Modify your expectations about people and situations: If you have no expectations, you won't be disappointed.

4. **Avoid self-medication,** such as alcohol or over-the-counter drugs. The ability to cope with stress comes from developing strategies that work for you.

5. **Get enough sleep and rest.** Eat the right foods and schedule "down time" to give your mind some space and distance from stressful situations.

6. **Do something for others.** Another way of getting your mind off your own problems is to help someone else.

7. **Take one thing at a time.** Don't over-obligate yourself. This creates even more demands that may be out of your control. Distance yourself from stressful environments.

8. **Make yourself available.** Don't isolate yourself from others and feel sorry for yourself. You aren't the only one experiencing stress.

Carefrontation

People need to hear you care about their well-being. It must be a genuine concern if confronting is to be effective; hence, a better term is *carefronting*. State the behavior, how you feel, and then reiterate your caring and concern:

- *"The concerns I have about you are because I care about you and our relationship."*

- *"I care about you too much to let this go and not say anything about what I see happening."*

Other guidelines include these:

Maintain a sense of calm. Be simple and direct. Speak to the point. Don't become emotional. It is all right to show your feelings, but anger should not be directed at the person.

Keep on the subject and be specific. Talk about the problem and specific ways it has affected the person's behavior.

Be prepared for promises, excuses, and counter-accusations, especially when confronting drinking behavior. Denial and resistance to receiving help may occur.

Ask permission.

Gently point out discrepancies in the person's thoughts, feelings, or actions.

Help identify important relationships and behavioral patterns that promote self-defeating behavior.

For example: *"Doug, can I share something about you that I'm concerned about?"* If Doug says yes, proceed. *"Every Monday you tell me that you aren't going to drink on the weekends anymore, but by Friday you have already connected with someone to buy you beer. I care about you, and I don't want you to become dependent."*

Describing Feelings and Empathizing

Describing feelings is putting your emotional state into words so that others can understand what you are experiencing.

1. Get in touch with the feelings you are experiencing. Identify them specifically (e.g., anger, embarrassment, helplessness, hopelessness).

2. Acknowledge and confirm those feelings.

3. Make a statement that contains the emotion you feel.

4. Share the feeling and your reaction. *"I felt rejected and alone when you broke your date with me."*

Empathizing is identifying what someone else is feeling and responding to it as if the feeling were your own.

1. Listen attentively to what the person is saying and try to understand the feeling behind the words.

2. Imagine what you would feel in the same situation.

3. Respond with the appropriate feeling words to share your own sensitivity to the person's circumstance:

"I feel so stupid in Herr Bradshaw's class, everyone is passing his German vocabulary test but me."

"Yeah, I understand the feeling. I had to stay after school a couple days last year to really catch on to what he wanted in class. I felt embarrassed."

Self-Disclosure

Self-disclosure is sharing personal thoughts, feelings, or experiences that are unknown to another person. Self-disclosure enhances interpersonal relationships if it reciprocated. Refrain from revealing intimate self-disclosures to short-time acquaintances.

1. Determine the level of risk. On a scale of 1 to 10, how risky is the information you will disclose?

2. If appropriate, move to a deeper level of self-disclosure.

3. Continue self-disclosure only if it is reciprocated by the other person.

4. Understand that everyone shares personal information differently.

For example, while being pressured to try cocaine, Bill responds, *"You know my stepfather is not my real dad. My real dad is doing time for dealing and doing drugs. I don't want to end up like him."*

Supporting

Supporting is a communication skill to help people feel better about themselves by soothing and reducing tension.

1. Listen to the message the person is sending, for the feelings behind the words.

2. Try to empathize with the person's feeling, try to walk in their shoes.

3. Paraphrase the other person's feelings.

4. Support them by indicating your willingness to be of help if possible.

For example: *"I've been on my fifth interview and I have yet to find a job."* Or, *"I can understand your disappointment; you've really worked hard. Let's practice an interview session and I'll record it. Then, we can play it back and see how you look in an interview situation."*

Expressing Anger

There is a special formula for expressing anger. It goes like this:

"I feel . . . when this happens . . . I would feel better if this would happen . . . "

Stressful Coping Statements

Upcoming stressful events can be broken down into stages: (1) preparing, (2) confronting, (3) coping, and (4) positive self-statements. The following stress coping statements for each stage can be used, modified, or developed:

Preparing

- I've succeeded with this before.
- I know I can do each one of these tasks.
- I'll jump in and be all right.
- Tomorrow I'll be through it.
- Don't let negative thoughts creep in.

Confronting

- I'm ready; I'm organized.
- Take it step by step, don't rush.
- I can do this, I'm doing it now.
- I can only do my best.
- Any tension I feel is a signal to use my coping exercises.
- I can get help if I need it.
- It's okay to make mistakes.

Coping

- Relax now; breathe deeply.
- There's an end to it.
- I can keep this with limits I can handle.
- I've survived this and worse before.
- Being active will lessen the fear.

Positive Self-Statements

- I did it right. I did it well.
- Next time, I won't have to worry as much.
- I am able to relax away anxiety.
- I've got to tell . . . about this.

Reflective Listening

Reflective listening is mirroring back to another person what he or she has said. To reflect back what was heard, use phrases such as these:

"Sounds like . . . "

"In other words . . . "

"What I hear you saying is . . . "

"Let me see if I understand this correctly . . . ?"

When you paraphrase, try to reflect both the content and the feeling the individual is trying to convey. The following formula is useful: *"Sounds like you feel . . . because . . . "*

This is a perception-checking technique that allows you to confirm or correct information that is presented. For example: *"Sounds like you feel frustrated because no one seems to understand how important it is to do this job right."*

Resent, Request, Appreciate

This is a highly structured technique that is particularly useful in cases of disagreement or conflict. The strategy consists of three steps: sharing resentment, request, and appreciation. First, in writing each person responds to each area.

Resentment. Each participant states what he or she dislikes about the other and outlines specific things that have been done to cause the resentment.

Request. Each participant tells the other what can be done to solve the problem.

Appreciate. Each participant identifies a quality they like or find admirable in the other.

For example: *"I resent when you come late to class. I requested that you leave earlier so we can get started and finish on time. I appreciate your sense of humor and your willingness to listen."*

Diffusing Anger in Others

The ability to diffuse anger can help prevent conflict from escalating into violence. In a potentially explosive situation, try not to overreact or take the issues personally. First, let the person verbalize and express his or her anger; don't debate, argue, interrupt, or bring up past experiences—just listen. Second, as you listen try to understand the person's perspective. Put yourself in his or her shoes. Third, paraphrase in your own words what you understood the person to say. The formula is as follows:

- **Listen**: Let the angry person verbalize. Don't argue or interrupt

- **Paraphrase content and feeling:** Make sure the other person knows you understand.

- **Problem solve and compromise:** Explore what can be done to make things better; try to compromise so that everyone's needs can be met.

Dealing with Anger

Here are some things to try when you are angry:

- Say something positive, if possible.

- Use appropriate internal dialogue and positive self-talk.

- Express how you feel and why.

- Ask to discuss how to solve the problem.

Seven Skills for Handling Conflict and Anger

There are seven skills that can be used when you are angry and in conflict. It is important to RETHINK to gain control of the situation:

1. **R**ecognize when you feel angry. Recognize what makes your parents, friends, or siblings angry. Recognize when anger covers up other emotions such as fear, stress, anxiety, embarrassment, or humiliation.

2. **E**mpathize with the other person. Try to see the other person's point of view; step into their shoes. Learn to use the "I" message: *"I feel . . . because . . . "*

3. **T**hink about it. Anger comes from our perceptions of situations or events. Think about how you interpreted what the other person said. What can you tell yourself about what you feel? Can you reframe the situation to find a constructive solution?

4. **H**ear what the other person saying to understand where he or she is coming from. Show that you are listening by establishing eye contact and giving feedback.

5. **I**ntegrate love and respect when expressing your anger. For example, *"I'm angry with you, but I want us to be friends."*

6. **N**otice your body's reaction when you are angry. How can you gain control of your behavior, and how can you calm yourself?

7. **K**eep your attention in the hear and now. Do not bring up the past. Bringing up the past is disrespectful (*Source*: Adapted with permission from *RETHINK,* p. 4, © 1995 by the Institute for Mental Health Initiatives, 4545 42nd Street, N.W., Suite 311, Washington, DC 20016).

Using Positive Self-Statements

When the conflict is resolved or coping is successful, be sure to give yourself positive feedback:

- I handled that one pretty well. It worked!

- That wasn't as hard as I thought it would be.

- I could have gotten more upset than it was worth.

- I actually got through that without getting angry.

- I guess I've been getting upset for too long when it wasn't even necessary.

Source: R. Novaco (1975). Anger control: The development and evaluation of an experimental treatment. In M. McKay, M. Davis, & P. Fanning (Eds.), *Thoughts and Feelings*. Reprinted with permission by New Harbinger Publications, Inc., Oakland, California.

Chapter 5

UNINTENDED PREGNANCY AND HIGH-RISK SEXUAL ACTIVITY

"It's harder than I expected it would be. Harder. I'm 18 now and pretty soon I'll be on my own . . . I want to go to college. I have to find somebody to keep my kids. And plus, I have to work—with two kids."

—Lakeisha, 18, mother of a 2-year-old son and an infant daughter

"She's 99% my responsibility and not 1% his . . . I assumed he would be there like every day . . . I'd really like him to get a job and help out with some money."

—Rachel, 17, mother of an infant daughter

While statistics on sexual behavior do not summarize adolescent sexuality, they do confirm that many adolescents initiate sexual activity during a developmental stage characterized by risk-taking behavior and a propensity to act without a full sense of the potential consequence of their actions. The United States continues to have an alarmingly high rate of teenage pregnancies and a concurrent increase in HIV-infected youth. In 1991, the pregnancy rate for females ages 15 to 19 was nearly twice that of Great Britain, which had the second-highest rate (Lawton, 1995).

There also is growing evidence that adolescent problem behaviors (e.g., sexual irresponsibility, alcohol and other drug abuse, delinquency, and school dropouts) are interrelated. Having an unintended pregnancy during adolescence can be viewed as a major developmental crisis. Potential negative outcomes include foregoing education, becoming dependent on welfare, and the dilemma of trying to deal with the developmental issues of adolescence while simultaneously trying to meet the needs of an infant. The following statistics further illustrate the dilemma:

- Of the 29 million adolescents over age 12 in the United States, about 12 million are sexually active. The mean age at first intercourse is under 15 years (Brooks-Gunn & Furstenberg, 1986).
- It is estimated that more than 1 million (11%) adolescent women become pregnant each year (Kiselica & Sturmer 1993); the majority of these pregnancies are unintended (White & White, 1991). The younger a female is at her first pregnancy, the more children she will have and the closer-spaced they will be (Edelman, 1994). The United States has by far the highest rate of teenage pregnancy of any industrialized nation (Christopher & Roosa, 1990; Kamerman & Kahn, 1980).
- Teenage girls with poor basic academic skills are five times as likely to become mothers before the age of 16; adolescent males with poor basic academic skills are three times as likely to be fathers as are those with average basic skills (U.S. Congress, 1986). Disadvantaged youth are three to four times more likely to give birth out of wedlock than are more advantaged teens (Robinson, 1988). Pregnancy is the most common reason that females leave school (Robinson, 1988).
- In actual numbers, more white than minority teenagers become pregnant, but disadvantaged minority youth account for a disproportionate number of teen pregnancies and births in the United States. While 27% of the teenage population is composed of minorities, they account for 40% of adolescent pregnancies and births (Edelman, 1988).
- The social costs of unintended teenage pregnancy are enormous. The Center for Population Statistics estimates that, over the next 20 years, society will have to pay $16 billion to support the first-born infants of teenagers (U.S. Congress, 1986).
- A strong relationship exists among teen pregnancy, poverty, and crime (Brookman, 1993). Census Bureau data showed child poverty in 1993 rose to its highest level in three decades, affecting 15.7 million children. Adolescent pregnancy and parenthood evolve from a complex and interrelated combination of factors such as culture, economy, family education, environment, and sexual development (Brewster, Billy, & Grady, 1993; Hofferth, 1991; Kiselica & Sturmer, 1993).

- Persons under the age of 20 account for 1 in 4 cases of gonorrhea, chlamydia, and genital herpes, and 1 in 7 cases of syphilis (Brookman, 1993).

As of 1993, 300,000 cases of AIDS had been reported in the United States (Brookman, 1993). Of these, more than one-fifth involved persons 29 years of age and younger. AIDS is the sixth leading cause of death among 15- to 24-year-olds. Despite the growing public awareness of HIV and AIDS, the rates of premarital intercourse among female teenagers between 1985 and 1988 grew from 44% to 52%, an increase not seen since the early 1970s (Centers for Disease Control, 1991).

According to the Alan Guttmacher Institute (1989), the United States now has higher teenage pregnancy, birth, and abortion rates than most developed countries in the world. The adolescent unintended pregnancy rate is 9.8% in the United States, while most European countries have shown an average of approximately 3.5% (Olson, 1989). Caught between peer values, parent values, and the image of sex portrayed in the media, adolescents frequently act impulsively, without thought to the consequences of their actions.

> The gross annual cost to society of adolescent childbearing and the entire web of social problems that confront adolescent moms and ultimately lead to the poorer and sometimes devastating outcomes for these kids is calculated to be $29 billion. (Maynard, 1996, p. 20)

There are a number of variables, however, that seem to predispose adolescents to risk-taking behavior. These factors have direct implications for school and community prevention and intervention initiatives.

PREDICTORS OF HIGH-RISK SEXUAL BEHAVIORS

Attitude and Expectations for the Future

Adolescents who see opportunities in their futures are more likely to delay pregnancy and childbirth than those who lack hope. Adolescent mothers often have a feeling of hopelessness about the future resulting from transgenerational poverty and economic deprivation. Codega (1990) found that some pregnant or parenting adolescents use indirect or avoidant-type responses more frequently as a means of coping with stress. Life skills in coping, problem solving, decision making, and conflict resolution could enhance feelings of self-worth and self-sufficiency in adolescents.

Poor Academic Achievement

There is a strong association between poor school achievement and pregnancy. Poor academic ability may influence the onset of sexual activity and early parenthood (Children's Defense Fund, 1986). A study conducted by Northeastern University revealed that females 16 years of age or older with poor basic skills are 2.5 times more likely to be mothers than their peers with average basic skills. Males with poor academic skills who were 16 years and older were 3 times more likely to be fathers than their peers with average academic skills. More than one-fifth of all girls who drop out of school do so because they are pregnant. No more than 50% of teenage parents eventually graduate from high school. In addition, teen parents are more likely to have difficulties getting employment. Finally, more than one-half of the money invested in Aid to Families with Dependent Children goes to families with mothers who first gave birth when they were teenagers (Black & DeBlassie, 1985).

False Assumptions About Reproduction

Misunderstandings, false assumptions, and ignorance surrounding reproduction play a large role in teenage unintended pregnancy. The belief that pregnancy will not occur as the result of first-time intercourse is particularly widespread. Further, adolescents often do not have the future orientation needed to understand their personal vulnerability to sexually transmitted diseases. They may engage in risk-taking behaviors such as sexual intercourse without the cognitive ability or abstract reasoning to see the consequences of their actions (Hofferth & Kahn, 1987).

Higher educational aspirations, better-than-average grades, internal locus of control, and high socioeconomic status are positively related to contraceptive use. Variables associated with responsible sexual behavior include older age of initiation of sexual activity; stability of the relationship with partner; knowledge of sexuality, reproduction, and contraception; higher academic aspirations; a realistic attitude toward personal risks; and the presence of parental supervision and support.

Family Influences

Girls who get pregnant often have mothers who gave birth in their teens. Parents of teen mothers and fathers often are considered by their own children to have "permissive attitudes" regarding premarital sexual activity and pregnancy (Robinson, 1988).

There also are cultural differences in the value placed on having children. For example, striking differences were found in a rigorous fieldwork study designed to compare values related to parenthood of white, middle-class and black, low-income adolescents. Gabriel and McAnarney (1983) found that, while teenage pregnancy was seen as detrimental and threatening to the goals of achieving adult status in the middle-class, white subculture, low-income African-American teenage girls saw motherhood and its concomitant responsibilities as a pathway to womanhood. In a study of 300 adolescents, Thompson (1980) found that African-Americans expressed stronger beliefs than whites that children promote greater personal security, marital success, and approval of others.

Young girls also become pregnant as an expression of rage against early deprivation or out of a need to find someone to belong to, all of which leads to a potentially precarious attachment relationship (Bolton, 1983). Within this context, for an adolescent who lives in poverty, a child represents the only tangible possession he or she truly owns.

Finally, children who do not have open, supportive relationships with their parents are at higher risk for unintended pregnancies. Fundamental problems in parent-child communication about sexual behavior include lack of knowledge, embarrassment, unclear values, fear that discussion will encourage sexual activity, and inability to initiate and sustain conversations related to sex. Parent education and religious orientation also affect their communication with their child about sex.

CHILD ABUSE AND SOCIAL DISORGANIZATION

A number of studies in the area of child abuse have linked youthfulness of the mother with child maltreatment (DeAnda, 1983). Adolescent mothers frequently have been described as emotionally deprived or rejected by their families. The term *affect hunger* has been used to describe the early impoverishment of the overprotective mother who tries to create a new childhood for herself through her child.

In an analysis of child abuse and neglect reports, DeAnda (1983) concluded that, although there is an association between teenage parenting and child maltreatment, child abuse may be a correlate of high levels of social disorganization in the family history rather than an outcome of youthful pregnancy. Further, Furstenberg, Brooks-Gunn, and Morgan (1987) found that teenage mothers have more than their share of out-of-wedlock births and marital upheavals, and their children are at increased risk for school and social failure.

HEALTH RISKS

Girls under the age of 16 are five times more likely to die during or immediately after pregnancy than women aged 20 to 24. Their infants have a higher incidence of toxemia, anemia, nutritional deficiencies, low birth weight, and retardation than infants of older women (Black & DeBlassie, 1985). A premature baby of a teenage mother can cost $158,000 in health care costs (U.S. Congress, 1986).

In addition, approximately 400,000 children are born annually to mothers who used crack or cocaine during pregnancy; many of these drug-using mothers are also teenagers (Yazigi, Odem, & Polakoski, 1991). Chasnoff, Landress, and Barrett (1990) reported that about 14% of pregnant women use drugs or alcohol that can cause permanent physical damage to a child during pregnancy. Add to this poor nutrition and low birth weight (variables that often affect teenage mothers and their child), and you find that infant survival and future potential are significantly diminished.

Extensive medical research has documented actual changes in the fetal central nervous system in response to alcohol, crack, and cocaine (Chasnoff, Burns, & Schnoll, 1985; Chasnoff, Landress, & Barrett, 1990; Chasnoff, Burns, Burns, & Schnoll, 1986; Chasnoff, Griffith, MacGregor, Dirkes, & Burns 1989; Lewis, Bennett, & Schmeder, 1989; Rodning, Beckwith, & Howard, 1989; Ryan, Ehrlich, & Finnegan, 1987). This has tremendous importance for schools, both academically and socially.

Teachers report that cocaine-affected school-aged children are impulsive and often violent. They are hyperactive, disruptive, and unresponsive to discipline and manifest learning and memory problems. Middle school teachers have reported that the cumulative and sequential nature of mathematics poses a substantial problem to cocaine-affected teens. Further, their social skills are impeded by their inability to set limits or to recognize appropriate limits for speech and behavior (Waller, 1992). Cocaine-affected children are unable to catch nonverbal cues, and their efforts to establish relationships with others suffer because they do not understand what another's smile or frown means in terms of their own behavior.

Other behavioral characteristics commonly seen in these cocaine-affected children include heightened response to internal and external stimuli, irritability, agitation, tremors, hyperactivity, speech and language delays, poor task organization, processing difficulties, problems related to attachment and separation, poor social and play skills, and motor development delays (Lumsden, 1990).

Waller (1992) maintained that social skills must be taught both verbally and by appropriate modeling. Direct instruction in sharing, greeting, and thanking are essential, and these are primary lessons children learn from play. But play has no intrinsic value to crack-cocaine children because they are disorganized and maintain little from their interactions and experiences with others. Play and games must be taught by direct instruction, through guided play, and under direct supervision. Without intervention, the impulsivity and inability to internalize rules of appropriate behavior will result in violence, early sexual activity, and drug and alcohol use (Waller, 1992, p.60).

ADOLESCENT FATHERS

> Intercourse is not a problem for males. . . . Pregnancy is defined by society as the problem. Males can have as much intercourse as they like . . . a problem occurs only when intercourse results in a pregnancy. But what transcends this issue is responsible behavior, responsible sex. (Elster & Panzarine, 1983, p. 700)

Teen fathers are underrepresented in the research literature. Far less is known about young unwed fathers than about young unwed mothers. Data from available studies indicate that young unwed fathers are demographically a heterogeneous group: They come from all regions of the country and all income and racial groups. Harvey and Spigner (1995) found that males who were sexually experienced reported more frequent use of alcohol, higher levels of stress, and more likely to engage in physical abuse.

African-American youth who father children outside of marriage are not very different in other respects from their peers who have not become fathers. However, Smollar and Ooms (1987) found that white unwed fathers are more likely than their counterparts to have histories of socially deviant behavior (e.g., alcohol and other drug use and juvenile delinquency). Pirog-Good (1995) found teen fathers more likely to come from poor and unstable families and to have family members who are less educated. Of infants born to teenage girls, 53% have fathers who are 20 years of age or younger (Sonenstein, 1986).

Research shows that young men in their early 20s who have earnings high enough to support a family of three above the poverty level are three to four times more likely to be married than are young men with below-poverty wages (Sullivan, 1988). As the educational requirements for entry into the labor market increase and the remuneration for entry-level jobs declines, the close relationship between fatherhood and providing support threatens to exempt increasing numbers of disadvantaged young men from being responsible parents and providers for the families they create.

Hendricks (1988), Hendricks and Montgomery (1983), and Hendricks and Solomon (1987) examined the concerns expressed by Caucasian, African-American, and Hispanic-American teen fathers and found that adolescent fathers desired the following: relationship counseling with their partners, the partners' families, and their families of origin; assistance with career counseling, employment, job training, and education; health care; instruction in childcare and financial planning; and emotional support. At this juncture, it is clear that the needs of teenage fathers are left out of the dialogue on adolescent unintended pregnancy.

An early pregnancy that is unplanned (as most are for adolescents) generally is a crisis not only for the young woman but also for her family and for the baby's father, and should be treated by helping professionals as such (Maracek, 1987). Brazzell and Acock (1988) found that a pregnant adolescent's choices about pregnancy resolution are influenced in part by her own attitudes toward abortion, by her perceptions of the attitudes of parents and friends, by her parents' and her own aspirations, and by how close she is to her boyfriend. This suggests that the process of resolving an unplanned pregnancy should include significant individuals in the adolescent's life whenever possible.

Activities promoting high self-esteem may help deter young males from fathering children in order to enhance their own self-image. Teen fathers have a more external locus of control and could benefit from being taught responsibility for their actions and for their children's welfare (Pirog-Good, 1995, p.15).

STRUCTURED INTERVENTIONS FOR HIGH-RISK BEHAVIORS

Therapeutic Initiatives

In the broadest sense, efforts to help American teens develop responsible sexual attitudes and behavior are hampered by society's ambivalence about sexuality. This ambivalence is shown in the odd contradiction between glamorization of sex in the national media (where sex is usually shown as bliss without consequences) and the unwillingness of many national television networks to advertise contraception. We're castigating our teenagers for what we ourselves are unwilling to talk about. (Elster & Panzarine, 1983, p. 703)

Today, high-quality family life education programs are offered in many schools. The literature suggests that successful programs focus on teaching the skills necessary for responsible and informed decision making and include the following aspects:

- They expose youth to good *decision-making* models and give them opportunities to make decisions in real or simulated situations.
- They encourage youth to *explore their values and behavior* and to confront discrepancies between the two.
- They give *accurate information* about acquiring and using contraceptives.
- They provide opportunities to explore *alternatives to sexual activity.*
- They expose youth to the *realities of teenage marriage and parenting,* about which they often have idealistic concepts.
- They teach that sexual thoughts, feelings, and emotions are normal, but *behavior must be monitored* for its appropriateness.
- They teach *effective communication skills* and provide opportunities to practice them.
- They teach new skills to *improve the students' sense of worth* and to help them understand their feelings and impulses.

Adolescents need structured experiences in building self-esteem and developing life management skills, as well as in understanding long-term consequences of high-risk behavior. They also need education on the consequences of sexual experimentation and on how to transform abstract information into potential long-term consequences. Other skills youth need are analytical reasoning, interpersonal communication skills, and skills in recognizing and avoiding high-risk behaviors.

Research indicates that youth who participate in life skill intervention programs have better problem-solving, negotiating, and communication skills; greater comprehension of reproduction and contraception; and more favorable attitudes toward family planning (Hofferth, 1991). Further, these youth place a higher value on sexual activity, pregnancy, and parenthood. When discussing sexual activity and parenthood, the message to teens is not simply, "don't do it," but a more subtle, "wait until you are better prepared." This message makes sense to teens whose futures hold promise, but for teens with poor academic skills, no high school diploma, and few job prospects, this message translates into an unacceptable, "don't ever have children" (Sullivan, 1988).

The school's role is not to stereotype single parents but, rather, to build on the resiliency the child and parent bring to the school. Single parents often experience increased stress linked to finding childcare, solving childbearing problems, and meeting basic economic needs. Offering comprehensive social and health services on school grounds can ease the burden for both educators and families. Schools and communities need to improve the social, educational, and wellness prospects of all youth.

Treatment Plan: Teen Parenthood Support Group.

Counseling Intention: To provide youth with a place to speak freely about their parenting concerns; to educate students in childcare and development; to aid youth in locating community services of benefit to them as parents; to promote good prenatal care; to impress upon youth the importance of staying in school for themselves and for their children's welfare.

Students who have children may be referred to the group by teachers, counselors, concerned others, parents, or by self-referral.

   Session 1: Family planning and adolescent sexuality. A local family planning agency provides a comprehensive workshop with discussion and pertinent literature for group recipients.

   Session 2: Enhancing self-esteem. This session focuses on participants' strengths. Positive reinforcement from other members is encouraged.

   Session 3: Finding social support. Local community agencies present resources available, such as social services, childcare organizations, and parenting groups.

   Session 4: Problem-solving skills. Members are guided through the problem-solving process, with repeated rehearsals and role-playing. The focus is on gaining control of life situations, to enhance the student's sense that he or she has the power to make things happen.

   Session 5: Developing an informal support network. Students are encouraged to develop a support network among themselves, to educate themselves in child development and child discipline.

   Session 6: Addressing concerns. Specific concerns of group members are addressed. The session focuses on enhancing coping skills and finding alternative solutions.

   Session 7: Strengthening self-sufficiency. Students are encouraged to build their self-sufficiency skills as parents and prospective employees, with a focus on responsibility, consistency, and encouragement.

Barnes and Harrod (1993) also developed a contemporary life issues clinic to work with teenage mothers. The program outlined these seven objectives:

1. increase the decision-making skills of youth;
2. encourage responsibility for one's actions;

3. encourage the development of coping skills;
4. foster emotional growth and maturation;
5. cultivate forward-looking, success-oriented attitudes;
6. provide information in areas of health-related, sexual issues (e.g., pregnancy prevention, sexually transmitted diseases, HIV/AIDS prevention);
7. provide information regarding the financial and legal implications of parenthood (p. 138).

Barnes and Harrod (1993) used a drop-in curriculum so youth were free to choose the sessions that appealed to their interests and concerns to enhance initiative and motivation. Topics included fitting in with the crowd, handling peer pressure, stress management, and self-esteem and date abuse.

Treatment Plan: Multimodal Group for Adolescent Mothers.

Modality	Problem assessment	Potential intervention
Behavior	Poor academic performance and attendance problems	Self-contracting; recording and self-monitoring
	Negative self-statements	Positive self-talk
	Discipline of children by yelling or hitting	Teach training principles in child management
Affect	Feelings of little self-worth	Increase range of positive reinforcement
	Anger toward significant others	Exercises in anger expression
	Conflict with others	Behavior rehearsal
	Role reversal	
Sensation	Anxiety and depression over present circumstances and future goals	Anxiety-management training goal rehearsal or coping imagery
Imagery	Unproductive fantasies	Positive imagery
	Image of self as incapable	Goal rehearsal
Cognition	Poor study habits	Study skills training
	Assertiveness training	
	Lack of educational or occupational information	Career counseling; assessment and information
	Sexual misinformation	Sex education; bibliotherapy
	Expectations of failure	Positive self-talk
Interpersonal relations	Poor relationships with peers	Social skills and assertiveness training
Drugs (biological functioning)	Poor dietary habits	Involvement in weight reduction program; nutrition and dietary information

Collective Community Initiatives

Developmental needs of adolescent mothers are to be assertive, to make good decisions, and to understand the consequences of high-risk behavior. Effective prevention programs must target multiple services and agencies to meet the needs of this high-risk population. The school, health department, social services, and court services should coordinate a systematic delivery of services.

A multifaceted counseling approach that focuses on strengthening the adolescent through this difficult developmental crisis should be paramount. Resources should include individual counseling, small-group counseling, and collaboration and consultation with family members. Intervention programs should raise awareness of the risk of unprotected sex and enhance skills related to sexual negotiations.

Intervention also should consider the adolescent's belief structures regarding alcohol use and accountability for high-risk behavior under its influence (Harvey & Spigner, 1995). For both males and females, the strongest predictor of sexual activity is alcohol consumption. Gender-specific strategies should be considered in more comprehensive intervention efforts. Finally, comprehensive family life education that encourages abstinence, teaches youth how to say "no," and provides contraceptive information has the potential to delay the onset of sexual activity.

CONCLUSION

Children and adolescents need to realize the emotional consequences of high-risk sexual behavior: emotional distress, guilt, anxiety, victimization, and sexual and physical abuse. They need to be aware of the physical consequences as well: sexually transmitted infections, HIV/AIDS infection, and cervical or genital cancers. Children and adolescents need life skills training in such areas as problem solving, assertiveness, impulse control, critical thinking, and peer-pressure resistance. Through a variety of experiential exercises, simulations, bibliotherapy, and structured discussions, adolescents can learn skills critical to developing a healthy, positive sense of self.

The goal is to prevent problems before they happen and to provide a framework of information to deal more effectively with challenges that arise throughout the life span. Several programmatic approaches to pregnancy prevention exist. The approaches cited most often in the literature include encouragement for use of birth control, school-based clinics, condom distribution, HIV-AIDS education, family life education, enhancing life options, and encouraging abstinence.

SOCIAL, EMOTIONAL, AND COGNITIVE SKILLS

Social Literacy Skills

Social literacy skills are *interpersonal skills* essential for meaningful interaction with others. Social skills are those behaviors that, within a given situation, predict important social outcomes such as peer acceptance, popularity, self-efficacy, competence, and high self-esteem. Social skills fall into categories such as being kind, cooperative, and compliant to reduce defiance, aggression, conflict, and antisocial behavior; and showing interest in people and socializing successfully to reduce behavior problems associated with withdrawal, depression, and fearfulness. Social skills include problem solving, assertiveness, thinking critically, resolving conflict, managing anger, and utilizing peer pressure refusal skills.

(*Note*: **Permission is granted to reproduce skills boxes for individual client use.**)

Being Assertive

A **"A" stands for "attention."**
Before you can solve your problem, you have to get the other person to listen to you. Find a time, place, or method that helps them focus their attention on you.

S **The first "S" stands for "soon, simple, and short."**
When possible, speak up as soon as you realize your rights have been violated. ("Soon" may be a matter of seconds, hours, or days.) Look the person in the eye, and keep your comments to the point.

S **The second "S" stands for "specific behavior."**
Focus on the behavior the person used, not on the person's personality. Otherwise, he or she will feel attacked. Tell the person exactly which behavior disturbed you.

E **"E" stands for "effect on me."**
Share the feelings you experienced as a result of the person's behavior: *"I get angry when ..."* Or, *"I get frustrated when ..."*

R **"R" stands for "response."**
Describe your preferred outcome, what you'd like to see happen, and ask for some feedback on it.

T **"T" stands for "terms."**
If all goes well, you may be able to make an agreement with the other person about how to handle the situation in the future. Or, you may "agree to disagree" (respectfully), or simply come to an impasse.

Even if no agreement has been reached, you've accomplished your goal of asserting yourself with dignity.

Assertiveness 1

Here are some ways to change someone else's undesirable behavior:

- Identify your needs, wants, rights, and feelings about the situation. Establish a goal for what it is you wish to accomplish.

- Arrange a meeting time that is convenient for you and the other person where a dialogue can take place.

- Define the problem clearly to the other person.

- Describe your feelings using "I" messages. "I" messages enable us to take responsibility for our feelings. "I feel . . ." "I need . . . "

- Express yourself in an assertive manner using a couple of clear sentences.

- Reinforce your statement by saying what the positive consequences will be when the other person makes the appropriate changes in the behavior.

Assertiveness 2

Assertiveness is the ability to state your position boldly and confidently, to clearly state how you think and feel about a situation or position.

1. Identify how you think and feel about a situation.

2. Analyze the source of those feelings.

3. Choose the appropriate skills necessary to communicate feelings such as, "I" messages (Thompson, 1996, p. 149) or DESC Script (Describe, Express, Specify, Consequences) (Thompson, 1996, pp. 153-155.

4. Communicate your thoughts or feelings to the source.

For example: *"I have never been charged a service fee before. Has there been a change in your bank's policy?"*

Rules for Assertive Requests

Assertive requests should be as clear, direct, and uncritical as possible. To make your request successfully, follow these basic rules:

1. Select a convenient time and place for your dialogue.

2. Make your request simple and manageable, limiting it to one or two specific actions.

3. Don't blame or attack the other person or bring up past experiences. Use "I" messages and stick to the facts.

4. Be specific. Describe the behavior, not the attitude, that you want to change. Don't make requests that are unreasonable or that have attached conditions.

5. Communicate assertively both verbally and nonverbally. Keep your tone of voice moderate, clear, and firm. Maintain eye contact, an erect posture, and a close proximity to the other person.

6. Keep the dialogue upbeat and positive by mentioning the positive consequences of giving you what you want.

Source: Adapted from M. McKay & P. Fanning (1987) *Self-esteem: A proven program of cognitive techniques for assessing, improving, and maintaining your self-esteem.* Reprinted with permission by New Harbinger Publications, Inc., Oakland, California.

Managing Anger

1. **Recognize angry feelings.**

    - Identify how your body feels.

    - Identify what you are saying to yourself.

2. **Calm down.**

    - Pause and take three deep breaths.

    - Count backward slowly from 10 to 0.

    - Tell yourself to stay calm and maintain control.

3. **Talk aloud to solve the problem.**

    - Express what you need and what you want.

    - See if you both can get what you want.

4. **Think about it later.**

    - What exactly made you angry?

    - Did you have maintain control over the situation?

    - Were you pleased with the outcome?

    - Could you have done things differently?

    - Did you do the best that you were capable of doing?

Speaking for Yourself

When you speak for yourself, you express your intentions and you clearly indicate that you are the owner of your thoughts and actions. The phrases "I think . . . ," "I feel . . . ," and "I want . . . " identify you as the owner. When you speak for yourself, you use "I," "me," "my, and "mine."

Statements such as these are good examples:

"It's important to me."

"I want more time to think about it."

"My perspective is different."

"I'm really pleased about our project."

These statements indicate that you recognize your feelings, intentions, and actions and that you are the owner of your perceptions and thoughts, feelings and wants. They also add to the accuracy and quality of communication.

Emotional Literacy Skills

Emotional literacy skills are intrapersonal abilities such as knowing one's emotions by recognizing a feeling as it happens and monitoring it; managing emotions (i.e., shaking off anxiety, gloom, irritability, and the consequences of failure); motivating oneself to attain goals, delay gratification, stifle impulsiveness, and maintain self-control; recognizing emotions in others with empathy and perspective taking; and handling interpersonal relationships effectively. Emotional skills fall into categories such as knowing the relationship between thoughts, feelings, and actions; establishing a sense of identity and acceptance of self; learning to value teamwork, collaboration, and cooperation; regulating one's mood; empathizing; and maintaining hope.

(*Note*: **Permission is granted to reproduce skills boxes for individual client use.**)

Validating Experiences with Sense Statements

Validating with sense statements means documenting what you perceive (i.e., see, hear, touch, taste, and smell). It clarifies sensations and intuition and serves as a perception check. It provides feedback and helps you avoid the pitfalls of making global statements, generalizations, or stereotyping. Validating with sense statements makes the dialogue of "yes, you are/no I'm not" harder to start and more difficult to continue. To validate sense statements:

1. Be specific about time, location, action, or behavior.
2. Document the behavior or action; do not stereotype or make a character assignation.
3. Engage in a perception check with the other person.
4. Avoid making global statements or generalizations.

Here is an example of how you might document time and behavior: *"This morning when you began to respond to my question, I saw you pause, look away, and then I heard you say . . . "*

Here is an example of *a perception check* and an opportunity to clarify the message:

> **Ryan:** *"I don't think you like my new shirt."*
> **Jessica:** *"That's bogus! What makes you say that?"*
> **Ryan** (documenting): *"When I tried it on for you, you were very quiet and you were grinning."*
> **Jessica:** *"Wait a second! I was quiet because I was thinking about how nice you looked. I guess I was grinning because it looked so cool on you."*

Finally, here is an example global judgments and overgeneralizing (i.e., what *not* to do), followed by an example of documenting (i.e., how to do it better):

"I get frustrated that you are so careless with our money." (global judgment; generalization)
"I got frustrated this morning when I noticed that you hadn't recorded the checks you had written over the weekend." (documenting)

Making Interpretative Statements

Interpretative statements express what you think, believe, or assume about a situation or experience. Identify your thoughts as your own, and avoid talking for others. For example:

"I think it's time to stop."

"It's my impression that you would be interested in going."

"I think it's the wrong way to go about it."

"I'm wondering if you're feeling what I'm feeling."

Atonement

Atonement is making up for what you've done. Four guidelines to help you choose an appropriate atonement.

1. **It is important to acknowledge that what you did was wrong.** This makes it clear that you accept responsibility for your behavior.

2. **You should atone *directly to the person you've wronged.*** Donating money to charity, becoming a big brother or big sister, or joining the Peace Corps will atone less effectively than directly helping the one you hurt.

3. **The atonement should be real, rather than symbolic.** Lighting candles or writing a poem will not rid you of guilt or responsibility. What you do to atone has to cost you something in time, money, or effort. It also has to be tangible enough so that it has an impact on your relationship with the person who is hurt.

4. **Your atonement should be commensurate with the wrong done.** If your offense was a moment of irritability, then a brief apology should be sufficient. But if you have been noncommunicative and cold toward someone for the past few weeks, then you'll have to do a little better than saying, "I'm sorry."

Source: Adapted from M. McKay & P. Fanning (1987) *Self-esteem: A proven program of cognitive techniques for assessing, improving, and maintaining your self-esteem.* Reprinted with permission by New Harbinger Publications, Inc., Oakland, California.

Acknowledgment

Acknowledgment means agreeing with a critic. Acknowledgment allows you to stop criticism immediately. When someone criticizes you, and the criticism is accurate, the following steps of acknowledgment may be helpful:

1. Say, "You're right," and let it go.

2. Paraphrase the criticism so that the critic is sure you heard him or her correctly.

3. Thank the critic for the observation, if appropriate.

4. Explain yourself, if appropriate. (Note that an explanation is not an apology).

Source: Adapted from M. McKay & P. Fanning (1987) *Self-esteem: A proven program of cognitive techniques for assessing, improving, and maintaining your self-esteem.* Reprinted with permission by New Harbinger Publications, Inc., Oakland, California.

The Compassionate Response

The compassionate response begins with three questions you should ask yourself to promote an understanding of a problem or behavior.

1. What need was (he, she, I) trying to meet with that behavior?
2. What beliefs or perceptions influenced the behavior?
3. What pain, hurt, or other feelings influenced the behavior?

Next, are three statements to remind yourself that you can accept a person without blame or judgment, no matter how unfortunate his or her choices have been.

4. I wish . . . had not happened, but it was merely an attempt to meet (his, her, my) needs.
5. I accept (him, her, myself) without judgment or feeling of wrongness for that attempt.
6. No matter how unfortunate (his, her, my) decision, I accept the person who did it as someone who is, like all of us, trying to survive.

Finally, there are two statements to remind you that it is time to forgive and let go.

7. It's over, I can let go of it.
8. Nothing is owed for this mistake.

Make a commitment to use the compassionate response whenever you notice that you are judging yourself or others. The basic thrust of the compassionate response is *understanding, acceptance,* and *forgiveness.*

Source: M. McKay & P. Fanning (1987) *Self-esteem: A proven program of cognitive techniques for assessing, improving, and maintaining your self-esteem.* Reprinted with permission by New Harbinger Publications, Inc., Oakland, California.

Conveying the Whole Message

Often, people need to better understand your perspective on a problem or situation. It may be helpful for them to know your feelings—how the situation or problem has affected you emotionally. The *whole message* means conveying your *thoughts* (how you perceived the situation), your *feelings,* and your *wants* as an assertive statement.

The formula is very simple:

"I think . . . (my understanding, perceiving, interpretations)."

"I feel . . . ('I' messages only)."

"I want . . . (an assertive request)."

For example: *"When you tease me in front of my friends, you make me sound pretty stupid. I am getting the feeling that that's what you really think of me. I feel embarrassed and angry. I'd really appreciate it if you would lighten up and not tease me or anyone else in our group."*

Source: M. McKay & P. Fanning (1987) *Self-esteem: A proven program of cognitive techniques for assessing, improving, and maintaining your self-esteem.* Reprinted with permission by New Harbinger Publications, Inc., Oakland, California.

"I Want" Statements

"I want" statements clarify to others what you want and how you want to fulfill your wants. They reduce the anxiety of being afraid to ask and of worrying whether the other person will know what you want. Many relationships have failed because needs and wants were unspoken.

For example, *"I want to know what I did to make you so angry, but I don't want you to call me names."*

"I want" statements can be framed as follows:

1. Say what you want: *"Instead of going to the theater, I want to stay home and rent a video."*

2. Rate your want on a scale of 1 to 10: *"I want to go to the movie theater, it's a strong preference—about an 8."*

3. State what your "I want" statement means and what it doesn't mean: *"I want to go to the movie theater sometime in the next two weeks. That's just for information; no pressure if you can't make it this weekend."*

Estimating Consequences

Look at a situation by logically evaluating the consequences. First, don't become emotional; be emotionally neutral. Second, when appropriate, use the following formula: *"When you . . .* (description of behavior), *then . . .* (statement of consequences). *You will have another opportunity to . . .* (statement of when this can occur). *"*

For example, *"When you continue to leave your car unlocked, you run the risk your stereo will get stolen. If stolen, you can get another stereo when you have saved enough money, because our insurance will not cover it."*

Chapter 6

LOSS, DEPRESSION, AND SUICIDE

> Money and privilege buy lots of things. They buy cars. They buy instant gratification. They buy all kinds of seeming opportunities to make oneself fill fulfilled. But what is missing is that families have lost the ability to teach coping skills, to teach calmness, to teach perseverance. Everybody on this earth is going to get depressed from time to time. Everybody's going to experience grave disappointments throughout life about how they see themselves and what goals they're not going to meet. And the busier, the more intense, our society is, the more people are going to be prone to grab what seem to be quick cures—drink, drugs, violence—as opposed to persevering through difficult times and doing the hard work one needs to do to sustain rich goals and relationships. (Smith, 1986, p. 36)

People often assume that adolescence is an exciting and carefree time of life; yet the stress of establishing self-identity, self-sufficiency, and autonomy is exceptionally difficult. The escalating rate of emotional disorders in our society can be attributed to several precipitating variables. For example, many teenagers from dysfunctional families live with alcoholism, violence, incest, and abuse. Add to these risk variables rapid social change, cultural pluralism, occupational diversity, and poor interpersonal skills, and a teenager's hopelessness and disillusionment with planning for the future are understandable.

Teenage suicide has reached epidemic proportions: It is now the second leading cause of death among this age group. The following data reflect the magnitude of the problem:

- Between 1960 and 1988, the suicide rate among adolescents increased much more significantly than in the general population, rising by 200% compared to approximately 17% (Garland & Zigler, 1993).
- The percentage of teens who have attempted suicide at least once rose from 6% in 1988 to 13% in 1993 (Jones, 1996).
- Suicide is second only to automobile accidents as the cause of death among American teenagers (Strother & Jacobs, 1986). In this country, 5,000 to 7,000 adolescents commit suicide each year (Papolos & Papolos, 1987; Snyder, 1986). Hafen and Frandsen (1986) asserted that depression is the most common factor in adolescent suicide.
- Depression in youth is viewed as a significant problem that affects approximately 30% of the adolescent population (Lewison, Hops, Roberts, Seeley, & Andrew, 1993). The *Diagnostic and Statistical Manual of Mental Disorders* (DSM-IV) (American Psychiatric Association, 1994) further recognized and differentiated aspects of adolescent depressive symptomology.
- Some 78% of teenage suicide victims gave some kind of warning within three months prior to the act (Tomlinson-Keasey, & Keasey, 1988).
- Among all age groups, the most common suicide methods are using firearms, hanging, and drug overdoses. In the past decade, the most frequent method for people between the ages of 15 and 24 was firearms (Brookman, 1993).
- Completed suicides are much more likely to be males, yet teenage girls are much more likely to attempt suicide than their male counterparts (Mehan, Lamb, Saltzman, & O'Carrol, 1992; Sandoval, Davis, & Wilson, 1987).
- In the United States, the Western states have the highest rates of adolescent suicide; the lowest rates are in the Southern, North Central, and Northeastern regions (Shaffer, Garland, Gould, Fisher, & Trautman, 1988).
- The highest suicide rate among Hispanics occurs among 20- to 24-year-olds. Data from five Southwestern states show that suicide rates for Hispanics are lower than for whites, but higher than for African-Americans. For young Native Americans, the suicide rate is the second leading cause of death (Brookman, 1993).

PREDICTORS OF TEEN SUICIDE

Depression

Increasingly, researchers and the public alike are acknowledging that depression is a serious disorder of children and adolescence and perhaps the most common impetus to suicide. Some researchers have estimated that depression affects nearly 30% of the adolescent population (Lewinsohn, Hops, Roberts, Seeley, & Andrew, 1993). According to Brookman (1993), 7 to 9 million American children have mental health problems requiring treatment—and 70% to 80% receive inadequate or no service. Brookman also estimates that 20% of teenagers have significant emotional disorders.

Recent clinical and research data on depression indicate an occurrence rate of 20% among school-aged children (Bauer, 1987; Worchel, Nolan, & Wilson, 1987), with a rate of 51% to 59% among children in psychiatric settings (McConville & Bruce, 1985). Inherently, the pattern of a teenager's life, and how he or she feels about it, affects all of his or her attitudes and actions.

Typically, major depression is diagnosed if a child or adolescent describes depressed moods or irritability or a loss of interest in normal activities for at least two weeks, accompanied by other symptoms such as weight loss, inability to concentrate, chronic pain, or insomnia that is not part of some other disorder such as schizophrenia (Forest, 1990). When applied to adolescents, depression describes behavior ranging from common mood swings or short-lived situational episodes to chronic recurring feelings of worthlessness, helplessness, and hopelessness (Garrison, Schuchter, Schoenbach, & Kaplan, 1989).

Depression often is characterized by withdrawal from normal social interactions, sleep disturbances, poor concentration, feelings of inferiority, and self-blame. Bartell and Reynolds (1986) suggested that depression can be considered primarily

- **affective** (characterized by worry and anxiety),
- **cognitive** (characterized by self-deprecation), and/or
- **motivational** (indicating withdrawal or decreased performance).

McConville and Bruce (1985) further delineated depression as follows:

The affective type: characterized by prominent sadness and helplessness.
The self-esteem type: characterized by prominent discouragement and negative self-esteem.
The guilt type: characterized by prominent guilt and self-destructive ideation or behavior.

The first two types typically are receptive to school/community/teacher/counselor support; the third type usually requires referral for clinical treatment.

Hopelessness and Helplessness

The severity of the depression often profiles this equation: *Severity = Distress × Uncontrollability × Frequency* (or FID: Frequency, Intensity, Duration).

Depression, hopelessness, and anxiety appear to be the important factors in both suicidal ideation and suicidal behavior in adolescents (Bernstein, Garfinkel, & Hoberman, 1989: Kazdin, French, Unis, Esveldt-Dawson, & Sherick, 1983). Research data also show that adults often do not recognize the signs of depression and suicidal ideation in adolescents. If significant figures in the adolescent's life do not perceive the child's despairing emotional state, they are not able to respond to it.

Family Dysfunction and Interpersonal Loss

Teenagers whose lives are disrupted by frequent changes in residence, schools, or parental figures show an increased risk for suicide (Davidson, Franklin, Mercy, Rosenburg, & Simmons, 1989). Perrone (1987) found that suicidal children and adolescents often have experienced more dysfunction in their families and loss of significant others, witnessed repeated traumas (e.g., family violence, chemical abuse), and were themselves subject to abuse and neglect. Gibbs (1985) found significant relationships between depression and three independent variables: parental occupation, number of household moves, and number of self-reported problems.

Compared to healthy youth, depressed youth reported more stressors and fewer social resources in the areas of family, extended family, school, friends, and support networks (Daniels & Moos, 1990; Feldman, Rubenstein, & Rubin, 1988). Most suicide victims experienced family disruption, and nearly half were functioning poorly in school (Allen, 1985). Functioning poorly in school should be recognized as a significant loss for many children and adolescents. Failure can be devastating.

Loss of Status

Hawton (1986) found that predominant problems immediately preceding adolescent suicide included school failure, a loss of status among family and/or friends, the feeling of letting others down, being publicly reprimanded or humiliated, and/or a significant love loss. Cohen-Sandler, Berman, and King

(1982), Gill-Wigal (1988), and Pfeiffer (1982, 1986) suggested that suicidal children and adolescents have experienced higher levels of stress than "normal" adolescents. Youth found most at risk for completed suicides are males who have an affective disorder, who abuse alcohol or other drugs, and who have experienced an acute proximal stressor that involves either a social loss or a blow to self-image (Crumley, 1990). Suicidal thoughts occur most frequently between the 7th and 9th grades (Perrone, 1987).

Isolation and Alienation

The adolescent suicide attempter often feels alienated from his or her family. Edwards and Lowe (1988) found some common issues that may trigger suicidal gestures in adolescents:

- Failure to successfully manage problems or stressors
- Failure to live up to expectations of self or others
- A wish to retaliate against adults or peers by making them feel guilty
- Desire to join a deceased loved one
- Desire to rid oneself of unacceptable feelings of guilt, failure, and despair
- Feelings of hopelessness
- Feelings of being emotionally overwhelmed
- Feelings of low self-esteem
- Desire to commit the ultimate act of self-destruction and abandonment

Adolescents who feel little control over their environment often experience their families and social institutions (such as the schools) as unavailable, rejecting, or overprotective. Sometimes in order to reach out for help, an adolescent may have to expose family secrets such as alcoholism, violence, or sexual victimization. This poses the additional stress of possible retaliation, or at least of further rejection from other family members (Gibbs, 1985).

All-or-Nothing Thinking

Suicide usually is the final act in a sequence of maladaptive behaviors. Central themes in assessing risk are the attraction death holds for the youth, the degree of isolation or alienation he or she feels in the family, his or her social status with peers, and his or her ability to express emotions and cope with problems. Escalating problems lead to an increasing sense of helplessness and impotence, eventually ending in a suicidal mindset.

Garland and Zigler (1993) studied cognitive and coping-style factors—generalized feelings of hopelessness and poor interpersonal problem-solving skills—as risk factors for adolescent suicide.

Capuzzi (1988) maintained that suicidal adolescents often distort their thinking patterns in conjunction with avoidance, control, and communication functions, so that suicide becomes the best or only problem-solving option. All-or-nothing thinking emerges in which no options for coping with or overcoming problems seem possible. Suicidal adolescents often have trouble developing solutions to troublesome situations or uncomfortable relationships. Expressing emotions is critical, because depressed adolescents generally suppress negative emotions at home, in school, and among peers. In addition, adolescents who abuse psychoactive substances—particularly those with any type of depressive disorder—appear to be at higher risk for suicidal behavior.

STRUCTURED INTERVENTIONS
FOR HIGH-RISK BEHAVIORS

Therapeutic Initiatives

Clients with depression can be treated successfully if better programs are developed for awareness, education, primary prevention, and intervention. Downing (1988) provided a multidimensional intervention system based on a learning theory approach for countering depression. Learning life skills to change debilitating behavior also is productive. In collaboration with therapist, parents, and counselor, children and adolescents can learn depression-coping and control techniques, such as recognizing depressive feelings and learning to increase their activity level, to relax, and to engage in positive self-talk.

Coping and control techniques lead to improved levels of functioning in all aspects of a child's or adolescent's life. Children learn these techniques best through a multifaceted support system involving the home, the school, and the child. Inherent in the intervention should be consistent, frequent, and regular monitoring of the process. Primary prevention and early intervention initiatives should be supported, since some research shows that children and adolescents seem to respond better than adults to techniques that prevent depression (de Shazer, 1982).

Helping professionals should concentrate on teaching adolescents specific skills to improve targeted symptom behaviors. These skills include positive self-talk, cognitive awareness strategies, study skills, time management, coping skills, assertiveness, guided imagery, relaxation techniques and increased physical activity. Downing (1988) also outlined several intervention strategies to counter depression in children and adolescents. These strategies are outlined below:

Ensuring Success Experiences. According to Downing (1988, p. 235), "to reverse the depression sequence, significant adults can systematically manipulate success and positive feedback for the child." Schaefer, Briesmeister, and Fitton (1984) reported similar findings, maintaining that one of the most important intervention strategies for children with self-defeating or self-destructive behaviors is ensuring daily successes in the child's life. It is critical that the child experience some feeling of control, however small, if he or she is to make a behavior change. Intervention team members should ensure successes by establishing small, attainable goals. As coach, the counselor can help the youth break down the goal into steps that can be made in small, success-assured increments. The child or adolescent, depending on his or her developmental readiness, should be actively involved in this process.

Improving Social Skills and Interactions. When subjected to environmental stress and situational pressures, children with poor social skills are more likely to succumb to depression. McLean (1976) illustrated this with the following equation: *Poor social skills yield marginal social interaction, resulting in less social recognition, which produces lower self-esteem and increased vulnerability to depression.* Techniques in assertiveness and self-confidence training can be used to improve social interactions skills.

Increasing Activity Levels. Supervised exercise with a partner or at a gym has been shown to produce positive changes in brain chemistry. Confidence and success in gaining control over one's physical well-being can be enhanced by jogging, aerobics, walking, or working out with free weights.

Cantwell and Carlson (1983) found that increasing a client's activity level helps control depression. Again, involving the client in selecting and planning the activities improves the likelihood of success. Enjoyable activities enhance the probability of a positive response. School attendance, however, should be a priority, and parents should insist that the child do chores and participate in family activities as well (Downing, 1988). The more commitments or obligations the child meets, the more he or she maintains a self-perception of normalcy, confidence, and control of feelings. The counselor also can encourage clients to develop a "pleasant events schedule by having them make a list of daily events, rank them according to enjoyment, and keep track of how often they do each one" (Forrest, 1990).

Creating Positive Team Support. Consistency, continuity, and commitment of all team members is critical to the success of any intervention. Everyone involved should be regularly reminded of their value and appreciated for their contributions of time and energy.

Limiting Inappropriate Attention. Sometimes family relationships become codependent—with individuals taking responsibility for another person's behavior and consequences. Members of the intervention team should not continually ask how the child is feeling. Response efforts should be focused on behaviors that gain attention in positive ways.

Teaching Coping and Change Skills. Children and adolescents can be taught to be aware of depressive feelings and thoughts when they occur, and can learn ways to avoid feelings or ideas that provoke depression. It might help to use *Matthew's Stress Management Formula* (Matthews, 1986) to teach this skill:

$$\text{Awareness} + \text{Benefits} + \text{Change} + \text{Dependency} = \text{Relaxation}$$
$$(A + B + C + D = R)$$

Essentially, the formula suggests that the awareness of stress plus the benefits of coping techniques leads to a changed response to stress. The child should also develop a repertoire of activities he or she can implement when feeling depressed. This repertoire might include the following:

- Increasing activity level
- Redirecting thoughts to pleasant experiences
- Using deliberate internal affirmations
- Using productive fantasies or imagery
- Using biofeedback to increase or decrease the pulse rate

All these strategies have one common denomination: They empower the youth with strategies that put him or her in control of making the change.

Using Classroom-Focused Strategies. Schloss (1983) identified several classroom-based strategies that can counteract a depressed youth's passivity and sense of helplessness by providing opportunities for success and experiences of control. These strategies include the following:

- Help the student avoid a sense of constant failure by providing work tasks in small, incremental steps that give him or her a sense of mastery and success.
- Neutralize helplessness by providing opportunities for choice and power (for example, in selecting work assignments or self-rewards).

- Provide increased verbal feedback and explanations for the depressed student, who may lack the ability to see cause and effect.
- Encourage depressed students to identify behaviors and outcomes themselves to encourage self-sufficiency.

Encouraging Positive Self-Talk. Cognitive therapists consider depression a result of the influence of negative, irrational beliefs. Clarizio (1985) recommended cognitive restructuring activities within the school or community, in which teachers or helping professionals incorporate instruction on the relationship between feelings and thoughts into lessons. Also useful are role-playing activities that focus on specific problems relevant to childhood depression, such as peer rejection, failure, and guilt.

Negative emotional reactions and behaviors can be changed by teaching children a thought-substitution process: First, they learn to become aware of negative thoughts; then, they learn to talk to themselves positively. So, instead of saying to themselves, *"Everyone thinks I'm a nerd,"* they might say, *"Chemistry comes easy to me, I really know my stuff. I can help others in the class by being on their study team."*

Teaching Communication Skills. Lack of communication skills and limited positive interpersonal feedback often precipitate depression. Intervention should emphasize increasing the quality, quantity, and breadth of the student's interpersonal communications. Counselor-prescribed contacts—such as making a personal phone call, writing a letter, or walking home with someone and talking to them—develop "internal competition" with the negative self-talk going on inside (Forrest, 1990, p. 7).

Teaching Decision-Making and Problem-Solving Strategies. Making clear decisions and coping with the sources of stress that precipitate depression are vital skills. The counselor can teach problem-solving skills by having the depressed client follow these basic steps:

- Clearly specify the problem.
- Entertain and list several alternative solutions.
- Evaluate the possible and likely outcomes of each solution in terms of time and money spent and short- and long-term effects.
- Think through time constraints, workload, resources, support networks, and coping skills to prevent stress as the client carries out the plan (Forrest, 1990, p. 7).

Helping the Client Assume Responsibility for Choices and Actions. To help students assume ownership of their own problems, direct them to think of an incident that made them angry or resentful and that they still have strong feelings about. Have them write about the incident, describing it as if others were completely responsible for causing it. In this exercise, the students are to blame others, making the problem clearly someone else's fault. Then, ask them to rewrite the incident as if *they* were solely responsible for starting, developing, and getting stuck with the problem. Insist that they take full account of what they could have done to change or avoid the situation. Process with them the issues of blame, responsibility, and victimization.

Other important strategies and techniques for classroom initiatives include *The Family Safety Watch* and *Post-Traumatic Loss Debriefing.* Treatment plans for a loss group and a divorce group also follow.

Treatment Plan: The Family Safety Watch.
Counseling Intention: Crisis intervention; to provide a collaborative intervention strategy for eliminating or decreasing self-destructive behavior or ideation.

The Family Safety Watch (Landau-Stanton & Stanton, 1985) is an intensive intervention strategy to prevent threatened self-destructive behavior. The safety watch also can be applied to such problems as self-mutilation, anorexia, bulimia, and alcohol or other drug abuse. The procedure is as follows:

1. Family members conduct the watch. They select people to be involved from their nuclear family, extended family, and network of family friends.
2. An around-the-clock schedule is established to determine what the adolescent is to do with his or her time over a 24-hour period: when he or she is to sleep, eat, attend class, do homework, play games, view a movie, and so on.
3. The intervention team leader (a counselor, parent, teacher, or principal) consults with the family to accomplish the following:

   • Determine family resources and support systems.
   • Find ways of involving these support systems in the effort. For example, "How much time do you think Uncle Harry can give to watching your child?"
   • Design a detailed plan for the safety watch.
   • Determine schedules and shifts so that someone is with the at-risk child 24 hours a day.

4. A back-up system is established so that the person on watch can get support from others if needed. A cardinal rule is that the child be within

view of someone at all times, even while in the bathroom or when sleeping. The family is warned that the at-risk youth may try to manipulate situations to be alone—for example, by pretending to be fine—and that the first week will be the hardest.

5. The family makes a contractual agreement stating that, if the watch is inadvertently slackened or compromised and the at-risk youth makes a suicide attempt or challenges the program in some way, the regime will be tightened. This is a therapeutic move that reduces the family's feeling of failure should a relapse occur during the year.

The primary goal of the watch is to mobilize the family to take care of their own and to help them feel competent in doing so (Landau-Stanton & Stanton, 1985). The family, adolescent, and helping professionals collaborate in determining what the adolescent must do in order to relax and ultimately terminate the watch. Task issues should focus on personal responsibility, age-appropriate behavior, and handling of family and social relationships, such as these:

1. Rising in the morning without prompting.
2. Completing chores on time.
3. Substituting courteous and friendly behavior for grumbling and sulking.
4. Talking to parents and siblings more openly.
5. Watching less TV and spending more time conversing with family, friends, and support networks.

The family and therapeutic team jointly decide to terminate the watch. It is contingent upon the absence of self-destructive behavior and the achievement of an acceptable level of improvement in the other behavioral tasks assigned to the adolescent. If any member of the team believes there is still a risk, full supervision with the safety watch is continued.

This approach appeals to families because it makes them feel empowered and useful and it lessens the need for (and so the expense of) an extended hospitalization. It also reestablishes intergenerational boundaries, opens communication within the family, reconnects the nuclear and extended families, and makes the adolescent feel cared for and safe. In addition, it functions as a "compression" move, pushing the youth and family members closer together and holding them there until the rebound or disengagement that almost inevitably follows. This rebound is a necessary step in bringing about appropriate distance within enmeshed subsystems, opening the way for a more viable family structure—a structure that does not require a member to exhibit suicidal or self-destructive behavior in order to communicate a need for attention.

After-care transition and support procedures for *The Family Watch* include the following:

1. Ascertaining the post-treatment plan for the youth and providing support at school.
2. Providing feedback to staff.
3. Monitoring student behavior.
4. Providing feedback to parent or guardian regarding adjustment concerns.

Treatment Plan: Post-Traumatic Loss Debriefing.
Counseling Intention: To help participants process loss and grief after the death of a loved one; to teach them about typical stress response reactions and their implications.

Each of the six stages of the debriefing takes two to six hours to complete, depending on need and available coping skills. Follow-up debriefing may be performed with the entire group, a portion of it, or an individual. More than one session may be necessary to process the collection of painful physical, emotional, and cognitive reactions. Once survivors come to terms with stress reactions, they can return to their precrisis equilibrium (Thompson, 1990, 1993).

1. **Introductory Stage:** Briefly introduce the debriefing process and establish rules for the process.

   - Define the nature, limits, roles, and goals of the process.
   - Clarify time limits, number of sessions, confidentiality rules, possibilities, and expectations to reduce unknowns and anxiety.

2. **Fact Stage:** This is the warm-up and information-gathering stage, when participants are asked to recreate the event for the leader. The focus of this stage is facts, not feelings.

   - Group members are asked to make brief statements about their role, relationship with the deceased, how they heard about the death, and circumstances surrounding the event.
   - Members take turns adding details to make the incident come to life again.
   - Members engage in a moderate level of self-disclosure. Questions such as, *"Could you tell me what that was like for you?"* encourage this process.

The counselor needs to be aware of members' choices of topics regarding the death to gain insight into their priorities for the moment. To curtail self-blaming, the counselor should help members see the many factors contributing to the death.

This low-level initial interaction is a nonthreatening warm-up and naturally leads into a discussion of feelings in the next stage. It also provides a safe climate for sharing the details of the death.

3. **Feeling Stage:** At this stage, survivors should have the opportunity to share the feelings they are experiencing in a nonjudgmental, supportive, and understanding environment. Survivors must be permitted to talk about themselves, to identify and express feelings, to identify their own reactions, and to relate to the immediate present. Thoughtful clarification or reflection of feelings can lead to growth and change, rather than to self-depreciation and self-pity.

   At this stage, it is critical that no one gets left out of the discussion, and that no one dominates the discussion at the expense of others.

   Members often will discuss their fears, anxieties, concerns, guilt, frustration, anger, and ambivalence. All of these feelings—positive or negative, big or small—are important and need to be expressed and heard. Most important, this process allows members see that subtle changes are occurring between what happened *then* and what is happening *now*— that things do get better, however small the changes may be.

4. **Reaction Stage:** At this stage, the counselor explores the physical and cognitive reactions to the traumatic event. There are two important steps to follow in this stage:

   • Ask such questions as, *"What reactions did you experience at the time of the incident or when you were informed of the death? . . . What are you experiencing now?"*
   • Encourage members to discuss what is going on with them in their peer, school, work, and family relationships.

5. **Learning Stage:** This stage is designed to teach members new coping skills to deal with their grief. It is also therapeutic to help survivors realize that others are having similar feelings and experiences:

   • Teach the group something about their typical stress response reactions.

- Describe how typical and natural it is for people to experience a wide variety of feelings, emotions, and physical reactions to any traumatic event. It is not unique but a universal, shared reaction.

It is critical in this stage to be alert to danger signals in order to prevent negative outcomes and to help survivors return to their precrisis equilibrium and interpersonal stability.

6. **Closure:** In this stage, the counselor provides final reassurances and follow-up, wrapping up loose ends and answering outstanding questions. Specifically, the counselor determines that initial stress symptoms have been reduced or eliminated, assesses survivors' increased coping abilities, and determines if participants need further intervention. The counselor also makes arrangements for follow-up contact once the sessions have been completed.

The group may close by planning a group activity—for example, going to a movie or concert or a similar outing—to promote a sense of purpose and unity.

Treatment Plan: Loss Group for Adolescents.
Counseling Intention: To assist members who have suffered the loss of a parent or other caregiver; to help them understand the stages of grief; to clarify and accept their feelings; to provide a supportive place to share their experiences with death.

Session 1: Getting-to-know-you exercise. This session focuses on helping students discover they are not alone in their loss and on getting acquainted with group members. Counselor should lead the group in a low-risk get-acquainted exercise that emphasizes similarities among group members.

Session 2: Explore the causes of death. Members identify the many ways people die: for example, accidents, murder, old age, illness, or suicide. The counselor leads the group in a discussion of how some causes of death are easier to accept than others. Each member shares his or her experience with the group.

Session 3: Stages of grief. The counselor explains the stages of grief—denial, anger, bargaining, depression, and acceptance—and discusses the progression to each stage. The group identifies which stages take longer to move through. Members determine what stages they are in now.

Session 4: Concerns and acceptance. The counselor helps determine concerns members have about death that interfere with their acceptance. Members draw pictures illustrating dreams they have had about their parent or caregiver since that person's death. Older students may prefer to describe their dreams. The counselor should look for similarities in themes such as fear, loneliness, wishing for the parent to return, or other unfinished business. The counselor also emphasizes the importance of talking about their concerns with someone they trust.

Session 5: Special personal achievement. Members are asked to write a letter to their late parent or caregiver, sharing something they are especially proud of and wish they could tell the person about. It is important to leave the group on a positive note. The counselor should briefly summarize the issues discussed and ask if the group would like to continue meeting as a support group.

Treatment Plan: Divorce Group for Children or Adolescents.

Counseling Intention: To clarify members' feelings toward divorce; to help members understand that others have similar feelings and concerns; to help them gain a realistic awareness of the situation; to teach them to cope with their feelings.

Wilkinson and Bleck (1977) outlined the following activities for a divorce group for children or adolescents:

Session 1: Introductions. Explain roles, expectations, and membership rules.

Session 2: Nondivorce-related self-disclosure. Pleasant and unpleasant feeling words are introduced so that the members can feel more comfortable about disclosing and discussing feelings.

Session 3: Bibliography on divorce and discussion. The counselor reads a story about parents getting divorced. Members discuss their reactions to the characters' feelings and behaviors.

Session 4: Divorce-related self-disclosure. A sheet of paper is divided into four quadrants. Members are asked to draw a picture of a good time they had with their families, an unpleasant time, why they think their parents got divorced, and what they would like to see happen to their families during the coming year. Members share their papers with the group (Omizo & Omizo, 1988).

Session 5: Role-playing the problems of divorce. Members brainstorm the problems of divorce, then pair off and select one problem to role-play for 3 to 5 minutes.

Session 6: Continued role-playing. Members role-play other problems. The counselor then leads an in-depth discussion.

Session 7: Positive aspects of divorce. The group discusses positive aspects of divorce (for example, parents no longer fighting). Each member completes a personal collage that reflects these positive attributes and shares it with the group.

Session 8: Building self-esteem. The counselor provides a checklist of positive adjectives; members select positive attributes of others to share in the group.

Sessions 9 and 10: Coping with parental divorce. The counselor introduces coping skills and techniques such as time management, stress management, communication skills, positive self-talk, and conflict resolution.

Session 11: Closure. The counselor solicits feedback on group learning and follow-up concerns.

Several group approaches are applicable to children and adolescents:

Situational and transition groups offer information, emotional support, shared feelings, and experiences within a group context, emphasizing the universality of experiences and feelings.

Structured groups teach children and adolescents how to deal with crisis situations through group discussions, role-playing, experiential activities, and expressive techniques such as art therapy.

Saturday workshops (for youth ages 10 to 17) focus on various themes regarding divorce, such as assertiveness training, learning to express feelings, boundary issues, communication skills, and joint custody issues.

The counselor's role is to provide a stable environment to discuss anxieties and concerns; to maintain consistent expectations and routines; to engage in a supportive, therapeutic alliance to encourage communication; and to inform parents about their child's progress or difficulties.

The counselor also provides instruction in specific social, emotional, and cognitive skills to improve targeted symptom behaviors, such as positive self-talk, cognitive awareness strategies, study skills, coping skills, assertiveness, opportunities to discharge emotions through increased physical activity, and biofeedback techniques to aide in relaxation or mood states (Downing, 1988; Hart, 1991).

Treatment Plan: Multimodal Treatment for Depression.
Counseling Intention: To provide a comprehensive intervention for behavior change.

Modality and referral problems	Related interventions
Behavior Reduced work performance Diminished activity Statements of self-denigration	• Implement a "pleasant event schedules" (ascertain behaviors, sensations, images, ideas, and people the student used to find rewarding) to ensure a daily sampling of pleasing activities
Affect Sadness, guilt, "heavy-heartedness" Intermittent anxiety and anger	• Standard anxiety-reduction methods (e.g., relaxation, meditation, calming self-statements combined with assertiveness training; a repertoire of self-assertive and uninhibited responses)
Sensation Less pleasure from food Diminished enthusiasm for life Easily fatigued	• A specific list of pleasant visual, auditory, tactile, olfactory, and gustatory stimuli is added to the "pleasant events schedule" to create a "sensate-focus" of enjoyable events
Imagery Visions of loneliness and failure Pictures himself or herself being rejected by important people in life	• Recalling past successes • Picturing small but successful outcomes • Applying coping imagery, the use of "time projection" (i.e., client pictures him- or herself venturing step-by-step into a future characterized by positive affect and pleasurable activities)
Cognition Negative self-appraisal Exaggerates real or imagined shortcomings. "I'm not good at anything." "Things will always be bad for me."	• Employ Ellis's (1989) methods of cognitive disputation, challenges categorical imperatives, "shoulds and oughts," and irrational beliefs • Identify worthwhile qualities and recite them every day
Interpersonal Decreased social participation	• Clients are taught four skills: saying "No!" to unreasonable requests; asking for favors by expressing positive feelings; volunteering criticism; and "disputing with style" (the client learns to ask for what he or she wants, resists unwelcome requests or exploitation from others, initiates conversations, and develops more interpersonal relationships) • Family therapy also may be recommended to teach family members how to avoid reinforcing depressive behavior and how to encourage the client to engage in pleasurable activities
Drugs/Biology Appetite unimpaired but has intermittent insomnia	• Issues pertaining to increased exercise, relaxation, appropriate sleep patterns, and overall physical fitness are addressed • Biological intervention, such as antidepressants, frequently are recommended in the case of bipolar disorders

Collective Community Initiatives

Young people need to develop coping skills and support networks and to be held in high esteem. A developmentally appropriate prevention model proposed by McWhirter, McWhirter, McWhirter, and McWhirter (1993) suggested that counselors follow these three steps:

1. Use generic skills-training and prevention programs for children in early elementary grades (e.g., programs on identifying feelings, dealing with conflict, and managing emotions).
2. Focus on topic-specific prevention and intervention efforts for youth during preadolescence.
3. Use more topic-specific preventions and interventions for adolescents (e.g., on dealing with loss, stages of grief, and seasonal affective disorders).

CONCLUSION

The causes of childhood and adolescent depression are uncertain, and probably differ from case to case. Adolescent depression may have its own distinct causes. Many researchers maintain that childhood and adolescent depressions often manifest themselves in other behaviors or symptoms, such as irritability, hyperactivity, aggressiveness, delinquency, somatic complaints, hypochondria, anorexia nervosa, substance abuse, obesity, poor school performance, school phobia, loss of initiative, social withdrawal, sleep disturbances, and attention deficit disorder (Angold, 1988; Carlson, 1981; Carlson & Cantwell, 1980; Carlson & Garber, 1986; Husain & Vandiver, 1984; Strober, McCracken, & Hanna, 1989).

The negative effects of divorce also are linked to depression and to excessive anger, aggression, self-destructive behaviors, decreased academic achievement, juvenile delinquency, thoughts of suicide, and sexual promiscuity (Benedek & Benedek, 1979; Bundy & Gumar, 1984; Farber, Primavera, & Felner, 1983). Kelly and Wallerstein (1976) found that children of divorce often experience feelings similar to those associated with death: shock, disbelief, and denial. Children of divorce also suffer from low self-esteem and feelings of abandonment, guilt, helplessness, and inadequacy. Omizo and Omizo (1988, p. 58) found that being aware of their feelings, being able to express them, giving and receiving positive feedback, and knowing that others experience similar feelings had a positive impact on adolescents in group counseling.

Depression is positively correlated to suicidal behavior, so recognizing the symptoms of depression is extremely important in preventing teen suicide. Adolescents, in particular, are likely to have little verbal communication with parents, turning instead to peers or other concerned individuals whom they trust. Therefore, a workable referral system that uses resources within the schools (counselors, social workers, and psychologists) and within the community (mental health professionals, private professionals, and treatment agencies) is crucial.

SOCIAL, EMOTIONAL, AND COGNITIVE SKILLS

Social Literacy Skills

Social literacy skills are *interpersonal skills* essential for meaningful interaction with others. Social skills are those behaviors that, within a given situation, predict important social outcomes such as peer acceptance, popularity, self-efficacy, competence, and high self-esteem. Social skills fall into categories such as being kind, cooperative, and compliant to reduce defiance, aggression, conflict, and antisocial behavior; and showing interest in people and socializing successfully to reduce behavior problems associated with withdrawal, depression, and fearfulness. Social skills include problem solving, assertiveness, thinking critically, resolving conflict, managing anger, and utilizing peer pressure refusal skills.

(*Note*: **Permission is granted to reproduce skills boxes for individual client use.**)

Giving Constructive Criticism

A formula for giving someone constructive criticism involves six steps:

1. Give the person two compliments. Be honest, sincere, and specific.

2. Address the person by name.

3. In a pleasant tone of voice, state your criticism in one or two short, clear sentences.

4. Tell the person what you would like him or her to do. Keep it simple. Set a time limit, if it's appropriate to do so.

5. Offer your help, encouragement, and support.

6. Thank the person for his or her time and for listening.

Helpful Feedback

Helpful feedback tells someone how his or her actions are affecting others. It is important to give feedback in a way that will not be threatening or lead to defensiveness. Some characteristics of helpful feedback are listed here:

- Focus your feedback on the person's behavior, not on personality.

- Focus your feedback on descriptions, not on judgments.

- Focus your feedback on a specific situation, not on abstract generalizations.

- Focus your feedback on the here-and-now, not on the there-and-then.

- Focus your feedback on sharing your perceptions and feelings, not on giving advice.

- Focus your feedback on actions the person can change.

Giving Constructive Feedback

To give constructive feedback, it is important to follow these guidelines:

1. **Ask permission.** Ask the person if he or she would like some feedback on behavior. (If no, wait for a more appropriate time; if yes, proceed.)

2. **Say something positive** to the person before you deliver sensitive information.

3. **Describe the behavior.** Be specific and verifiable. (Have other people complained?) Consider only behavior that can be changed.

4. **Focus on only one behavior at a time.** Include some suggestion for improvement.

    For example: *"Jessica, I've notice something about your behavior at our meetings. Would you like to hear it? . . . At the last two meetings of the homecoming committee, whenever Ryan suggested a theme, you interrupted him and changed the subject. It would be helpful if you would listen to him."*

Asking for What You Want

Asking for what you want involves making an assertive request. It is important to make clear statements so that others understand what you want. Here are the facts you need to include:

From . . . Write down the name of the person who can give you what you want.

I want . . . Be specific about what you want the other person to do, Specify exact behavior. For example, *"I want to have an equal vote on where we go on Friday night."* Or, *"I want the real reason why you don't include John in our plans anymore."*

When . . . State the deadline for getting what you want, the exact time of day, or the frequency with which you want something. For example, you may want extra help with chemistry. Be specific: *"Every Thursday night after dinner."*

Where . . . Write down the place where you want something; the location that will serve to precisely define what you want. If you want to be left alone when you are in your room, specify that place as your special place to be alone.

With . . . Specify any other people who have to do with your request. For example, if you want your brother to stop teasing you about your braces in front of his friends, spell out all the friends' names.

For example,

From: Ryan

I want: No more jokes or remarks about my clothes, my braces, or my friends. I want to be treated with respect.

When: When your friends come over.

Where: At home, at the mall, or at the burger place.

With: John, Ralph, and Bobby.

Source: M. McKay & P. Fanning (1987) *Self-esteem: A proven program of cognitive techniques for assessing, improving, and maintaining your self-esteem*. Reprinted with permission by New Harbinger Publications, Inc., Oakland, California.

Emotional Literacy Skills

Emotional literacy skills are intrapersonal abilities such as knowing one's emotions by recognizing a feeling as it happens and monitoring it; managing emotions (i.e., shaking off anxiety, gloom, irritability, and the consequences of failure; motivating oneself to attain goals, delay gratification, stifle impulsiveness, and maintain self-control; recognizing emotions in others with empathy and perspective taking; and handling interpersonal relationships effectively. Emotional skills fall into categories such as knowing the relationship between thoughts, feelings, and actions; establishing a sense of identity and acceptance of self; learning to value teamwork, collaboration, and cooperation; regulating one's mood; empathizing; and maintaining hope.

(*Note*: **Permission is granted to reproduce skills boxes for individual client use.**)

Positive Affirmations

Many people are limited by their negative thinking. They may be judgmental, opinionated, or highly critical of themselves. Positive affirmations can soften the self-imposed demands or criticisms. Guidelines for positive affirmations follow:

- Begin with the words, *"I am . . . "*

- Include your name in the affirmation.

- Choose positive words.

- Phrase it in the present tense.

- Keep statements short.

- Incorporate your strengths.

Once you have constructed an affirmation, close your eyes, repeat the affirmation several times (at least three), and notice what inner picture it creates. If the picture it creates matches your desired outcome, your affirmation is a good one.

For example: *"I, Jessica, am capable, conscientious, and intelligent. I will be successful in what I attempt to do."*

Paraphrasing

To convey to other people that you understand the meaning of what they said, paraphrase what you heard them say in your own words. Follow these guidelines:

- Listen attentively.

- Pause to determine what the message means to *you*.

- Restate the meaning you got from the message, using your own words.

- Obtain a confirmation from the other person that the meaning you conveyed was correct.

   For example, *"My history teacher just assigned three more chapters for the test tomorrow and I am scheduled to work tonight."*

   Jessica replies, *"You must feel stressed and overwhelmed about what you need to do."*

Dealing with Perfectionism

Some people are driven to perfectionism, so much so that the anxiety interferes with their performance. Panic attacks, self-doubt, and negative self-talk are common. Below are some thoughts to counteract the need to be perfect:

- I would like to do my best, but I do not have to be perfect.

- Making a mistake doesn't mean I have failed.

- I can do something well and appreciate it without it being perfect.

- I will be happier and perform better if I try to work at a realistic level rather than demanding perfection of myself.

- It is impossible to function perfectly every time.

- It is important to stop and smell the roses.

Expressing Intentions

Expressing intention lets others know more about your immediate or long-range expectations. Expressing intentions is a way of being direct about what you would or would not like to do. Intention statements begin with words like these:

"I want . . . "

"I'd like . . . "

"I intend . . . "

For example, *"I want to be with you today, but I don't want to spend all our time shopping."*

"I'd like to do my studying in the afternoon, then catch the game this evening."

"I'd like to be with you, but I want to be with my family tonight too, because it's my brother's birthday.

Perception Checking

Perception checking is a verbal statement that reflects your own understanding of the meaning of another person's nonverbal cues. The process for perception checking is as follows:

1. Pause and observe the behavior.

2. Describe the behavior mentally.

3. Ask yourself, "What does the behavior mean to me?"

4. Put your interpretation of the nonverbal behavior into words to check whether your perception of the situation is accurate.

For example, Ryan, speaking in an abrupt tone of voice, gives Jessica the assignment she missed in class.

Jessica (using a perception check) says, *"From the sound of your voice, Ryan, I get the impression you're upset with me. What's going on?"*

Chapter 7

CONFLICTED YOUTH, DELINQUENCY, AND VIOLENCE

These bondless men, women, and children see those around them as objects, targets, stepping stones. Most lie, steal, cheat without a concern about the consequences on others. They have no conscience and they feel no remorse for their actions. If the suppressed rage ever surfaces, they are capable of much more than a con. The sickest commit the senseless murders so prevalent in the newspapers today. And they do it just for kicks. (Magid & McKelvey, 1987, p. 26)

The homeboys call him Frog. . . . He rakes in $200 a week selling crack, known as "rock" in East Los Angeles. He proudly advertises his fledgling membership in an ultra-violent street gang: the Crips. And he brags that he used his drug money to rent a Nissan Z on weekends. He has not yet learned how to use a stick shift, however, and at 4ft. 10 in., he has trouble seeing over the dashboard. Frog is 13 years old. (Lamar, 1988, p.37)

The United States has the highest rate of interpersonal violence of any industrialized country. The homicide rate for men ages 15 to 24 in this country has increased at an alarming rate in the past two decades (Prothrow-Stith, 1991) with more than half of all serious crimes (murders, rapes, assaults, and robberies) committed by youth ages 10 to 17 (Winbush, 1988). Media images, violent films, and music (e.g., "gangster rap" and "death metal") often glorify interpersonal violence. Violence has become a crisis of epidemic proportions for children in urban centers in the United States (Pynoos & Nader, 1988).

Violence is most prevalent among the poor, regardless of race. And the victims and perpetrators of the carnage are getting younger and more violent. Socioeconomic inequity fosters a sense of relative deprivation among the poor, and the lack of opportunities to improve their life circumstances manifests itself in higher rates of violence and a lack of hope about the future.

The increase in juvenile violent crime over the last decade should serve as a wake-up call to the nation that current policies have not worked to diminish violence among young people. The corridors of the juvenile courts are increasingly populated with parents who are still children themselves, children who have no parent but the state, and baby-faced teenagers charged with crimes worthy of the most hardened criminals.

Today, it is painfully clear that children are committing more serious crimes at ever younger ages. The most common crimes committed by adolescents are vandalism, motor vehicle theft, burglary, larceny, robbery, and stolen property. Vandalism and theft often correlate with drug and alcohol use; children steal in order to pay for a drug habit.

Statistics paint an alarming picture:

- Law-enforcement agencies made 129,600 juvenile arrests for violent crimes in 1992, a 55% increase from 1983, when there were 83,400 arrests (Portner, 1995).
- Today, homicide is the third leading cause of death for all children between the ages of 5 and 14; the second leading cause of death for all young people between the ages of 10 and 24; and the leading cause of death among African-Americans of both sexes between the ages of 15 and 34. Teenagers are more than twice as likely to be victims of violent crime than those over the age of 20 (Sautter, 1995).
- Juvenile arrests for violent crimes increased by 50% between 1983 and 1992—double the adult increase; juvenile arrests for murder rose 85%— four times the increase for adults. Today, 3 of every 10 juvenile murder arrests involves a victim under the age of 18. National surveys repeatedly show that people under the age of 20 account for a disproportionate percentage of violent-crime victims, and that teenage victimization is most likely to occur at school (Gallop International Institute, 1994).

- Juvenile arrests for murders, forcible rapes, robberies, and other violent crimes have reached an all-time high, accounting for 17 percent of all arrests for such crimes. One in 20 persons arrested for a violent crime today is under the age of 15 (Brookman, 1993).
- Researchers contend that the increase in the murder rate of young men is linked, in part, to the recruitment of youths into drug markets, where guns are used to settle disputes (Lawton, 1994). In 1991, 88% of all homicides among 15- to 19-year-olds were firearm-related (Portner, 1994).
- In larger, more urban communities, 20% of all males belong to gangs (Brookman, 1993).
- Homicide is the leading cause of death among African-American youths (Lawton, 1994).
- In 1994, there were more than 1 million people in federal prisons, and an additional 500,000 in local jails. The annual cost of incarcerating federal prisoners has been estimated at $20,072 per inmate (Charles Stewart Mott Foundation, 1994).
- As the crime rate rose during the 1980s, so did the number of children living in poverty. In 1992, 14.6 million juveniles lived below the poverty level, a 42% increase from 1976 (Portner, 1995).

Violence also has a psychological impact. Post-traumatic stress experienced by victims of and witnesses to violence "includes intrusive imagery, emotional constriction or avoidance, fears of recurrence, sleep disturbance, disinterest in significant activities, and concentration difficulties (APA, 1993; Thompson, 1990, 1993). Violence and post-traumatic stress interfere with normal development, with learning in school, and with a child's inherent right to a happy childhood. All fall victim to the fear, the anger, the guilt, and the helplessness that follow an act of violence.

PREDICTORS OF VIOLENT BEHAVIOR

The American Psychological Association (APA, 1993, p. 4) found that "the strongest developmental predictor of a child's involvement in violence is a history of previous violence." Being a victim of abuse also is a factor. About 70% of men involved in the criminal justice system were abused or neglected children. The long-range implications and overt ramifications of abuse are documented in violent crimes. The criminal profiles below illustrate how dysfunctional and abusive relationships in childhood can play out tragically in adulthood:

"My future is small, my past an insult to any human being. My mother must have thought I was a canoe, she paddled me so much" (Arthur Bremer, who, on May 15, 1972, attempted to assassinate Governor George Wallace of Alabama).

Sirhan Sirhan, the man who assassinated Robert Kennedy, was beaten by his father with sticks and fists, and had a hot iron held to his heel because he was disobedient.

James Earl Ray lived under chaotic conditions as a child, drifting from foster home to foster home after having been abused by an alcoholic father. He alledgedly shot and killed Dr. Martin Luther King, Jr.

Lee Harvey Oswald was a troubled child, brought up by a single mother who physically abused him. He spent much of his youth in a children's training institution for deprived children. On November 22, 1963, he assassinated the President of the United States, John F. Kennedy (Fontana, 1985, p. 22).

The APA also found that "children who show a fearless, impulsive temperament very early in life may have a predisposition for aggression and violent behavior" (APA, 1993, p. 4).

The single strongest predictor of violence in adolescence and adulthood, however, is antisocial behavior (aggression, stealing, lying, or dishonesty) during late childhood and early adolescence. Having an antisocial parent is the next best predictor of adult antisocial behavior. The association between parental criminality and delinquency is especially strong when the parent is a repeat offender and when parental criminal activity occurred during the child-rearing period (Charles Stewart Mott Foundation 1994, p.16).

The impetus for violence is born of distorted emotions and depraved values—unbridled anger, unyielding vengeance, cold-hearted retribution, mis-led loyalty, false bravado—skewed motivations that continue to perplex educators, counselors, social workers, probation officers, police officers, law makers, juvenile courts, judges, and others as they try to devise strategies to arrest the momentum of youth violence.

Child advocates and social workers also warn that relentless poverty, inequitable educational opportunities, latchkey homes, child abuse, domestic violence, and family disintegration, as well as the general abandonment of children to a constant barrage of televised chaos, will result in escalating real-world violence (Edelman, 1994; Sautter, 1995). The typical adolescent of any ethnic or economic group witnesses on television more than 8,000 murders and more than 100,000 other violent acts by the time he or she enters 7th grade

(Charles Stewart Mott Foundation, 1994; Sautter, 1995). Without the opportunity to process random acts of violence in the media, youth become desensitized and begin to have destructive social expectations and a proclivity for aggressive behavior.

Well-established antecedents of serious, violent, and chronic juvenile crime, then, are neglect, weak family attachments, a lack of consistent discipline, poor school performance, delinquent peer groups, physical and/or sexual abuse, residence in high-crime neighborhoods, economic inequity coupled with lack of opportunity, media influences, and emotional and cognitive deficits (APA, 1993).

Finally, violence may also have a chemical factor. Recent studies of the brain suggest that fluctuations in the availability of the neurotransmitter serotonin can play an important role in regulating our self-esteem and our propensity for violence. Researchers have associated high serotonin levels with high self-esteem and social status, and low serotonin levels with low self-esteem and low social status. Behaviorally, high serotonin levels are associated with calm assurance. Low levels are associated with irritability that leads to impulsive, reckless, aggressive, violent, suicidal behaviors that often are directed at inappropriate targets (Sylwester, 1995).

YOUTH AT RISK FOR GANG MEMBERSHIP

Youth gangs are groups of adolescents and young adults who interact frequently with one another; are frequently and deliberately involved in illegal activities; share a common collective identity that is usually, but not always, expressed through a gang name; and typically express that identity by adopting certain symbols and claiming control over certain turf (Goldstein & Huff, 1993, p. 4).

Spergel (1989) suggested the following working definition for a gang: "juvenile and young adults associating together for serious, especially violent, criminal behavior with special concerns for 'turf.' Turf can signify the control of a physical territory, a criminal enterprise, or both."

Conflicted youth are likely candidates for gang membership. Marginally adjusted in school, they may be perceived as withdrawn and passive or as sullen and intense. They often show problems with anger and are sensitive to humiliation or teasing. A family history of abuse or mistreatment—with the residual outcomes of low self-esteem, resentment, and substance abuse—often

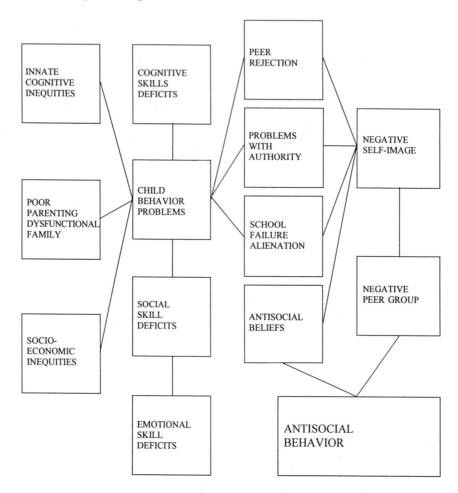

Figure 7.1.   Development of antisocial behavor.

is present. Rejected by family, school, and peers, conflicted youth repeatedly experience failure, stress, depression, hopelessness, and alienation.

Conflicted youths often join gangs because they don't find caring and mutual support in the home environment. They might join out of a need for family, to gain acceptance from someone else, or to get peer approval. A gang also fulfills status and esteem needs, as well as providing material wealth from the drug trade.

Many immigrant children—those dealing with the transition from one culture to another—are also vulnerable to the attractions of gangs of youth in similar situations. Young men from single-parent families and female-dominated homes often are attracted to gangs as well, because the gang provides male-bonding experiences. There are varying debates about why youth join gangs, but the predominate factors include these:

- A lack of caring and mutual support in the home (family) environment, feeling neglected by parents, a need for a family
- A need for acceptance, a need to gain approval from peers, a need for status or self-esteem
- A need for money available through drug trade or other illegal methods

The National School Safety Center (1988) found reported these findings:

- Once in a gang, the odds are overwhelmingly against a boy or girl leaving it.
- Gang membership, while dangerous, often provides the best protection available to inner-city youth.
- Most violent crimes are committed by youth in "packs" of three or more.

To help identify young people most at risk, several recent publications have included lists of behaviors that, when seen in definite patterns, are strong indicators of possible gang involvement (National School Safety Center, 1988). The warning signs include these:

- Rumors or reliable information that a youth has not been home for several nights
- Evidence of increased substance abuse; abrupt changes in behavior and personality
- Newly acquired and unexplained "wealth," often showered on or shared with peers (from sharing bags of candy with younger children to a flurry of extravagant spending by older youth)
- Requests to borrow money
- "Hanging around," but being unable to discuss problems
- Evidence of mental or physical child abuse
- A dress code that applies to a few: wearing a color, a style, an item of clothing, a particular hairstyle, or symbols of identification (National School Safety Center, 1988, p. 10)

Gangs and Criminal Behavior

For several years crack-cocaine has been the principle commodity for large-scale gang drug trafficking. Youth participation in such activity has changed the character of many gangs. Youth gangs have become increasingly involved with controlling drug markets, often far beyond their original territories.

In this context, several reasons for the crushing wave of youth violence emerge: the escalation of drug wars and the engagement of young "soldiers" to conduct the street battles, society's desensitization toward violence, the deterioration of family bonds, and the lack of cohesiveness in communities nationwide.

Keeping Youth Out of Gangs

Some states are beginning to crack down on teenage law-breakers with new "parent-liability" laws. In Arkansas, California, and Florida, for example, parents can be fined or jailed for their child's offenses.

However, many leaders in the field of child and adolescent development believe that stable parent-child relationships, not stronger juvenile laws, are the best way to prevent teens from breaking the law. They believe parents should encourage their children's participation in community organizations, such as the YMCA, sports, music, and other activities, so that the children develop self-esteem and a sense of responsibility to their community.

In their study *Violence & Youth: Psychology's Response*, the APA maintained that early childhood intervention to prevent future violence is critical. Children who show signs of antisocial behavior need to be targeted early for school and family intervention, not only to teach them alternatives for resolving conflicts but also to ensure that their aggressive tendencies do not interfere with reaching their full academic potential (APA, 1993).

STRUCTURED INTERVENTIONS FOR HIGH-RISK BEHAVIORS

Therapeutic Initiatives

To help conflicted youths resist the temptations of gang membership, Goldstein, Glick, Irwin, Pask-McCartney, and Rubama (1989) advocate aggression-replacement training that focuses on interpersonal skills, anger control, and moral education. Interpersonal skill training would center on such social skill deficits as these:

- Listening and maintaining a conversation
- Asking for help and giving instructions
- Apologizing and expressing feelings
- Dealing with someone's anger, negotiating, using self-control
- Assertiveness and keeping out of fights
- Responding to persuasion and to failure
- Dealing with an accusation and group pressure

Components of an anger-control training curriculum might include keeping a "hassle log" to record angry situations, identifying more effective coping skills, training in self-awareness of anger, and learning relaxation techniques. Group discussions of moral dilemmas and role-playing alternatives also are important components.

In addition, the APA (1993) found that school programs that promote social and cognitive skills seem to have the greatest impact on attitudes about violent behavior among children and adolescents. Such skills include "perspective taking, alternative solution generation, self-esteem enhancement, peer negotiation skills, problem-solving training, anger management, and the cognitive skill of thinking things through" (APA, 1993, p. 34.) One such curriculum was developed by the National Institute on Alcohol Abuse and Alcoholism (1990) to teach a think-first model, in which students go through four steps:

1. **Keep cool.** Violent offenders often are "hot reactors" (i.e., quick to anger) This step teaches the difference between being cool-headed and being hot-headed.
2. **Size up the situation.** Violent offenders define a problem in a hostile way and automatically treat other people as adversaries. This step seeks to show alternative ways of viewing problems. The way an individual defines a problem influences the solution he or she chooses.
3. **Think it through.** Violent offenders simply do not think things through; they are concrete in their thinking and cannot see consequences. The emphasis of this step is on thinking of alternative solutions and thinking about the consequences of actions.
4. **Do the right thing.** Students are taught to pick the response that is most likely to succeed and be effective in solving the problem and preventing violence.

Violence is a learned behavior—one that can be unlearned or prevented altogether. Children and adolescents need to be taught how to think of alternatives clearly and how to prevent violence. These are cognitive skills that can be taught by the classroom teacher and reinforced in the classroom setting. Johnson and Johnson (1991) promoted integrating social and cognitive skill training in the classroom, maintaining that cooperative learning, in addition to contributing to academic improvement, teaches social and mediation skills that enable young people to interact with others more positively.

Further, children and adolescents should be given the strategies and information to integrate various conflict resolution styles. Helping them differentiate between conflict resolution approaches also is helpful. Most conflicts can be defined as issues resulting from circumstances that affect both parties. Conflict is perceived as a challenge to personal beliefs, opinions, actions, and authority.

The key to making conflict work in a positive way is to remember that conflict, like other problems, is solvable. This assumption tends to bring about solutions. Collectively, there are at least 12 conflict resolution, mediation, or management styles:

Mediation is a structured process in which a neutral third party facilitates an agreement between two or more parties. The disputing parties have responsibility for making recommendations, determining final decisions, and finding mutually agreeable solutions (Girard, Refkin, & Townley, 1985).

Conciliation refers to an informal voluntary negotiation process in which a third party brings the disputing parties together and facilitates communication by lowering tensions, carrying information between parties, and creating a safe environment to share issues. Conciliation may be a prerequisite to formal mediation (Messing, 1993).

Alternative Dispute Resolution (ADR) is intended to facilitate settlement of civil cases before they go to trial by encouraging voluntary agreements as a result of informal sessions with magistrates or judges (Messing, 1993, p. 67).

Arbitration is submission of a dispute to a neutral third party, who presents a decision after hearing arguments and evaluating evidence. In binding arbitration, the parties agree to an assigned arbitrator and are legally bound by the decision (Girard, Rifkin, & Townley, 1985; Messing, 1993).

Confrontation is a direct conflict of issues or persons. Power strategies includes the use of physical force, bribery, extortion, or punishment.

Gang behavior would be an example of this approach. The intention is to provide a win/lose situation, in which one person wins and the other person loses something of value. The limitation of this approach is that it produces feelings of hostility, anxiety, and/or physical damage to self, others, or personal property (Johnson & Johnson, 1991).

Competition can be viewed as self-serving or assertive about a conviction. It is self-serving when an individual is pursuing personal concerns or goals at another person's expense. In this form it is uncooperative, unyielding, and power-oriented. Selling poor merchandise to unsuspecting consumers would be an example of this type of behavior. It is assertive when it is portrayed as standing up for a conviction or defending a position a person believes is right. Being patriotic about one's country during war is an example of this approach. The user's intention often is to secure immediate resources or to stand up to beliefs. The limitation of this approach is that it often intimidates other people.

Collaboration involves attempting to work with the other person to find some solution to the dilemma, negotiating the best fit between individuals or groups by exploring disagreements and generating alternatives. The user's intentions are to learn from another person's perspective and to identify all issues or concerns to a dilemma. The limitations are that it is time-consuming and not applicable to crisis situations (Johnson & Johnson, 1991).

Compromising is assertive and cooperative when parties seek a middle ground. The goal is to find some expedient, mutually acceptable solution that partially satisfies both parties. The user's intention is to reach expedient decisions on minor disagreements. The limitation is that everyone's ultimate goal may not be reached. Revision, reevaluation, and reinvention may be the next step.

Accommodation is unassertive but cooperative. The individual or group yields to another point of view. It means obeying another person's order when one's preference would be otherwise. The user's intention usually is a self-check on his or her perspective by yielding that he or she may be wrong. Critical personal concerns that may be neglected or tabled for the time being are the main limitations.

Diffusion is an approach that delays immediate action or confrontation. The individual or group uses strategies to try to cool off the situation or to keep the issues so unclear that attempts at confrontation are inhibited. The intention often is to delay a discussion of a major problem or to postpone a confrontation until a more auspicious time. The limitation is that it avoids clarification of the salient issues underlying a conflict, typically resulting in dissatisfaction, anxiety about the future, and concerns about self or others.

Avoidance is withdrawing from the situation or not addressing it, attempting to avoid conflict situations altogether or to avoid certain types of conflict situations. The user's intentions may be to avoid situations in which confronting is dangerous, to afford an opportunity to cool down, or to provide more time to prepare for the situation. Individuals repress emotional reactions or escape conflicting situations with this approach, and often are left without much satisfaction.

Negotiation attempts to promote an encounter in which both parties win. The aim of negotiation is to resolve the conflict with a solution that is mutually satisfying to both parties. Negotiation provides the most positive and least negative consequences of all conflict resolution strategies. Negotiation skills include a clear identification of the conflict, effectiveness at initiating a carefronting solution, an ability to hear the other person's point of view, and the ability to use problem-solving processes to bring about a consensus decision. This resolution style is a component of most peer-mediation programs today.

Nattive, Render, Lemire, and Render (1990) defined conflict resolution as a complex skill built on the practice and mastery of simpler communication skills that promote positive interaction. The ability to interact requires several things:

- Awareness of others
- Awareness of the distinction between self and others
- Skills in listening and hearing
- Awareness of one's feelings and thoughts
- An ability to respond to the feelings and thoughts of others

Social and emotional skills necessary for conflict resolution include active listening, empathy, critical thinking, problem solving, and communicating with "I" messages. Effective and continued communication is vitally important in conflict resolution. It is quite common, however, for the individuals in a conflict to refuse to communicate with one another. Only when communication is aimed at an agreement fair to all parties involved is it helpful in resolving conflict. It is important to help others realign their attitudes toward conflict so they can view it constructively.

Mediation characteristics that align with counseling include confidentiality, acceptance, active listening, development of rapport and empathy, role-playing, clarification, and emphasis on the here-and-now (Kelly, 1983; Messing, 1993). Other useful counseling techniques include the following:

Ivey's (1988) five-stage interview process, which includes defining the problem, defining a goal, exploring alternatives, confronting incongruity, and generalizing to daily life.

Verbal reframing, in which clients rephrase negative descriptions in positive ways. Reframing is an influencing skill that offers another way of seeing how a situation or event happened (Cormier & Cormier, 1985; Ivey, 1988; Messing, 1993).

Selective reinforcement to develop desired cooperative behaviors and problem-solving strategies like brainstorming.

Mediation contracts to reinforce expectations for compliance by each party, to attest the belief was fair, and that external consequences related to the failure of a negotiated agreement serve as the motivation to maintain the agreement (Egan, 1982; Messing, 1993).

Treatment Plan: Conflict Resolution and Anger Management.
Counseling Intention: To teach a framework for resolving conflict in a systematic way; to provide conflict resolution skills for adolescent and adults.

Johnson and Johnson (1991) outlined the following steps in negotiating resolutions to conflicts. This process is most appropriate with adolescents and adults who possess a mature cognitive reasoning ability. Participants need to follow the following steps:

1. **Agree on a definition of the conflict.**

   - Describe the other person's actions.
   - Define the conflict as a mutual problem to be solved, not as a win/lose struggle.
   - Define the conflict in the smallest and most specific way possible.
   - Describe your feelings about, and your reactions to, the other person's actions.
   - Describe your actions (what you are doing and neglecting to do) that help create and continue the conflict.

2. **Exchange proposals and feelings.**

   - Present your proposed agreements and feelings.
   - Listen to the other person's proposals and feelings.
   - Clarify, evaluate, refute one another's proposals.
   - Stay flexible, changing your position and feelings when persuaded to do so.
   - Focus on needs and goals.

- Find out about the differences between your underlying needs and goals and those of the other person.
- Communicate cooperative intentions.
- Clarify your motivation and the motivation of the other person to resolve the conflict.

3. Understand the other person's perspective.

- Do not second guess the other person's intentions.
- Do not blame the other person for your problem. It is counter-productive and will make the other person defensive and closed-minded.
- Discuss one another's perceptions.
- Look for opportunities to act inconsistently with the other person's negative perceptions.
- Give the other person a stake in the outcome by making sure he or she participates in the process.

4. Invent options for mutual gain.

- Focus on needs and goals, not on positions.
- Clarify differences before seeking similarities.
- Empower the other person by staying flexible and giving choices.
- Avoid obstacles to creative thinking.
- Avoid judging prematurely.

5. Reach a wise agreement.

6. Keep trying, over and over again.

Younger children can be empowered with mediation training to serve as peer mediators. It is important to start prevention programs in the early elementary grades in order to circumvent gang influence.

Treatment Plan: Mediation Training.
Counseling Intention: To teach mediation skills to pre- and early-adolescents; to empower them to handle their own conflicts; to provide the necessary skills so that peers can resolve their own conflicts in a systematic way.

Teaching children mediation skills empowers them to have control over their own behavior. The following guidelines can be posted in the classroom, the team room, or the clubroom and are most appropriate for preadolescents:

1. **Introduction:** Disputants are welcomed and people introduce themselves. The mediation process is explained. Mediators explain the ground rules:

   - Do not interrupt when someone is talking.
   - Do not call anyone names.
   - Disputants must tell the truth.
   - Disputants must try to solve the problem.

2. **Help disputants define the problem:** Ask the first party to define the problem briefly, as he or she sees it, and to express feelings about it. Then ask the second party to define the problem and express feelings about it. Ask questions after each person speaks to help them focus on the issues and identify feelings. Finally, summarize the problem as each person stated it.

3. **Help parties understand each other.** Ask each person to summarize the other's feelings and concerns about the problem. Ask if there is a way they could have handled the problem differently.

4. **Help parties find a solution to the problem.**

   - Ask the first party what he or she likes or dislikes about the solution.
   - Ask the second party what he or she likes or dislikes about the solution.
   - Ask the second party what would be a fair solution.
   - Ask the first party to respond.
   - Help disputants find a solution to which they can both agree.
   - Summarize the solution and check with disputants for accuracy.

5. **Write up agreement.** Read the agreement out loud. Make changes if necessary. When both parties are satisfied, have them sign the agreement. Congratulate them for coming to the agreement.

Treatment Plan: Anger-Reduction Technique.

Counseling Intention: To channel angry feelings into socially acceptable directions; to foster an environment in which the norm is cooperation, respect, and nonviolence instead of aggression and exploitation.

Anger from another, if responded to skillfully, can broaden interpersonal learning and strengthen a relationship. The following steps (RACN) are important:

- **Recognize** and affirm the other person's feelings. Acknowledge that you hear him or her and that you are willing to respond. Not recognizing feelings intensifies the situation.
- **Accept** your own defensiveness.
- **Clarify** and request specific feedback. Distinguish between what you want and what you need. When needs and wants are clarified, the resolution of the conflict becomes more probable. Give and receive specific feedback.
- **Negotiate** or renegotiate the relationship. Plan together how you both will deal with similar situations in the future. Acknowledge regret and exchange apologies. Establish a verbal or written contract about practicing new behavior.

Throughout the resolution process, it is important to be open, to be willing to generate alternatives, to search for a solution, and to commit to the solution after extensive dialogue. Maintaining anger and discord, refusing to listen, and being defensive do not help resolve conflicts or improve relationships. The following treatment plans could be useful for working with angry or conflicted youth.

Treatment Plan: The Win/Win Support Group.
Counseling Intention: To teach the separation of people from the problems they are having; to help youth learn to respond instead of merely reacting; to offer an opportunity to practice the skills taught; to teach positive human interaction skills.

Youth participating in this support group have the opportunity to learn how to achieve a "win-win" situation, to improve relationship skills, to increase self-esteem, and to reduce intensity and frequency of conflict in their lives. Dysinger (1993, p. 307) outlined the following conflict resolution strategies to use with adolescents:

Session 1: Conflict and People. Introduce the technique of separating people from problems so that, in negotiating conflicts, people understand the differences between personal interest, individual wants, and human rights and responsibilities. List examples of situations such as ganging up, forming alliances, or being left out. Encourage youth to watch for these situations in the coming week and to jot down how they felt and reacted.

Session 2: Conflicts, Feelings, and Reactions. Ask for reports on feelings or reactions noted in the previous week. Listen for inclinations to report reactions erroneously. Discuss how conflict resolution requires acceptance of the equal value of each person, and how individuals *must* resolve problems differently because their feelings, wishes, wants, and reactions are different. Point out the value of considering options instead of reacting. Encourage youth to be aware of problems, feelings, reactions, and consequences in the coming week.

Session 3. Discussing a Problem. Introduce several roadblocks to communication, such as labeling another person, listening to hearsay, or magnifying a situation. Encourage a discussion of a designated problem, describing feelings, thoughts, and opinions on it.

Session 4. Responding Versus Reacting. Introduce specific responses useful in conflict situations, such as using "I" messages.

Session 5. Making Choices. Have youth practice learning from criticism, and ask them to separate the harmful messages from possible truths.

Session 6. Considering Options. Ask youth the following questions: *"Have you noticed any changes in the frequency or intensity of conflict in your life? . . . If so, what do you believe you did to bring about those changes? . . . If not, what do you believe you need to do to cause positive changes?"* Distribute bookmarks listing these truisms:

- Problems can be defined and thought about carefully.
- Problems are different for people, and people's problems are different.
- Roadblocks of communication and problem solving can be removed.
- Specific skills can help resolve conflict: "I" messages, using helpful criticism, changing chain reactions, and choosing the best option are four of them.
- Friendliness helps reduce conflict.

Session 7. Friendship. Describe levels of friendship. Brainstorm relationship skills, such as complementing sincerely, inviting, listening and responding, telling the truth, considering feelings, allowing differences, understanding mistakes, and supporting someone in need.

Session 8. Conclusion. Plan a reunion in 4 to 6 weeks to check on members' progress.

Treatment Plan: Self-Disclosing and Expressing Anger.
Counseling Intention: To identify feelings associated with anger.

Each member completes the following open-ended sentences on index cards (one per card). They are to write down the few responses that occur to them without censoring or modifying the responses.

- *I feel angry when others . . .*
- *When others express anger toward me, I feel . . .*
- *I express my anger by . . .*

Members pin their responses to their shirts. Process the experience by focusing on the personal impact of sharing their feelings about anger with the group. Provide feedback on the extent to which each individual's responses to anger seem congruent or incongruent. The processing phase may be followed by a practice session on expressing anger.

Johnson and Wilborn (1991) provide the following treatment plan for managing anger:

Session 1: Ask members to describe an experience when they were angry and to focus on the feeling connected with the anger. Have them recall how their parents expressed anger and decide which parent they most resemble in their experience and expression of anger. For homework, ask them to be aware of their own anger and that of others during the following week.

Session 2: Begin the group with members sharing their anger experiences of past week and their observations of other people's expression of anger. Explain Ellis's *Rational Emotive ABC Theory* (Walen, DiGuiseppe, & Wessler, 1980). Talk about how many people have trouble with "C" (their emotion) because of underlying beliefs about the emotion. Explain that all emotions are justified simply because they exist. Help group members distinguish between thoughts and feelings.

Session 3: Relate an anger-provoking incident and ask members to respond to it in terms of the degree of anger experienced and how they would feel and react in such a situation. Introduce the "push-button technique" (Mosak, 1984), in which group members are asked to close their eyes and see themselves in a pleasant experience. Ask them to remember how they felt, and to feel the same feeling in their bodies. Then ask them to change and remember an unpleasant experience, to remember how they felt, who was there, and so on. Then have them remember the pleasant experience again. This helps participants experience the changing of feelings and their power to create the feeling they choose. Members are led to see the control they have over events and experiences in their lives.

Session 4: Ask members to recall how anger was expressed in their families of origin and to discuss the differences between the male and female experience and expression of anger. Introduce reflective listening and "I" messages as tools for dealing with anger. During the week ask them to observe anger expressions by men and women with whom they associate and as portrayed on television to compare observations at the next meeting.

Session 5: Ask members what advice they would give their parents about helping their children deal with anger, and what general advice they would give to today's teenagers about expressing anger. Ask them to discuss the most stressful events in their lives and how they dealt with those events.

Session 6: Introduce the concept of anger experienced as a task and problem-solving technique (Novaco, 1975). Summarize the content of the group discussion and provide an opportunity for follow-up.

Individual Multimodal Treatment Plan for Conflicted Youth.

Counseling Intention: To provide a comprehensive intervention for behavior change.

Modality	Problem assessment	Potential intervention
Behavior	Poor academic performance and attendance problems Negative self-statements Aggressive acting out	• Self-contracting; recording and self-monitoring • Positive self-talk • Aggression Replacement Training
Affect	Feelings of little self-worth Anger toward significant others Conflict with others	• Increase range of positive reinforcement • Exercises in anger-expression • Behavior-rehearsal • Role-reversal
Sensation	Anxiety and depression over present circumstances and future goals	• Anxiety-management training goal rehersal or coping imagery
Imagery	Unproductive fantasies Image of self as incapable	• Positive imagery • Goal rehearsal
Cognition	Poor study habits Lack of educational or occupational information Sexual misinformation Expectations of failure	• Study skills training • Assertiveness training • Career counseling; assessment and information • Sex education; bibliotherapy • Positive self-talk
Interpersonal relations	Poor relationships with peers	• Social skills and assertiveness training
Drugs (biological functioning)	Poor dietary habits; substance abuse	• Nutrition and dietary information; alternative "highs"

Collective Community Initiatives

Young people need to know how to communicate effectively, to resolve conflicts, and to manage anger. It also is critical to teach our young people interpersonal communication, leadership, problem solving, and assertiveness to enhance self-esteem. Slovacek (1993) suggested that comprehensive prevention or early intervention programs must include the following areas:

- Drug/gun/gang policy awareness
- Drug and gang prevention education
- Racial and cultural sensitivity development
- Before- and after-school alternative programs for structured supervision with recreation, remediation, and enrichment opportunities
- Mentoring role models and partnerships
- Community service opportunities
- Career and education awareness
- Early intervention counseling
- Childcare and parent education

Moreover, the media, community leaders, and high-profile role models must join forces with educators and helping professionals to promote nonviolence.

Concurrently, the flight of businesses—and employment opportunities—from the urban core has created a climate of hopelessness, loss of discipline, and diminished self-confidence, undermining the moral structure of those neighborhoods. People tend to be more aggressive when they are deprived of basic needs. Poverty, deprivation, and adverse conditions affect a growing proportion of American children and adolescents. These pervasive conditions provide fertile ground for aggressive conduct and subversive activities. Until these trends are reversed through collective intervention, it unlikely that violence among youth will decline.

The ramifications of youth violence are not limited to urban communities. Domestic violence, hate crimes, sexual violence, and violence among peers have jeopardized the safety and well-being of children and adolescents in every community.

CONCLUSION

Conflict can serve many purposes: to escalate already tense situations, to motivate another person to action, or to inhibit new ideas. It often is a struggle for power. It can be intimidating. It can create ideas or estrange previous relationships. Within multicultural and diverse settings, conflicts can expand exponentially. Our typical response to conflict is to compete, collaborate, compromise, accommodate, or avoid. The ability to resolve conflicts successfully is one of the most important social and emotional skills an individual can possess.

SOCIAL, EMOTIONAL, AND COGNITIVE SKILLS

Social Literacy Skills

Social literacy skills are *interpersonal skills* essential for meaningful interaction with others. Social skills are those behaviors that, within a given situation, predict important social outcomes such as peer acceptance, popularity, self-efficacy, competence, and high self-esteem. Social skills fall into categories such as being kind, cooperative, and compliant to reduce defiance, aggression, conflict, and antisocial behavior; and showing interest in people and socializing successfully to reduce behavior problems associated with withdrawal, depression and fearfulness. Social skills include problem solving, assertiveness, thinking critically, resolving conflict, managing anger, and utilizing peer pressure refusal skills.

(*Note*: **Permission is granted to reproduce skills boxes for individual client use.**)

Dealing with Conflict without Violence

Here is a list of things to try when you are faced with a conflict situation:

- Share or take turns.

- Ignore what someone says or does.

- Ask for help from someone else.

- Use assertive behavior and "say no"

- Negotiate and work out a mutual plan.

- Compromise; give up something.

- Apologize, explain, and try to understand.

- Postpone and get some distance from the situation; sleep on it.

- Change the subject or suggest doing something else to avoid a conflict.

- Find humor in the situation.

Anger Management

Here is a checklist of steps for dealing with anger:

- Stay in control.

- Stay calm and cool.

- Stand in the other person's shoes; try to see his or her perspective.

- Give the other person a way out.

- Lighten up and relax.

- Apologize or excuse yourself.

Rules of Conflict Resolution

Here is a list of rules to follow when you are engaged in conflict resolution:

- I agree to work to solve the problem.

- I will not call the other person names, use put downs, or "dis" the other person.

- I will not interrupt when the other person is talking.

- I will be honest and follow through on resolving the problem.

The Peer Mediation Process

Here is a process for mediating conflicts:

1. **Introduction and Ground Rules**
   - Introduce yourselves
   - Ask if the parties want to solve the problem with you.
   - Explain that what is said will be kept confidential.
   - Get agreement to the four rules:
     - Do not interrupt
     - No name calling or put-downs
     - Be as honest as you can
     - Work hard to solve the problem
2. **Defining the Problem**
   - Decide who will talk first.
   - Ask person #1 what happened. *Restate.* Ask person #1 how he or she feels and why. *Restate feeling.*
   - Ask person #2 what happened. *Restate.* Ask person #2 how he or she feels and why. *Restate feeling.*
   - Ask both persons if they have anything to add.
3. **Finding Solutions**
   - Ask person #1 what he or she can do to solve the problem.
   - Ask person #2 if he or she can agree to the solution. If he or she cannot, ask person #2 if he or she has a solution to the problem.
   - Ask person #1 if he or she can agree to this solution. Go back and forth until agreement is reached.
4. **Final Agreement**
   - *Restate* the final solution to make sure both parties agree to the same thing and hear all the parts.
   - Ask each what he or she can do to keep the problem from happening again.
   - Ask the disputants if they feel the problem is solved.
   - Ask the disputants to tell their friends that the conflict has been solved to prevent rumors from spreading.
   - Congratulate the students for their hard work.
   - Fill out the mediation agreement form.
   - Have the disputants sign the agreement form.

Source: P. S. Lane & J. J. McWhirter (1992). A peer mediation model: Conflict resolution for elementary and middle school children. *Elementary School Guidance and Counseling, 27,* pp. 124-127. Published by the American School Counselor Association (ASCA). Reprinted with permission.

Negotiating

Negotiating is an important skill for managing conflict when both people feel strongly about their position or circumstance.

1. Determine whether activities in conflict can both be accomplished in time. (i.e., Can you create a win/win situation?)

2. Are negotiable elements of equal importance?

3. Are words or phrases used that indicate or imply that one position or circumstance is superior to the other?

4. If so, reframe the position or circumstance in a more equitable banner.

5. Suggest a compromise or another plan of action. For example, if one person's idea is followed first, the second activity will fulfill the other person's needs.

For example: *"You need a ride to your choral concert, and I need someone to type my paper for English class. I'll give you a ride and help you set up if you will type my paper in the morning."*

Emotional Literacy Skills

The model of emotional literacy was first proposed by Salovey & Mayer (1990). Emotional literacy skills are intrapersonal abilities such as knowing one's emotions by recognizing a feeling as it happens and monitoring it; managing emotions (i.e., to shaking off anxiety, gloom, irritability, and the consequences of failure; motivating oneself to attain goals, delay gratification, stifle impulsiveness, and maintain self-control; recognizing emotions in others with empathy and perspective taking; and handling interpersonal relationships effectively. Emotional skills fall into categories such as knowing the relationship between thoughts, feelings, and actions; establishing a sense of identity and acceptance of self; learning to value teamwork, collaboration, and cooperation; regulating one's mood, empathizing; and maintaining hope.

(*Note*: **Permission is granted to reproduce skills boxes for individual client use.**)

How to Let Someone Know
He or She Is Bothering You

Here are some steps to follow for letting someone know his or her behavior is bothering you:

1. Keep a serious facial expression and maintain eye contact. In a serious tone of voice, ask if you could talk to the person for a moment.

2. Say something positive: *"I like . . . "*

3. Tell the person what's bothering you using an "I" message:

   "When you . . . (specify behavior), *I feel . . . because I . . .* (consequences)."
   Listen attentively—let the other person know you heard what he or she said.

4. Paraphrase. Repeat what the other person said in your own words.

5. Check for understanding: *"Do you mean . . . ?"*

6. Reflect feelings. Say how you think they feel: *"You really seem angry."*

7. Ask for more information (how, what, when, where).

8. Problem solve. Give the person suggestions for changing. Be specific. Ask for a small behavior change. Work toward a compromise.

9. Discuss positive and negative consequences, and give the person a reason for changing.

10. Thank the person for listening.

Chapter 8

ALIENATION, UNDERACHIEVEMENT, AND DROPPING OUT

> If education ever gets to the place where there are no dropouts, we can feel secure that we're getting the job done in our schools. People rarely drop out when they experience a sense of purpose, success, and growth. What will it take for us to realize that the dropout issue is a symptom of an unwellness in our schools? It will not require long-term studies and extensive funding to eliminate the dropout problem. It will take making sure that our young people experience success instead of failure in our schools. (Wright, 1989, p. 47)

Statistical manipulations often have the effect of trivializing a significant social and educational problem. For example, dropout rates in nearly all large U.S. cities are tabulated annually, rather than according to how many high school freshmen actually receive diplomas four years later. One reliable estimation is provided by the U.S. General Accounting Office (GAO). To count dropouts, the GAO uses the all-inclusive definition adopted by the Current Population Survey (CPS), which polls a national sample of households representative of the working-age civilian population. The CPS defines dropouts as "persons neither enrolled in schools nor high school graduates." This definition does not exclude such categories as "pregnant teenagers" or "needed at home." It simply assumes if you aren't in school and you haven't graduated, you're a dropout.

The most common reason for leaving school is poor academic performance. The National Center for Educational Statistics (1995) found "didn't like school" and "couldn't get along with teachers" as significant social and emotional variables. Being older than average for one's grade level also is a strong predictor of dropping out. The ramifications are extensive:

- Nearly 700,000 youth drop out of school each year in the United States.
- Dropouts will earn $237 billion less during their lifetimes than high school graduates; state and local governments will collect $71 billion less in taxes.
- Welfare, unemployment, and crime prevention costs for dropouts will total $6 billion.
- In some areas, 30% of inner-city students never complete the 8th grade.
- Dropouts are more likely to engage in other high-risk behaviors, such as premature sexual activity, unintended pregnancies, crime and delinquency, alcohol and other drug use, and attempts at suicide (Asche, 1993).

McKinlay and Bloch (1989) listed these factors as contributing to dropping out

- **Socioeconomic factors,** such as cultural isolation, ethnicity, and a language other than English
- **Home and family factors,** such as poor family relationships or lack of parental encouragement
- **Psychosocial development factors,** such as substance abuse, lack of goals or career decisions, lack of motivation, and poor self-concept
- **Academic development factors,** such as lack of basic academic skills, alienation from school, and academic failure
- **Institutional factors,** such as inadequate programs, youth "falling between the cracks," and lack of counseling services (p. 8).

Low regard for self seems to be present in all studies on underachievement, no matter what else is involved. Several special populations should be specifically targeted for dropout prevention:

- Pregnant and parenting youth
- Substance abusers
- Disruptive students
- Truants
- Students who lack motivation

The profile that often emerges from the data is not an unconcerned, un-motivated, disruptive youth, but one with high levels of stress-related anxiety who lacks adaptive ways to reduce that stress and methods to increase self-management skills.

Gage (1990, p. 280) maintained that reducing the national dropout rate would verify our dedication to social justice and to an enlightened and humane national self-interest. Intervention and prevention, however, require change in social organizations on a grand scale: families, schools, communities, business and industry, and local, state, and federal governments. Any dropout prevention program should plan for the success of *all* youth. The fact is that the further a child moves from competing with his or her peers academically, the greater his or her chance of competing with peers in less constructive ways, such as joining gangs, doing drugs, or dropping out of school.

SKILLS FOR THE 21ST CENTURY

An adolescent's decision to drop out of school often is the end result of a long series of negative school experiences: academic failure, grade retention, and frequent suspensions. Yet today's dropouts will be at an even greater disadvantage tomorrow than ever before. Today, information seems to multiply exponentially. Communication, mathematics, science, and computer literacy skills have been identified as the basic academic skills required of high school graduates. In addition, changes in the U.S. economy now require youth to have a substantial knowledge base and higher-order thinking skills. These skills include the ability to solve complex problems, to function in an uncertain environment, to think and reason abstractly, and to apply this knowledge in creative and imaginative ways.

New performance standards and advanced technologies have changed the workforce's educational requirements. International competition and new technologies dictate the need for a well-educated workforce. Participatory management, sophisticated quality control, decentralized production services, and increased use of information-based technology are common in both large and small businesses. These new workforce skills are categorized as follows:

1. **Academic skills:** reading, writing, computing
2. **Adaptability skills:** learning to learn, creative thinking, problem solving
3. **Self-management skills:** self-esteem, goal setting, motivation, employability, and career development.

4. **Social skills:** intra- and interpersonal, negotiation, and team work
5. **Communication skills:** listening and communicating well
6. **Influencing skills:** organizational effectiveness and leadership

Advanced technology also has changed the organization of the workplace from pyramidal to more participatory structures, increasing the need for skills in conflict resolution, interpersonal facilitation, problem solving, and cooperative learning. Employability skills for the 21st century include these:

Individual competence: communication skills, comprehension, computation, and tolerance of diversity

Personal reliability skills: personal management, ethics, and vocational maturity

Group and organizational effectiveness skills: interpersonal skills, organization skills, and skills in negotiation, creativity, and leadership (Gainer, 1988)

The vast changes in the workplace have increased the autonomy, responsibilities, and value of personnel at all organizational levels. These changes, in turn, call for workers with higher levels of academic competencies and broader technical knowledge. Prerequisite social skills for the potential worker may include working as a team, being a leader in building consensus, being able to see things from the perspective of others, and being able to persuade and promote cooperation while avoiding conflicts. Prerequisite emotional skills for the potential leader may include taking initiative, managing and coordinating the efforts of a network of people, being self-motivated to take on responsibilities above and beyond one's stated job, and self-management in regulating time and work commitments. High scores on measures of intelligence may secure enrollment into a prestigious university and a comparative career; however, doing well in the corporate culture may be more dependent on social or emotional intelligences not yet measured quantitatively.

STRUCTURED INTERVENTIONS
FOR HIGH-RISK BEHAVIORS

The emphasis on higher-order thinking and not on *just basic skills* is a key concern in addressing the education of at-risk youth. Keeping lesser-achieving youth only in the realm of the basic may mean they will be dependent thinkers all their lives. Given the experience of thinking skills programs, teaching metacognition behavior may be one of the most important goals to pursue in the education of at-risk youth. These children and adolescents are episodic in their learning, fail to make connections that others may see more spontaneously, and too often they miss the central meaning that is key to learning. . . . Educators and helping professionals of at-risk youth should be mindful of the emphasis on metacognition in teaching thinking and learning. (Presseisen, 1988, p. 48)

Therapeutic Initiatives

Intelligence is not a simple thing, but a compound of influence. The circumstances can be summarized with the following equation:

Intelligence = power + tactics + content. (Perkins, 1986, p. 5)

Research has increased our knowledge of how children learn and retain information (Armstrong, 1994). Because problems in academic performance relate to study skills deficits and to emotional and personal problems, the complex needs of a child with academic difficulties are best served by an interactive learning system consisting of primary strategies (study skills) and support strategies (counseling). Successful study skills programs that enhance cognitive deficits incorporate a dual approach by including the following components:

1. Study skills instruction combined with counseling
2. Group rather than individual counseling
3. High levels of warmth, empathy, genuineness, and acceptance
4. Skills instruction related to content material (i.e., different approaches to studying different subjects)
5. Structured rather than unstructured formats
6. Programs of 10 hours or more

Specific skill development can be integrated and reinforced at all educational level around specific themes such as these:

- **Locating information and reference materials** such as reader's guides, tables of content, catalogues, and computerized information
- **Organizing information** such as note-taking, summarizing, listening, and recognizing patterns
- **Understanding graphic aids** such as tables, charts, or graphic organizers
- **Following both oral and written directions**
- **Reading strategies** such as rapid reading for the main idea and techniques to improve comprehension

- **Remembering information** with use of mnemonic devices, peg words, and memorization strategies
- **Studying effectively** and efficiently, and managing time

In addition, direct thinking skills instruction—that is, instruction that introduces a skill, then provides guided practice and reinforcement in using the skill in a variety of settings with a variety of media—helps with retention of information. Direct instruction uses a five-step process as an introduction to a thinking skill (Beyer, 1983):

1. The instructor introduces the skill by describing an example of it in action or by having the student actually do it.
2. Referring to the examples, the instructor explains the specific steps and rules for the skill.
3. The instructor demonstrates how the skill works with the content being studied.
4. Working in pairs, under the instructor's supervision, youth apply the skill procedures and rules to similar data.
5. Restating and explaining the basic components of the skill as it has been used thus far with follow-up experiences reinforces learning.

Thinking skills instruction should be direct and frequent, introduced in small pieces, and adequately reinforced. It also should be developmental in approach, increasingly more complex as children progress. Providing systematic, developmental instruction in thinking skills builds on the cognitive development of youth.

Further motivation studies (Alderman, 1990; Alderman & Cohen, 1985; Ames & Ames, 1989; Dweck, 1986) and cognitive learning studies (Gardner, 1993, 1991, 1983; Pressley & Levin, 1987; Weinstein & Mayer, 1986) offer counselors and educators an abundant repertoire of strategies to foster success and enhance self-worth. To acquire a high degree of motivation, one must know how he or she personally contributes to his or her success. There must be a link between what the student does and the outcome that follows. Drawing from research on motivation and learning strategies, Alderman (1990) developed the *links-to-success model* for helping the *helpless* student become successful and, in turn, developing an increased sense of self-worth.

Link 1: Proximal Goals. The first link to success is setting goals for performance. Goal setting provides the mechanism for self-assessment and promotes self-monitoring. To be effective, the goal setting should be specific rather than general, attainable, and short-term. Pre-intervention assessments (such as study skills inventories and feedback forms from teachers on student performance) should set a baseline of performance and list deficits in study and social skills in the classroom that inhibit academic achievement.

Link 2: Learning Strategies. Low-achieving youth are often "inefficient learners" (Pressley & Levin, 1987) because they fail to apply a learning strategy that could enhance their performance. The goal here is for youth to identify the learning strategies that will help them accomplish their goals. Examples of learning strategies are basic and complex rehearsal strategies; comprehensive-monitoring strategies (Weinstein & Mayer, 1986); task-limited and across-domains strategies, with metacognitive knowledge about when to use them; and various reading comprehension strategies, such as summarization, clarification, prediction, and asking the right questions.

Link 3: Successful Experience. A learning goal rather than a performance goal ensures greater success. Dweck (1986) maintained that focusing on the learning goal in relation to performance improvement and goal attainment produces more lasting effects.

Link 4: Attribution for Success. Youth should be encouraged to attribute success to their personal efforts or abilities. Abilities are skills that have been learned (e.g., reading comprehension skills, time-managed study, or composition writing). Increased self-efficacy leads to increased confidence about goal accomplishment. Failure should be reframed within the context of not using the proper strategy. Within this context, students are more likely to try again (Alderman, 1990, pp. 28–29).

This four-link approach helps youth take responsibility for their learning, which enhances motivation and performance. Low-achieving youth need to know exactly what they are expected to do and be given criteria for measuring their success. This link-to-success model provides a framework for beginning the cycle of progress that fosters self-responsibility for learning and self-efficacy in achievement.

Cooperative Learning: Enhancing Cognitive Skills and Promoting Teamwork. To compete in the 21st century, children and adolescents need good interpersonal skills. Cooperative learning fosters these skills. The variety of cooperative learning models provide a repertoire of strategies educators can use to accommodate wide-ranging differences in skill and achievement levels in mixed-ability classrooms, including classrooms in which special education and general education students are integrated. Research indicates that these approaches have many possible advantages over traditional instructional models, and may have especially important benefits for more culturally diverse classroom environments. Documented cognitive and affective benefits include the following:

- Higher achievement for all youth, especially for the most vulnerable
- Greater use of higher-level reasoning
- More on-task behavior and increased motivation and persistence in completing a task
- Greater peer interaction, teamwork, and development of collaborative skills; better rapport between students
- Better attitudes toward school, peers, and educators
- Higher personal and academic self-esteem
- More positive relationships among youth of various races and ethnic backgrounds and between handicapped students and their nonhandicapped peers
- A lessening of the importance of intergroup distinctions, less stereotyping, less grouping, and more complex perceptions of members of other groups

Children and adolescents mature intellectually in reciprocal relationships with other people. Vygotsky (1978) maintained that higher functions actually originate in interactions with others. Every integration of cultural development appears twice: first on the social level, and later on the individual level. This is applicable to voluntary attention, to logical memory, and to the formation of concepts. All higher functions originate as actual relationships between individuals (Vygotsky, 1978).

Cooperative learning promotes the skills needed to collaborate. It is important to determine which interpersonal skills youth need. What follows is a list of some of the most important:

Forming skills: moving into groups quickly and quietly; sitting face-to-face; talking in quiet voices; using names and making eye contact when speaking to each other

Functioning skills: carrying out assigned tasks; staying on task; being sure everyone understands the task

Communication skills: paraphrasing what another team member said; asking for explanations

Brainstorming skills: asking questions; generating alternative answers; giving evidence for conclusions

Trust-building skills: praising others; encouraging participation; showing respect for others' ideas; avoiding put-downs

Conflict-management skills: clarifying disagreements within the group; asking questions to help understand another's point of view

Cooperative learning helps young people feel successful at every academic level: low-achieving youth can make contributions to a group and experience success, and all students can increase their understanding of ideas by explaining them to others. Cooperative learning also has been shown to improve relationships among youth from different ethnic backgrounds (Slavin, 1987).

A variety of social and communication skills are involved in cooperative work groups. These skills can transfer to the classroom and later to the workplace. Students working in groups perform better and achieve more if they receive training in group process skills. These skills can be grouped in five different categories such as:

1. Be a Team Player

- Follow directions.
- Use each other's names.
- When you are working together, don't work ahead of the others.
- When you are unsure, ask for help or say you don't understand.
- Participate: Share an idea, take your turn answering, suggest ways the group could solve a problem or complete an assignment.

2. Be an Attentive Listener

- Look at the person who is talking.
- Politely tell someone when you agree or disagree. *"I respect your opinion, but I disagree."*
- Let others finish. Wait to see if their idea is wrong or just different.
- Listen for the other group members points of view.
- Check to make sure you understand what someone said or how it relates to the assignment: *"Do you mean . . .?" "Are you saying . . .?"* A T-Chart can teach this interpersonal skill.

  1. Identify the interpersonal skill that will be emphasized in the cooperative learning activity.
  2. Create a T-chart by asking what this skill "looks like." (See the T-chart that follows for "Attentive Listening.") List responses and add others if necessary.
  3. Ask what this skill "sounds like." List their responses and add others if necessary. Hang the chart in a place where all groups can see it during the activity.

Attentive Listening

Sounds Like	Looks Like
Say "uh-huh" as speaker talks	Nod
Use open-ended questions to keep the speaker talking	Make eye contact
Paraphrase what the speaker says	Lean forward
Use encouragement to keep the speaker talking	Smile
Accept what the speaker says rather than give your opinion	Relaxed posture
Summarize the speaker's comments	Hands unclenched Arms not crossed

3. Be a Team Supervisor

- Check to see if everyone can see, has the materials needed, has space to work, and is working and making progress.
- Make sure everyone understands: Ask each member for an answer; ask someone to demonstrate how to find an answer; call for an "answer check," in which everyone individually works a problem and shows his or her answer; ask someone to summarize what was said or what the problem is.
- Check back with other group members on ideas and points that were discussed earlier in the period or week. Don't have a group member learning something new and without check to see that he or she remembers it.

4. Be a Cooperative Teacher

- Explain how you found an answer or worked a problem.
- Show how to do the same type of problem using different numbers. Don't be satisfied with correct answers; think of new problems that relate to the lesson.
- Help concentrate the group's efforts by watching the time.
- Make up a similar problem or an easier problem to help students who are having trouble understanding. Don't stop when they finally do a problem right. Have them do three or four more to help them remember.
- Help your group get the main idea by having group members say it in their own words, summarize the main idea, or give an example.

5. Be a Group Manager

- If members of your group are off-task, tell them what they should be doing.
- Encourage the group to solve problems on their own rather than asking the teacher for help.
- Help the group stay on task by saying, *"We are supposed to be doing . . . "* or *"We better get back to work."*
- Summarize what the group has decided at the end of a discussion.
- Set goals and challenge the group to do its best: *"Can the group do better than last time?"* *"Can we finish problems 1 through 5 by 10:15?"*

Building relationships in the classroom is perhaps the most advantageous way to empower students. Cooperative learning teaches critical social skills that can be experienced, observed, and integrated. With cooperative learning strategies, one educator has the power to significantly change the relationship skills of thousands of youth during his or her career.

Treatment Plan: Study Improvement Program.
Counseling Intention: To improve study skills, organizational skills, time management, goal setting, and decision making.

This study improvement program was adapted from Malett (1983) and consists of 11 half-hour group sessions. Seven sessions are technique-oriented, directed primarily to teaching behavioral self-control as a study technique; three sessions are semi-structured discussions of personal factors affecting academic performance.

Session 1: Introductions and self-control techniques. Behavior modification techniques are used to teach youth to control their own behavior and to change undesirable habits. Self-observation and self-monitoring are used to chart current study behaviors to establish a baseline for evaluating change.

Session 2: Time management. Universal components of time management instruction include record keeping procedures (daily schedules or diaries to identify self-defeating habits), schedule planning, life support activities, leisure time, study time blocked out to allow a commitment for each course, realistic goals for each study session, study breaks coordinated with individual energy periods, and planned use of short study intervals (distributive versus mass practice).

Session 3: Textbook reading efficiency skills. Underlining, outlining, highlighting, and the use of graphic organizers are standard methods for focusing attention and increasing understanding of written texts. *SQ3R* and *REAP* methods are useful for processing and retaining information. The SQ3R technique for reading and studying textbooks involves five steps:

- Survey: glance at chapter headings, read summaries, review questions, and determine organization
- Question: formulate questions about each section
- Read: while reading, actively search for answers to formulated questions
- Recite: answer questions without reference to the text
- Review: list major points under each heading

The REAP reading and study method has four basic steps:

- Read to discover the message
- Encode the message in one's own words
- Annotate by writing the message notes
- Ponder the message by processing it through thinking and discussion

Session 4: Discussion of the importance of grades. Show the relationship between grades, achievement scores, aptitude, and interests. Identify strengths and weaknesses.

Session 5: Stimulus control. This technique involves changing the environment. Finding a new, less-distracting place to study is an example of environmental change. Identify optimum study environment at school, home, and library.

Session 6: Test taking and anxiety management. Instruction counseling in this component should consist of the following steps:

- **Test preparation:** frequent, scheduled and organized study void of distractions
- **Test strategies:** strategies for taking objective and essay tests
- **Test wiseness:** following instructions, scanning, pacing, making educated guesses, eliminating the obvious wrong answer, reviewing
- **Managing test anxiety:** replacing negative self-statements with positive self statements, deep breathing techniques, progressive relaxation, and systematic desensitization for test anxiety

Session 7: Discussion of academic and nonacademic pressures. Discuss life balance between academic and leisure activities, along with part-time work schedules; the need to be with peers; and the need to succeed academically for oneself, for family, and for the future.

Session 8: Taking lecture notes. Note-taking often is an individual study style. However, one strategy for keeping notes, developed at the Cornell Study Center, incorporates the basic process of effective reading in a "5-R process":

- **Record**: pick out main ideas
- **Reduce**: summarize, note key terms
- **Recite**: repeat key ideas to oneself
- **Reflect**: think about content
- **Review**: recall and commit information to memory

Session 9: Discussion of values. Exercises from Chapter 11 are helpful here, according to group needs and developmental stages.

Session 10: Writing papers. Enlist the help of colleagues in the English Department and use style books.

Session 11: Problem solving. Graphic organizers for problem solving are included in this chapter, as well as in Chapter 11.

Treatment Plan: Succeeding in School.

Counseling Intention: To improve study skills, to encourage help seeking behavior, and cooperation with peers and adults.

This exercise involves 10 50-minute sessions and was developed by Gerler and Herndon (1993).

Session 1: Successful people. The first meeting consists of the following elements:

1. Purpose of the group and discussion of ground rules
2. Discussion of common traits of successful people; what it takes to be successful
3. Sharing of successes in and out of school
4. Exploration of successes members expect to experience in the future

Session 2: Being comfortable in school. Group leaders present material on relaxation methods, with practice exercises. Members discuss times they felt comfortable and relaxed in school.

Session 3: Being responsible in school. Leaders review how to feel relaxed and comfortable at school. Members discuss the meaning and importance of behaving responsibly, define responsibly, and give examples of how they have behaved responsibly in and out of school.

Session 4: Listening in school. Leaders review how to be responsible in school, giving examples of responsible behavior. Members discuss how listening to others may influence behaving responsibly and define a good listener. Members role-play to sharpen their listening skills.

Session 5: Asking for help in school. Leaders introduce exercises to improve listening skills. Members discuss the importance of asking appropriate questions and list situations when listening and asking for help from teachers had positive outcomes.

Session 6: How to improve at school. Leaders review listening skills. Members identify school subjects that needed improving and brainstorm strategies that will lead to improvements. The session closes with members identifying improvements already made in school.

Session 7: Cooperating with peers at school. Leaders review reactions from the previous session. Members discuss the importance of getting along and cooperating with peers, role-play cooperative behaviors, and discuss personal experiences of cooperating with peers.

Session 8: Cooperating with teachers. Leaders review the importance of cooperating with peers and teachers. Members complete the following sentences:

- *"If I were teacher for a day, I'd . . . "*
- *"I wish my teachers would . . . "*
- *"I would like would like to talk with a teacher about . . . "*

Blank cards are distributed, and members are asked to finish the statement: *"I would like to get along better with my teacher, but my problem is . . . "* The session concludes with members sharing how they have cooperated with their teachers.

Session 9: The bright side of school. Leaders review the value of cooperating with others and encourage members to consider how cooperation might improve the atmosphere at school. Members identify some things about school they dislike and consider what might be positive about those things. The session ends with members describing some positive aspects of being in the classroom and at school.

Session 10: The bright side of me. Leaders review some of the highlights of the previous sessions. Members share what they have learned about themselves and their strengths. The session concludes with the opportunity for members to receive positive feedback.

Another format for delivering necessary study and time management skills was highlighted in *The Study Improvement Program* (Malett, 1983) offered to college freshmen at the University of New York, Rochester. Training consisted of three-hour seminars held once a week in basic counseling skills, study skills, and self-control techniques. The seminars offered didactic presentations, modeling, practice, and videotape feedback, with the goal of teaching attending, paraphrasing, questioning, reflection of feelings, interviewing, and related small-group discussion techniques. The session topics are as follow:

1. Introduction/self control techniques
2. Time management
3. Textbook reading efficiency skills
4. Discussion of the importance of grades
5. Stimulus control
6. Test taking and anxiety management
7. Discussion of academic and nonacademic pressures
8. Lecture note-taking
9. Discussion of values
10. Writing papers
11. Problem solving

Proponents of multimodal counseling and psychotherapy maintain that cognition and learning are affected by what happens in other domains of individual functioning as well. Young people who manifest behavior problems such as emotional disturbances, attention deficits, or interpersonal difficulties also are likely to experience learning problems. To promote cognitive development and academic success, educators and helping professionals are beginning to infuse regular classroom instruction with innovative approaches, such as creative physical fitness programs (Carlson, 1990), social skills programs (Stickel, 1990), and computer interventions (Crosbie-Burnett & Pulvino, 1990).

In addition, helping professionals can positively influence learning through the use of encouragement (Rathvon, 1990), video-assisted study skills training (Heldenbrand & Hixon, 1991), interpersonal communication training (Asbury, 1984), and stress-reduction and relaxation methods (Danielson, 1984; Omizo, 1981).

Treatment Plan: Multimodal Counseling for Children.
Counseling Intention: Keat (1990), changing the acronym *BASIC ID* (Lazarus, 1992, chapter 2) to HELPING to meet the developmental needs of children, offers a pragmatic and technically eclectic way of helping children learn skills to help themselves.

In this program, the developmental needs and problems of children are presented from a multimodal point of view.

H E L P I N G Children Change

Mode	Rank	Concern number	Concern	Intervention
Health	5	H1	Pain	Avoid/Relief
		H2	Sickness	Wellness
Emotions	2	E1	Anxiety	Stress Management
		E2	Anger	Madness Management
		E3	Feeling	Fun Training
Learning	5	L1	Deficiencies	Life Skills
		L2	Failing	Study Skills
		L3	Sensory shallowness	Music
Personal Relationships	1	P1	Getting along (adults)	Relationship Enhancement (RE)
		P2	Lacks friends	Friendship Training
Imagery	4	I1	Low self-worth	IALAC
		I2	Lacks coping skills	Heroes (cartoons)
Need to Know	7	N1	Despair	Hope Cognitive Restructuring
		N2	Mistaken ideas	Bibliotherapy
		N3	Lack of information	
Guidance of Actions, Behaviors, and Consequences	3	G1	Behavior deficits	Modeling
		G2	Motivation	Contracts

Treatment Plan: Multimodal Treatment Plan for Students with Deadline Disorder.

Counseling Intention: To empower students who procrastinate with essential cognitive skills.

Students who procrastinate usually have not learned the strategies to approach and complete a task or an assignment in an organized way. Incomplete assignments or frantic last-minute efforts often leave a student with feelings of frustration, anxiety, failure, and low self-esteem. Morse (1987) provided the following multimodal profile for procrastinators:

Multimodal Group Intervention for Deadline Disorder

Mode	Group activities	Procrastinator characteristics
Health	Participate in relaxation exercises	Locus of control
Emotions	Brainstorm and discuss feeling words	Fear of failure Fear of success
	Share common fears	Fear of failure Fear of success
	Discuss and share feelings of frustration	Perfection
	Discuss power and the power one feels	Locus of control
Learning/ School	Share feelings about school, favorite subjects, performance levels	Self-concept
	Discuss problems in completing assignments	Rebellion against authority; fear of failure; fear of success
	Complete worksheet "Getting Work Done Survey"	Perfection; fear of failure
People/ Personal Relationships	Share feelings about family and friends	Rebellion against authority
	Discuss relationships with classmates and the ability to function in the classroom group	Rebellion against authority; locus of control
Imagery/ Interests	Discuss strengths and weaknesses	Fear of failure; Self-concept
	Share likes and dislikes	Self-concept
	Discuss put-downs by others	Self-concept
	Discuss put-downs by self	Fear of failure; Self-concept
	Participate in guided imagery to develop positive self-image	Self-concept
Need to Know	Discuss differences between thoughts and feelings	Self-concept; Rebellion against authority
	Identify thoughts and feelings under positive or negative categories	Self-concept; Rebellion against authority
	Practice positive self-talk	Self-concept
	Role-play positive and negative aspects of of putdowns	Self-concept

(Table continues on next page)

Multimodal Group Intervention for Deadline Disorder (*Continued*)

Mode	Group activities	Procrastinator characteristics
Keed to Know (*Cont.*)	Discuss how choices are made	Lack of skill Locus of control
	List choices students make during their day	Locus of control
Guidance of Actions	Identify "putting-off" behaviors	Perfection; Fear of failure; Fear of success
	Discuss ways time is wasted and saved	Lack of skill
	List activities to be done in a day and time required to accomplish them	Lack of skill
	Set priorities for completing tasks	Lack of skill
	Write short-term goals and implementation strategies	Lack of skill
	Record progress toward goals	Lack of skill
	Write long-term goals (1, 5, & 10-year) and implementation strategies	Lack of skill

Strategy: Partnerships to Assist Academically Resistant Youth.

Counseling Intention: To provide a more comprehensive solution focused intervention for specific classroom behaviors

Teaching problem solving, goal setting, and time management is helpful, but a more comprehensive intervention that addresses the fears and negative feelings procrastinators often experience may have more long-term benefits. Focusing on the structured modalities of emotions, learning, interpersonal relationships, interests, and guidance of actions in a group setting may be the pivotal link to behavior change.

It is often overwhelming to attend to all the behaviors that may emerge in a typical classroom or group setting. Fundamentally, every behavior is a communication about needs, expectations, goals, and aspirations. Table 8.1 provides a brief glimpse of behaviors that may interfere with the progress of any group (i.e., the classroom), which are paired with suggested interventions.

Collective Community Initiatives

Young people have a fundamental need to achieve, solve problems, and establish long-range goals. Educators, helping professionals, and community

Table 8.1
Partnership to Assist Academically Resistant Youth

Behavior Manifestations	Suggested Interventions
1. Truancy/absenteeism	Weekly contingency contracting for attendance; focus on the benefits of attending school (e.g., increased income and worth); visualize the future and describe what it would be like without an education; establish an attendance card and weekly reward schedule; reframe the perception about school through cognitive restructuring.
2. Impulsiveness	Teach ways to delay responding (e.g., count to 10 or one minute pause for *think time*); model slow and careful problem solving and decision making; instruct how to scan alternatives and use different problem solving methods; encourage verbalization to solve the problem (e.g., "I need to take time to look at all possible answers not just the first one that comes along"); limit overstimulation and distractors (listening to music, however, often may enhance attention, concentration, and memory providing a sense of predictability and consistency); contract for the completion of short assignment.
3. Inattention	Use a cue or signal that means it is time to pay attention; structure seating arrangements based of sociometric ratings with team leaders chosen to be the most influential peer of least attentive youth; train to self-monitor; teach self-questioning strategies (e.g., "What am I doing? How is that going to affect others?"). Develop mechanisms to enhance control and integrate successful strategies for paying attention—strategies such as stopping to define a problem, considering and evaluating various solutions (critical thinking) before acting on one, checking for accuracy, persisting in using every strategy to solve it, and congratulating for a job well done. "Stop, listen, think, do."
	The following three sentence stems are often helpful ("I-message"):
	"(Name of child), when you _____, I feel _____, because _____."
	"I feel this way when this happens _____; I would feel better if this happens _____."
	"I resent your inattention when I _____; what I need from you is _____; what I appreciate in you is _____."

(Table continues on next page)

Table 8.1
Partnership to Assist Academically Resistant Youth (*Continued*)

Behavior Manifestations	Suggested Interventions
4. Poor academic performance	Instruct in goal setting; instruct in self-recording of study intervals and rates; establish accountability logs; instruct in time management; write down all assignments to take home; involve parents in checking assignments; cooperatively develop a learning plan.
5. Low self-esteem	Share personal success experiences; keep a personal journal of successes during the week; start each day with positive affirmations; create a climate that stresses strengths rather than weakness; teach assertiveness skills; structure opportunities for success; change self-dialog from "I can't" to "I will try"; enhance social skills such as conversation skills, making and responding to comments or questions.
6. Unable to follow-up or follow through on assignments	Instruct in goal setting and problem solving; show how to break large jobs into achievable parts; establish dates and timelines for work completion; provide examples and specific steps to accomplish each part.
	Assist student in setting long-range goals; break the goal into realistic parts.
	Use a questioning strategy—"What do you need to be able to do this?" Keep asking that question until the child has reached an obtainable goal.
	Have the child set clear timelines (i.e., what he or she needs to do to accomplish each step (monitor student's progress frequently).
7. Attention seeking behavior	Model how to gain others' attention appropriately.
	Highlight others who are behaving appropriately; move the attention seeker out of the spotlight; distract the attention seeker with a question about the current topic; attend to the attention seeker only when he or she is on task.
8. Prioritization of most to least important tasks	Provide a model hierarchy to demonstrate least to most important tasks that can be generalized to other situations; post the model around the room and refer to it often.

Table 8.1
Partnership to Assist Academically Resistant Youth (*Continued*)

Behavior Manifestations	Suggested Interventions
9. Unable to maintain effort and accuracy consistently	Reduce assignment length; increase the frequency of positive reinforcements; teach specific methods of self-monitoring such as double checking written work; encourage proofreading.
10. Unable to complete assignments on time	List, post, and repeat all steps necessary to complete each assignment; develop a checklist and timeline for completing components of an assignment; reduce the assignment into manageable sections; make frequent checks for work/assignment completion; implement a "study buddy" program where students team up to maintain academic responsibilities.
11. Power-seeking behavior	Ignore the behavior in the moment and elicit feedback from the power seeker during a less confrontational time; ask how he or she might handle a similar situation; express your feelings regarding the behavior (e.g., *"I feel this way when this happens . . .; I would feel better if this would happen. . . ."*).
	Place the power seeker in a leadership role; discuss roles and responsibilities of a good leader; contract with the power seeker regarding expectations; evaluate follow through of desired behavior; reinforce the positive leadership.
12. Difficulty with taking tests	Teach test-taking skills and strategies; allow extra time for testing; use clear, readable, and uncluttered test forms; use the test format with which the student is most comfortable.
13. Revenge-driven behavior	Clearly define acceptable and unacceptable behavior; form a positive relationship through cooperative trust-building strategies (e.g., think-pair-share) and creative problem-solving activities; find ways to encourage group members to show that they care for the member; improve self-esteem and base group activities that encourage the processing of feelings such as *"Today, I felt _____ in the group"*; set up a "graffiti board" in the room for writing out feelings or recording positive things people have done or said.

(*Table continues on next page*)

Table 8.1
Partnership to Assist Academically Resistant Youth (*Continued*)

Behavior Manifestations	Suggested Interventions
14. Poor reading comprehension skills (e.g., difficulty finding main idea from a paragraph)	Provide student with copy of reading material with main ideas underlined or highlighted; outline of important points from reading. Teach outlining, main-idea concepts. Provide audio tape of the text.
15. Unable to follow oral instructions or directions	Accompany oral directions with written directions; give one direction at a time; repeat directions and check for understanding; strategically place general methods of operation and expectations on charts around the room; provide a copy of presentation notes; allow peers to share carbon-copy notes from presentations (have student compare own notes with copy of peer's notes); provide framed outlines of presentations (introducing visual and auditory cues to important information); encourage use of tape recorder; teach and emphasize key words (*"the following," "the most important point is,"* etc.).
16. Withdrawal or shyness	Lower the student's anxiety about mistakes; build the student's confidence by breaking the group task into smaller chunks; remind the student of past successes; ask what the student could do to ensure a repeat of that success; use self-concept strategies ("me bag" or "me collage") with the help of the group; give *extra* recognition for individual contributions to the group; arrange for a study buddy.
17. Sloppiness and carelessness	Teach organizational skills. Introduce the importance of daily, weekly, and/or monthly assignment sheets; list materials needed daily; require consistent format for papers; have a consistent way for students to turn in and receive back papers; reduce distractions. Give reward points for notebook checks and proper paper format. Provide clear copies of handouts and consistent format for worksheets; establish a daily routine; provide models for what you want the student to do. Arrange for a peer who will help him or her with organization.

Table 8.1
Partnership to Assist Academically Resistant Youth (*Continued*)

Behavior Manifestations	Suggested Interventions
	Assist student in keeping materials in a specific place (e.g., pencils and pens in pouch).
	Repeat expectations.
18. Poorly developed study skills	Teach study skills specific to the subject area—organization (e.g., assignment calendar), textbook reading, note taking (e.g., finding main idea/detail, mapping, outlining), skimming, summarizing.
19. Poor self-monitoring	Teach specific methods of self-monitoring (e.g., stop-look-listen).
	Proofread finished work after some time has elapsed.
20. Difficulty maintaining effort to complete tasks or assignments	Allow for alternative method for completing assignment (e.g., oral presentation, taped report, visual presentation, graphs, maps, pictures, etc. with reduced written requirements).
	Allow for alternative method of writing (e.g., typewriter, computer, cursive or printing).
21. Disruptive class participation; inappropriate attention seeking; interference with the progress of the group	Seat student in close proximity to the teacher. Reward appropriate behavior. Use study carrel if appropriate.
22. Frequent excessive talking	Provide hand signals to indicate when and when not to talk; reinforce listening.
23. Difficulty making transitions from activity to activity; tendency to give up; refusal to leave previous task; appearance of agitation during change	Program for transitions (e.g., give advance warning of when a transition is going to take place [*"Now we are completing the worksheet; next we will. . . ."*] and the expectations for the transition [e.g., *"and you will need. . . ."*]); list steps necessary to complete each assignment; arrange for an organized helper [i.e., peer]).
24. Inappropriate responses in class often blurted out; answers given to questions before they have been completed	Seat individual in close proximity to teacher to visually and physical monitor behavior; state what appropriate behavior is desired.

(*Table continues on next page*)

Table 8.1
Partnership to Assist Academically Resistant Youth (*Continued*)

Behavior Manifestations	Suggested Interventions
25. Tense, anxious, or panicked when pressurized to perform athletically or academically	Teach techniques of desensitization, relaxation, cognitive restructuring, anxiety management, assertiveness, disputing irrational beliefs, gradual step-by-step role-playing, meditation (counted breathing); increase actual exposure to anxiety-producing situation.
	Use yoga to reduce tension, relieve stress, improve vitality, increase calmness, and enhance a sense of well-being; bibliotherapy; cognitive restructuring; classical music to reduce test anxiety.
	Lessen the pressure to compete and excel; teach deep breathing exercise to promote relaxation and control; establish a learning contract that is realistic and manageable; stress effort and enjoyment for self rather than competition with others; minimize timed activities.
26. Inappropriate behaviors in a team or group setting (e.g., difficulty waiting turns in group situations, unable to give members "equal air time")	Assign a responsible job or leadership role (e.g., team captain, care and distribution of the materials); put in close proximity to teacher or group leader.
27. Poor interactions with adults or authority figures	Provide positive attention; outline appropriate versus inappropriate behavior, (e.g., *"What you are doing is . . . ; a better way of getting what you need or want is to. . . ."*)
28. Difficulty using unstructured time— recess, hallways, lunch-room, locker room, library, assembly, etc.	Define the purpose of unstructured activities (e.g., *"The purpose of doing this _____ is to get this ___"*); encourage group games, participation, and team building.
29. Losing things necessary for task or activities at school or at home (e.g., pencils; books; assignments before, during, and after completion of a given task)	Teach organization skills; frequently monitor organizational habits with *"A place for everything and everything in its place"*; provide positive reinforcement for good organization.

Table 8.1
Partnership to Assist Academically Resistant Youth (*Continued*)

Behavior Manifestations	Suggested Interventions
30. Poor use of time (e.g., daydreaming, staring off into space, not working on task at hand)	Establish periodic eye contact; teach designated reminder cues (e.g., a gentle touch on the shoulder); outline expectations of what paying attention looks like (e.g., *"You look like you are paying attention when _____")*; give a time limit for a small unit of work with positive reinforcement for accurate completion; tape an index card on the desk and place a check mark to reward on task behavior; use a contract or timer for self-monitoring.
31. Depression and anxiety	Teach depression-coping and control techniques such as recognizing depressive feelings, ways to increase activity level, positive self-talk, and redirecting thoughts to pleasant experiences.
	Use cognitive restructuring techniques to enhance coping skills; teach how to dispute irrational thoughts about expectations; keep a journal of success experiences in highly anxious situations; learn biofeedback techniques and anger management strategies.

agencies can use a variety of methods to encourage youth to stay in school. Successful programs often separate youth from the mainstream, accelerated curriculum, and provide counseling and supportive services. Many programs emphasize flexibility and a curriculum tailored to the learning needs of the individual and integrate vocational education or GED preparation. Successful programs also involve a broad range of special services for at-risk youth that focus on enhancing self-esteem, tutoring, childcare services, medical care, substance abuse prevention, bilingual instruction, and employment training in collaboration with community agencies, such as juvenile and family services, the courts, the health department, social services, and the community services board.

Breaking Ranks, the latest report on the restructuring of high schools from the National Association of Secondary School Principals, in partnership with the Carnegie Foundation for the Advancement of Teaching, found that young people on the brink of adulthood must contend with a whirlwind of destabilizing forces that undermine their scholastic potential (Maeroff, 1996). The report recommended that high schools restructure to reduce in size and personalize the educational experiences for youth to promote identification and connectedness.

Each adolescent also should have a "personal adult advocate," an adult in the school or community who meets with the youth individually on a regular basis to serve as a liaison between the youth and others in and out of school. The report also called for every adolescent in high school to have a "personal learning plan" to identify and accommodate individual learning styles and to encourage adolescents to achieve.

CONCLUSION

Nationally, over 25% of high school students drop out before graduation, including a disproportionate number of males and minorities. Once a child is behind one grade level at grade 4, 2 grade levels by grade 7, and does not pass grade 9, his or her chances of graduating are significantly diminished. Trends in the evolution of the information age make primary prevention and intervention strategies imperative.

Successful programs often separate underachieving students from other students, accelerate the curriculum, relate work to education, and provide counseling and supportive services. Effective programs include a broad range of special supportive services, such as remediation programs, tutoring, childcare, medical care, substance abuse awareness programs, bilingual instruction, and employment training.

SOCIAL, EMOTIONAL, AND COGNITIVE SKILLS

Cognitive Literacy Skills

Educators no longer can conceptualize the process of learning as the result of rote memory and mnemonic strategies that merely link meaningless bits of information to one another (Anderson, 1980; Armstrong, 1994; Gardner, 1991, 1993; Resnick, 1984). The productive workers of the next millennium must *think for a living.* Youth with poor cognitive literacy will not have the skills to function in a society that increasingly demands higher-order thinking skills such as inference, analysis, interpretation, problem solving, decision making, critical and creative thinking, and time and stress management. It is paramount that we teach students to construct meaning from reading; solve problems; develop effective reading, thinking, and learning strategies; and transfer skills and concepts to new situations.

Cognitive skills fall into categories such as *knowing how to problem solve, describe, associate, conceptualize, classify, evaluate,* and *think critically.* Cognitive psychologists advocate teaching at-risk youth a repertoire of cognitive and metacognitive strategies using *graphic organizers, organizational patterns, monitoring, self-questioning, verbal self-instruction, self-regulation,* and *study skills.* Inherently, social, emotional, and cognitive skills can be taught and cultivated giving youth advantages in their interpersonal adjustment and their academic/vocational success, as well as enhancing their resiliency through life's ultimate challenges.

(*Note*: **Permission is granted to reproduce skills boxes for individual client use.**)

Higher-Order Thinking Using Analysis

Analysis involves breaking down an issue, problem, or situation into its component parts. Identifying characteristics and components; recognizing attributes and factors; comparing and contrasting; and ranking, prioritizing, and sequencing are all skills that promote analysis. Examples of these skills include the following:

Compared to . . . , these attributes are similar.

On the positive/negative side . . . , these attributes are present.

A logical sequence would be . . . .

What are the parts of . . . ?

Classify . . . according to . . . .

How does . . . compare with . . . ?

What evidence can you list for . . . ?

Compare/Contrast Frame

	Name 1	Name 2
Trait 1		
Trait 2		
Trait 3		

Higher-Order Thinking Using Synthesis

Synthesis is the combination of ideas, facts, or principles to form a new perspective. For example:

What would you predict if . . . happened?

How would you design a new . . . ?

What might happen if you combined . . . with . . . ?

What solutions would you propose for . . . ?

I.N.F.E.R.

Identify literal, face-value interpretation, facts

Note indicators of further meaning; verbal and nonverbal clues

Feeling Nuances: analyze nuances and indicators, subtle shades of meaning, feelings

Extend original interpretation based on inferences made from "hidden clues"

Restate revised interpretation

Higher-Order Thinking Using Evaluation

Evaluation is developing opinions, judgments, or decisions after careful study. For example:

What did the study reveal about . . . ?

What are the points of view about . . . ?

What is the best and worst about . . . ?

One point of view is . . . .

Affective Processing of a Lesson

PMI = Talk about the pluses and minuses about a particular lesson

What I liked (+)	P	
What I didn't like (−)	M	
Questions or thoughts I found interesting	I	

Higher-Order Thinking Using Application

Application is the use of facts, rules, or principles to a issue, concept, or situation. For example:

How is . . . related to . . . ?

What can . . . also apply to?

I think this applies to . . . .

A connecting idea is . . . .

A situation like this reminds me of . . . because . . . .

Graphic Organizer for Analyzing

Goal:		
What to look for:	Evidence or Examples of	Connections (+) (-)
1.		
2.		
3.		
4.		
5.		
Other Possible Clues/ Criteria Found:		
6.		
7.		

Higher-Order Thinking
Using Critical Thinking Skills

Using **critical thinking skills** involves identifying point of view, determining the accuracy of presented information, judging the credibility of a source, and determining warranted and unwarranted claims. For example:

This is reality . . . . This is fallacy . . . .

This is a warranted claim backed by empirical evidence. This is an unwarranted claim backed by hearsay.

These are the benefits . . . and these are the drawbacks . . . .

This is essential evidence . . . and this is incidental evidence . . . .

This . . . is a value judgment.

This . . . is a point of view.

Graphic Organizer: Fact/Opinion Chart

Statement(s)	Fact(s)	Opinion(s)	Evidence

Analysis for Bias

Analysis for bias involves reading, listening, and acting as a critical thinker when viewing advertising, political candidates, and other perspectives for possible misrepresentation.

- **Be** aware of point-of-view

- Indicate examples of bias clues (EOIOC):

  Exaggeration *("never," "always")*

  Overgeneralization

  Imbalance (one-sided story)

  Opinion as fact *("They say . . . ")*

  Charged words *("You don't have to be a rocket scientist to know")*

- Account for possible bias by citing proofs

- State opinion based on "reasoned judgment"

Source: *Catch Them Thinking*, by James Bellanca and Robin Fogarty. © 1986 by IRI/Skylight Training and Publishing, Inc., Palatine, IL. Reprinted with permission.

Analyzing for Assumptions

An **assumption** is an unproven claim, a broad assertion without proof, or a generalization that lacks specific backup. For example, *"Choosey people choose . . . "* Or, *"Nine out of 10 doctors recommend . . . "*

Assume assertions are present.

Search deliberately for the hidden message.

Sense gaps in logic.

Use linking statements to check validity.

Make revisions to clarify.

Express revised statement.

Source: *Catch Them Thinking*, by James Bellanca and Robin Fogarty. © 1986 by IRI/Skylight Training and Publishing, Inc., Palatine, IL. Reprinted with permission.

Analyzing for Personification

Analyzing for personification means separating text into its parts (articles or stories into paragraphs, sentences, clauses, and phrases) to distinguish the figures of speech and personification.

Here are some rules for using this skill:

1. Keep the purpose for analysis clearly in mind.
2. Identify "parts" to look for, clues helpful to your analysis, and questions to guide your analysis before you begin.
3. Examine each sentence or clause by asking the following clue questions.

   - What is the sentence or clause talking about?
   - Is that subject an object or thing?
   - Is that subject behaving as if it were a person?

1. **What if the clues prove inadequate?** Consult reference books for definition, examples, and so on. Rewrite clue questions.
2. **What if I don't find evidence of the author's use of personification?** Reevaluate the purpose and redesign the clues. Lack of evidence may be as important as evidence in supporting an opinion.

In order to analyze for personification, you need to know two things:

1. Sentence structure and personification.
2. Classifying and generalizing skills.

Steps involved include these:

1. Divide the article into paragraphs, sentences, and clauses.
2. Run a sentence or clause through the gamut of clue questions; record results; repeat.
3. Draw inference and make generalizations to satisfy your goal. Did the author use personifications in his or her writing? Does this use (or disuse) support an opinion of the writing?

Source: Daisey E. Arredondo & Robert J. Marzano. "One district's approach to implementing comprehensive K-12 thinking skills program." *Educational Leadership, 43(*8), 28-32. Copyright © 1986 by ASCD. Reprinted with permission. All rights reserved.

Teaching for Thinking

A code of silence regarding classroom conduct seems to permeate the halls of today's high schools. Irrational fears of being wrong or ridiculed often inhibit active involvement. Bellanca and Fogarty (1992) developed a number of strategies to promote positive behavior. They maintained that the DOVE guidelines are helpful:

Do accept other's ideas. (Avoid criticism and put-downs.)

Originality is okay. (We need to examine lots of ideas. The way each individual looks at an idea will vary. Share your view.)

Variety and vastness of ideas provide a start. (After we explore many ideas, we can become critical thinkers. Put your brain to work.)

Energy and enthusiasm are signs of intelligent and skillful thinkers. (Put your brain to work.)

Source: *Catch Them Thinking*, by James Bellanca and Robin Fogarty. © 1986 by IRI/Skylight Training and Publishing, Inc., Palatine, IL. Reprinted with permission.

Drawing Conclusions from Evidence

Drawing conclusions from evidence can only be done with sufficient proof. This means differentiating between soft data and hard data. Soft data include opinions, bias, and personal views. Hard data are reliable facts that can be observed and measured. In order to debate or support an argument, it is helpful to follow the five "prove" rules:

1. Pick as much data as you can for evidence.

2. Review the facts to make sure they logically support the argument.

3. Organize the data to show the pattern.

4. Validate the data by checking for accuracy.

5. Evaluate the reliability of the data source.

To make generalizations from the data, use the RULE acronym:

Round up specific data.

Uncover the patterns.

Label the patterns.

Evaluate the validity of the generalizations with the 80-20 rule: Do at least 80% of the randomly selected samples fit the pattern?

Source: *Catch Them Thinking*, by James Bellanca and Robin Fogarty. © 1986 by IRI/Skylight Training and Publishing, Inc., Palatine, IL. Reprinted with permission.

Dealing with Deadline Disorder

What is deadline disorder? When you inappropriately put off doing something that you could do now, should do now, and would do now if you just knew how to begin, you are exhibiting deadline disorder. Some strategies to prevent procrastination include these:

- **Divide and conquer.** Divide the big task into manageable parts.

- **Start with a believable part.** Start with the part you think you can complete.

- **Make a game of doing it.** See if there are any new ways to approach the project.

- **Make it ridiculous.** Use your imagination. Make it amusing. Pretend it is something greater than it actually is.

- **Reward yourself.** Choose a part of the task that you have been putting off. Do it. Give yourself a big reward.

- **Put it on automatic.** Just do it. Don't question it; don't judge it. Just do it, and get over it.

Academic Growth Group and Mentoring Program Study Habits Survey

Name _____ Date _____

My improvement goal for this quarter is: _____

I can and want to improve these study habits:

Attend school every day that I am not sick.

Be more attentive in class.

Have paper and pencil, books, and other necessary supplies in class.

Ask questions when I don't understand.

Turn in my daily work.

Complete all homework.

Organize my notebook with sections for each subject, clean paper, and everything fastened in place.

Stay after school with my teacher for extra help.

Review all notes before a test.

Have the following supplies with me in all classes and at home for my study:

- Three-ring loose-leaf notebook
- Loose-leaf notebook paper
- Index sheets or dividers
- Sharpened pencils
- Eraser
- Ballpoint pens

Source: D. J. Blum & L. A. Jones (1993). Academic growth group and mentoring program for potential dropouts. *The School Counselor, 40*, 3. Published by the American School Counselor Association (ASCA). Reprinted by permission.

Note-Taking

The Cornell University Note-Taking Method is a systematized method for recording and remembering notes. The major steps involve the five Rs, as listed below.

Make a vertical line on a piece of paper 2½ inches from the left edge. Use the right side for taking notes in class. Loose-leaf paper works best for this procedure.

1. **Record.** Write down the main ideas presented by the teacher. Write on one side of the page only.

2. **Reduce** the notes you have taken into fewer words. This should be a summary of the ideas on the right side of your page.

3. **Recite.** Cover the Record column with a piece of paper and attempt to recite an explanation of the words in the Reduce column. In this stage you will be expanding to yourself what you reduced. If you have any difficulty during this step, refer to the Record column for help. Reciting in this manner will help you learn and remember the material. You are actually testing yourself on a regular basis.

4. **Reflect.** After you test yourself, you should reflect on the material. How does it relate to what you already know and understand?

5. **Review.** This should be done on a regular basis. The more often you review, the easier it will be to prepare for tests. Regular short reviews will strengthen your memory and improve your test performance.

For example:

Reduce	**Record**
Organization	Good organ. is cent. to learning, & mem. To learn w/eff, we need to be organ.

The SQ3R Method for Reading

1. **Survey:** Before you start to read, take a minute or two to read the chapter title and the section headings. Also, be sure to read the summary paragraph and any review questions at the end of the chapter.

    Your survey takes only a minute, but it will give you a good idea about what your reading is going to be.

2. **Question:** Now go back to the beginning of your assignment and turn the first heading into a question. You can do this by asking how, what, why, or who about it.

    If you turn the heading into a question, you'll know what you're trying to find out when you start reading.

3. **Read:** Now read the section to find the answer to your question.

4. **Recite:** First, ask yourself the question about the section that you've just read; then, tell yourself the answer you've learned from your reading.

    Reciting is the step that most helps you learn what you've read. The best way to recite is to take brief notes in an outline form. Why?

    -   Writing something down on paper helps you to remember it better than simply saying it to yourself.

    -   Writing down the SQ3R questions and answers takes only a few minutes and gives you a record of what you've read that you can use later.

    Below is an example of a good way to organize these notes:

    1. Question.   1. Main idea of section
                                     A. Detail
                                     B. Detail
                                     C. Detail

    Write your question on the left side of your paper, your notes on the right side. Taking notes in this way will help you later, when you want to review.

    When you have finished taking notes for the first section, go on to the next section and follow the same steps:

5. **Review:** When you've finished the question, read, and recite steps for all the sections in your assignment, it's time to review. Cover up the right-hand side of your notes. Ask yourself the questions on the left-hand side, and see if you can tell yourself the answers.

Emotional and Social Literacy Skills

Initial school success is more dependent on emotional and social factors than a child's precocious ability to read. A child's readiness for school is more dependent on the following emotional and social measures: being self-assured and interested; knowing what kind of behavior is expected and how to rein in the impulse to misbehave; being able to wait, to follow directions, and to turn to teachers for help; expressing needs while getting along with other children; a sense of control, mastery, and competence over one's world; and the ability to verbally exchange ideas, feelings, and concepts with others (Brazelton, 1992; Gallamine, 1995).

Emotional literacy skills are *intrapersonal* abilities such as knowing one's emotions by recognizing a feeling as it happens and monitoring it; managing emotions (i.e., shaking off anxiety, gloom, irritability, and the consequences of failure; motivating oneself to attain goals, delay gratification, stifle impulsiveness, and maintain self-control; recognizing emotions in others with empathy and perspective taking; and handling interpersonal relationships effectively. Emotional skills fall into categories such as knowing the relationship between thoughts, feelings, and actions; establishing a sense of identity and acceptance of self; learning to value teamwork, collaboration, and cooperation; regulating one's mood; empathizing; and maintaining hope.

Social literacy skills are *interpersonal* skills essential for meaningful interaction with others. Social skills are those behaviors that, within a given situation, predict important social outcomes such as peer acceptance, popularity, self-efficacy, competence, and high self-esteem. Social skills fall into categories such as being kind, cooperative, and compliant to reduce defiance, aggression, conflict, and antisocial behavior; and showing interest in people and socializing successfully to reduce behavior problems associated with withdrawal, depression, and fearfulness. Social skills include problem solving, assertiveness, thinking critically, resolving conflict, managing anger, and utilizing peer pressure refusal skills.

(*Note*: **Permission is granted to reproduce skills boxes for individual client use.**)

Turning Negative Thoughts
About Studying into Positive Thoughts

Brainstorm with students all the possible negative thoughts they might tell themselves about studying. Turn the negative thoughts around or replace them with positive thoughts.

There are three steps to this process:

1. Identify your goals.
2. Try to figure out the negative messages you are giving yourself.
3. Rephrase the message in positive terms.

For example, here are some negative thoughts:

- The work is too hard.
- I'm dumber than everyone else.
- I don't know how to begin.
- I'm tired.
- This is boring.
- I can't stand the teacher.
- My teacher doesn't like me.

Here are some affirmations:

- I am bright and capable.
- My teacher and friends like me.
- I know how to ask questions and get started.
- I am ready for action.
- Ask for volunteers to share their goals, and go through the process with them, following these steps:
- Have each student practice writing affirmations.
- Lead a "go around," so that all students can practice saying their affirmations aloud.
- Have the students pick the affirmation they like best.
- Tell them to write it 10 times and say it to themselves as they write it.
- Have them practice it every night and at the beginning of every class.

Source: Campbell, C. A. (1991). Group Guidance for Academically Undermotivated Children. *Elementary School Guidance and Counseling, 25*(1).

Overcoming Public Speaking Anxiety

There are five steps to follow in overcoming the fear of speaking in public.

1. **Identification.** Identify exactly what you are most afraid of. For example, is it getting up in front of class to give a report or leading a discussion?

2. **Self-talk.** Verbalize your "fearful self-talk" aloud. Write it down. For example,: *"I could stutter. I could faint. I might get laughed at for sounding stupid."*

3. **Action plan.** Write down a plan of action for your greatest fear. For example, read a self-help book on effective presentations, join the debate team, practice a talk in front of the mirror, or tape a talk and play it back.

4. **Rehearse.** Rehearse doing what you fear in your mind; visualize it. Practice and prepare your talk. Use a tape recorder to record your voice and play it back. Ask a friend to listen to a practice session. Practice your talk in front of the mirror. Become comfortable with your public self.

5. **Positive self-talk.** Tell yourself to relax. Tell yourself that no one else has prepared as well as you did. Tell yourself that your presentation will be your best.

Academic Growth Group and Mentoring Program Evaluation to Be Completed by Teachers

To the teachers of . . .

This student will participate in group counseling to improve his or her academic work and grades. It would be helpful if you would complete this questionnaire before the student begins the group sessions and again after he or she has completed eight group sessions. I will send you another copy of this form after the group sessions. Please keep me informed of this student's academic progress as we work together to help him or her improve his or her written work and performance in class. Thank you.

Directions: Please indicate by circling A if you agree and D if you disagree.

This student:

1. Is self-confident.   A   D

2. Is aware of his or her strengths.   A   D

3. Is aware of his or her assignments.   A   D

4. Completes his or her assignments.   A   D

5. Does satisfactory work in class.   A   D

6. Uses good study skills.   A   D

7. Gets along well with other students.   A   D

8. Gets along well with me and other adults. A   D

Source: D. J. Blum & L. A. Jones (1993). Academic growth group and mentoring program for potential dropouts. *The School Counselor, 40*, 3. Published by the American School Counselor Association (ASCA). Reprinted with permission.

Chapter 9

ISOLATION, VICTIMIZATION, AND ABUSE

Miranda did suffer repeated childhood beatings at the hands of both parents, especially her father. But Miranda also remembers his frequent neglect, and somehow that was even worse. "I now see that I did a lot of things to get my father's attention," she admits. "If I was good, daddy ignored me. So I stayed out late, stole from stores, and didn't go to school; that got his attention." And a beating. Miranda learned that the kind of attention she "deserved" was violent. When she later became involved with abusive lovers, she believed she had caused—deserved—those beatings too. The fact that men hit her convinced Miranda that they cared about her. (Baker, 1983, p. 313)

The National Center of Child Abuse and Neglect (NCCAN) recently released its third National Incidence Study, reporting 1993 statistics, the most recent data available. An estimated 1,553,800 children in the U.S. were abused and neglected in that year. This data reflects a 67% increase since the last study in 1986 and a 149% increase since the last study in 1980. When these children were classified according to the degree to which they were injured, the estimated number of seriously injured children escalated from 141,700 in 1986 to 565,000 in 1993. This increase demonstrates that too many families see violence against children as an option (Prevention Update, 1997). Compared to other industrialized countries, the United States lags far behind in the development of human resources to address this crisis. The list below gives an idea of the magnitude of the problem:

- In the United States, 1 out of 3 girls, and at least 1 out of 5 boys will be sexually abused before they are 18 (Buel, 1993).
- A million adolescents run away from home every year. Most are victims of abuse, and a majority of them become prostitutes or delinquents (*Education Week,* 1990).
- Statistics show that 1 out of 8 women in the U.S. have been raped (Martin, 1992), and that 29% of rape victims are younger than 11; another 32% are between 11 and 17. This means that, in 61% of all rapes in this country, the victim is 17 years old and younger. (Martin, 1992).
- Domestic violence is even more prevalent: Researchers estimate that 21% to 34% of women in this country are physically assaulted by an intimate partner at some time in their lives—an astonishing 3 to 4 million every year (Biden, 1993).
- Some 350,000 newborns each year are exposed prenatally to drugs, including alcohol.
- The incidence of pediatric HIV infection has risen dramatically in recent years, affecting some 15,000 to 30,000 infants (Burgess, & Streissguth, 1992).

Because of the vast range of maltreatment behavior, this phenomenon is perhaps more readily understood if classified into categories presenting both acts of commission (i.e., physical abuse) and acts of omission (i.e., emotional neglect). Acts of commission include these:

1. **Physical abuse:** Infliction of physical injury (e.g., burns, bites) on a child.
2. **Sexual abuse:** Subjection of a child to sexual acts by an adult.
3. **Physical neglect:** Failure to provide a child with a nurturing home environment that supplies the basic necessities of life (i.e., food, clothing, shelter, supervision, and protection from harm).
4. **Medical neglect:** Failure of a caretaker to provide medical treatment in cases of suspected or diagnosed physical ailments.

Acts of omission include these:

1. **Emotional abuse:** Speech and actions by a caretaker that inhibit the healthy personal and social development of a child.
2. **Emotional neglect:** Failure of a caretaker to show concern for a child or his or her activities.
3. **Educational neglect:** Failure of a caretaker to ensure that a child is provided with the opportunity to learn.

4. **Abandonment:** Failure of a caretaker to make provisions for the continued sustenance of a child.
5. **Multiple maltreatment:** A severe and complex combination of several types of abuse and/or neglect.

It is estimated that 60% of domestic violence victims and 80% of batters come from families with a history of violence (Buel, 1993). Low self-esteem and feelings of inadequacy can result in problems ranging from low productivity on the job to delinquency, character disorders and mental illness (Dean, 1979). Furthermore, the problems are often self-propagating in that they may be passed on from one generation to the next (Schrut, 1984). Children who have been psychologically abused throughout their lives often act out once they become adolescents. For example, Foreman and Seligman (1983) stated:

> In the courts, the abused adolescent is once again the loser; he or she may be punished as an offender rather than treated as a victim. Such responses from legal or social authorities tend to reinforce adolescents' own negative self-images and encourage them to view themselves as offenders and provokers, to be blamed for their own abuse. (p. 19)

SEXUAL ABUSE IN THE FAMILY

In an extensive study, Alter-Reid (1992) found that the majority of child abuse victims had been sexually abused by a family member, including natural parents (19%); surrogate parents, such as step-fathers or live-in boyfriends (21%); and other relatives (22%). Only 3% were victimized by strangers. Alter-Reid (1992) also found that children at the highest risk of incest are those with step-fathers. A stepfather is 6 times more likely than a biological father to sexually abuse a daughter. Children under the age of 9 are abused more frequently by relatives and acquaintances than are older children (those from 9 to 16). Therefore, sexual abuse prevention programs should not be limited to stranger abduction.

The news that the effects of abuse are long-lasting is not new. Children report post-abuse fear, poor self-esteem, guilt, and a sense of being "damaged goods." As adults, they report depression, fear, and problems in sexual relationships. The impact of physical and sexual abuse is not easily quantifiable, but it is clearly seen in school and clinical settings and supported by the clinical experience of counselors and others. Some effects include these:

- Loss of trust, security, and the innocence of childhood
- Ambivalence and conflict of feelings: love and hate, rage and guilt, stoicism and fear
- The creation of defenses: walls of denial, repression, and dissociation; the armors of anorgasmia, anorexia, and obesity; the weapons of the fist, the tongue, and the belt; the retreat to the bottle, the pill, and depression; escape from family, society, and reality
- Death—frequently invisible, unnoticed, unmourned—by overt or covert suicide (Alter-Reid, 1992, p. 16)
- Several studies have suggested that child sexual abuse victims may internalize their victimization to such a degree that they *expect* further abuse, resulting in a choice of partners who continue to abuse them and/or their children (Gillman & Whitlock, 1989).

INDICATORS OF ABUSE

In terms of impact, there is little difference between physical, sexual, and emotional abuse. All that ultimately distinguishes one from the other is the abuser's choice of weapons on the victim. What emerges from such a punitive relationship is pervasive sadness, a severely damaged self-concept, difficulty with other relationships, and a lifelong quest to gain the approval of others. This quest for approval often is eclipsed by the notion that one does not really deserve it. Self-defeating, self-destructive behaviors often manifest themselves in obesity, drug addiction, anorexia, bulimia, alcoholism, domestic violence, child abuse, attempted suicide, and depression.

Most counselors and practitioners are aware of the physical indicators of abuse, including these:

Physical abuse: unexplained bruises, burns, bites, fractures, lacerations, or abrasions

Physical neglect: abandonment, unattended medical needs, lack of supervision, hunger, poor hygiene

Sexual abuse: torn, stained underclothing; vaginal pain or itching; venereal disease

Emotional abuse: speech disorders, delayed physical development, substance abuse, ulcers, asthma, severe allergies

Many, however, may not recognize behavioral indicators. Figure 9.1 provides behavioral indicators of abuse in checklist form for educators, counselors, and other helping professionals.

Physical Abuse

☐ self-destructive

☐ arrives at school early or stays late

☐ withdrawn and aggressive

☐ chronically running away

☐ uncomfortable with physical contact

☐ wears clothing inappropriate for age

Physical Neglect

☐ regularly displays fatigue

☐ reports no caretaker at home

☐ self-destructive

☐ falls asleep in class

☐ frequently absent or tardy

☐ steals food, begs from classmates

Sexual Abuse

☐ withdrawn, chronic depression

☐ lack of confidence

☐ peer problems

☐ sudden school difficulties

☐ threatened by physical contact

☐ excessive seductiveness

☐ hysteria, lack of emotional control

☐ promiscuity

☐ poor self-esteem

Emotional Maltreatment

☐ habit disorders (sucking, rocking)

☐ sleep disorders

☐ developmentally delayed

☐ antisocial, destructive

☐ passive aggressive

☐ delinquent behavior

Source: Adapted from T. Bear, S. Schenk, & L. Buckner. "Supporting victims of abuse." *Educational Leadership, 50*(4), 44. Copyright © 1993 by ASCD. Reprinted by permission. All rights reserved.

Figure 9.1. Behavioral Indicators of Abuse

Children from violent homes are likely to show several emotional reactions, according to their coping skills and developmental age:

1. **Feeling responsible for the abuse.** *"If only I had been a good girl, Daddy would not have hit Mommy."*
2. **Anxiety and guilt.** Anxiety about the next violent situation and guilt about good feelings the child may have toward the abuser.
3. **Fear of abandonment or abduction.** When children are removed from one parent because of violent acts, they often have fears that the other

parent will abandon them or that the abuser will abduct them or retaliate.

4. **Shame, embarrassment, and uncertainty about the future.** Sensitivity to the stigma of abuse may result in shame, uncertainty in interpersonal relationships, and anxiety over future planning.

Reactions also vary according to the type of abuse a child experiences and
whether the child internalizes or externalizes blame for the abuse:

- The results of sexual abuse include self-blame, confusion about sexuality, and distorted, negative views of self and others.
- Pynoos and Eth (1985) maintained that children who witness extreme
acts of violence are at "significant risk of developing anxiety, depression, phobic conduct, and post-traumatic stress disorder (p. 19).
- Children and adolescents who internalize blame for abusive situations
may manifest the following symptoms: self-destructiveness, depression,
suicidal thoughts, passivity, withdrawal, shyness, constricted communication, nervous habits, nightmares, and somatic complaints (Blume,
1990).
- Children and adolescents who tend to externalize blame manifest a different set of symptoms: anxiety, aggression, hostile behavior, overactivity,
impulsivity, readiness to strike back, and fearful responses.

RAPE

Rape has been declared a social disease of epidemic proportions. McCann,
Sakheim, and Abrahamson (1988) estimated that 46% of women in the United
States will be raped at least once in their lives. Other researchers place the
figure at 22% (Koss & Oros, 1982; Koss, Gidycz, & Wisniewski, 1987; Russell, 1984).

Rape victims constitute the largest single group of post-traumatic stress
disorder (PTSD) sufferers (Steketee & Foa, 1987). Rape-related symptoms that
are consistent with PTSD include intrusive and unpleasant imagery, nightmares,
exaggerated startle responses, disturbance in sleep pattern, guilt, impairment in
concentration or memory, and fear and avoidance of rape-related situations (Steketee & Foa, 1987). The aftermath of sexual trauma is a major mental health
problem with both short- and long-term effects (Roth & Lebowitz, 1988).

In recent years, researchers and the media have raised new awareness of a
kind of rape that has gone unreported for years: date rape. Victims of date rape

often have serious concerns about their self-perceptions and view themselves as weak, helpless, and out of control.

Armsworth and Holaday (1993, p. 51) examined the cognitive, affective, behavioral, and somatic-physiological effects of sexual assault on children and adolescents. Cognitive effects of trauma in children and adolescents that meet the criteria of PTSD include these:

- time distortion regarding the event
- inability to recall details of the event in sequence
- intrusive imagery and thoughts with conscious suppression and avoidance
- a foreshortened sense of the future
- no goals or altered goals
- hypervigilance
- alertness to reminders
- guardedness against attack

Affective effects of trauma in children and adolescents include these:

- labile affect, including anxiety, panic, and irritability
- fears, including excessive worry, generalized phobias, and fears of re-traumatization
- tension
- constricted emotions
- inability to express or fear of expressing feelings
- distress at reminders of objects, situations, or people
- traumatic dreams
- avoidance of pleasurable activities
- reexperiencing the event emotionally

Several behavioral effects meet the criteria for PTSD, including these:

- post-traumatic play
- regressive behaviors
- loss of previously learned skills (academic and social)
- reenactment of the events
- retelling the event without affect
- poor concentration, inattentiveness, hyperactivity, and impulsivity
- no regard for consequence of actions
- alteration of behavior to avoid activities, people, situations, and objects that are reminders of the events

- alterations of behavior that results from feeling alone, estranged, left out, or different (Armsworth & Holaday, 1993, p. 53)

Physiological and somatic effects of trauma noted in the literature that meet the criteria of PTSD include these:

- autonomic response to traumatic reminders
- hyperarousal
- low tolerance for stress
- startle response to reminder stimuli alternating with numbing
- sleep disorders
- fatigue

RUNAWAYS AND HOMELESS YOUTH

Without a systematic, centralized system for collecting information about runaways, the number of young people who run away is difficult to determine with certainty. Estimates range from 700,000 to almost 1 million each year, and one study indicated that 12% of all American youth have run away at least once before the age of 18 (Jones, 1988). The significant fact is that many of these young people are refugees from unbearable situations or circumstances.

Furthermore, current research shows a trend toward long-term homelessness for runaway youth. This is caused by such factors as family breakdown, rejection, physical, and sexual abuse (Jones, 1988; McCormack, Burgess, & Hartman, 1988). Kufeldt and Nimmo (1987) found that as many as 30% of long-term runaways no longer even knew where their parents lived, and that 6% of sporadic runaways had lost track of their parents. These researchers also noted that the tendency to assume a pattern of street life is associated with the length of time away from the family and the distance from the home.

Runaway behavior seems to reflect a multidimensional problem. The reasons for running away are multiple and complex, as the following list indicates:

- **Negative psychological or social adjustment** (Ferran & Sabatini, 1985; Kammer & Schmidt, 1987)
- **An attempt to find a value system that the runaway can accept** (Adams & Munro, 1979; Loeb, Burke, & Boglarsky, 1986)
- **An attempt to "find" oneself or gain control over one's life** (Adams & Munro, 1979)
- **Poor self-image and low self-confidence** (Englander, 1984; Miller, 1981)

- **Family disturbance, including poor communication, alcoholism or drug abuse, and parent-child conflict** (Ferran & Sabatini, 1985; Kammer & Schmidt, 1987; Kogan, 1980; Morgan, 1982; Stiffman, 1989)
- **Parental rejection or expulsion** (Adams, Gullotta, & Clancy, 1985; Levine, Metzendorf, & Van Boskirk, 1986)
- **A rational and appropriate reaction to detrimental circumstances** (Aptekar, 1989)
- **Economic stress, including a lack of adequate resources to sustain a stable pattern of life** (Aptekar, 1989; Ferran & Sabatini, 1985).
- **Sexual and physical abuse** (Daly & Wilson, 1985; McCormack, Burgess, & Hartman, 1988) (When the definition of sexual abuse is widened, up to 73% of female runaways report having experienced some form of sexual abuse; Stiffman, 1989.)
- **Engaging in confrontations in school** (Zieman & Benson, 1980)
- **Difficulty with school authorities** (Nielsen & Gerber, 1979; Zieman & Benson, 1980)
- **Lack of academic success** (Levine, Metzendorf, & VanBoskirk, 1986; Miller, 1981)

Compared to nonrunaways, runaways have lower self-esteem, less self-confidence, and more difficulty with interpersonal relationships, including a lack of social poise. Generally, runaways feel less control of their environments, which perhaps accounts for research findings that they are more likely to be anxious, to be defensive, and to exhibit suicidal tendencies.

In a study by Roberts (1982), the runaway population sample also manifested inadequate problem-solving methods. They attempted to deal with stressful situations by sleeping, crying, turning to drugs or alcohol, forgetting about major elements in their lives, or attempting suicide. All these coping strategies involve removing oneself from the situation rather than confronting it. This pattern of destructive thinking has been labeled *cognitive confusion* by Janus, Burgess, and McCormack (1987).

STRUCTURED INTERVENTIONS
FOR HIGH-RISK BEHAVIORS

Therapeutic Initiatives

Eliminating victimization and abuse takes a school/community multidisciplinary approach to helping children and adolescents. Networks and resource centers can operate in a wide variety of local settings: hospital, schools, community mental health centers, recreation centers, libraries, community colleges, civic centers, daycare centers, social service agencies, and churches. Network members should be drawn from the medical, educational, law enforcement, and social work disciplines and include key leaders from business, political, and volunteer segments of the community. Committees of network members should concentrate on such areas as these:

- **Mental health services for sexually abused children:** Interviewing techniques that provide potential cues through toys, materials, and photographs can elicit much more information than verbal questioning alone.
- **Family life education programs** that teach adolescents about the social aspects of sexuality, including the importance of sexual consent. These programs also should teach parenting skills and address such areas as self-esteem, coping skills, decision making, communication, developmental issues, and parental control.
- **Systematic teacher education:** Because of their daily contact with children, teachers often are the first finders of child abuse. They need to learn to recognize the warning signs of child abuse, including aggression, withdrawal, poor personal hygiene, low self-esteem, or reluctance to dress for physical education activities.
- **Self-help groups** at churches and community centers.
- **Volunteer teachers** as facilitators of school-based sexual abuse prevention programs.
- **Helping families** search for solutions to problems such as parental conflict, divorce, alcoholism, legal problems, and sexual or emotional abuse.

Helping Abused Children in the Classroom. Children who have been abused usually attempt to keep the abuse a secret and to control the emotional turmoil they feel inside. When they do confide the abuse, it often is to a teacher. In addition to reporting the abuse, classroom teachers have a unique opportunity to identify abused children and to start the healing process that will restore safety to their lives, Bear, Schenk, and Buckner (1993, pp. 46-47) outlined the following suggestions for helping:

1. **Expectations.** Set reasonable goals and provide the support needed for the child to feel confident in his or her abilities. School can be a place where children rebuild their self-esteem, assert themselves, and see themselves as successful.
2. **Structure.** To help the child feel a sense of control in a positive manner, give accurate information and build trust. Allow expression of feelings when appropriate through art, music, drama, or creative writing to help the child release pent-up emotion.

3. **Identity.** Point out the child's strengths: *"You are a hard worker."* *"You are a good team leader."* Ask questions that help the child formulate a position on issues. Administer interest inventories and teach decision-making and problem-solving skills to enhance interpersonal relationships and self-understanding.

4. **Self-esteem.** Help children learn they are valued, accepted, and capable by fostering an environment that honors each child's uniqueness. Valuing their differences enables children to begin seeing themselves as having something to contribute that others appreciate.

5. **Sense of belonging.** To facilitate a sense of belonging, provide designated places for possessions, display work in the classroom, and make a conscious attempt to include abused children in classroom activities. Teach social skills individually, in small-group settings, and through cooperative learning to help children gain experience in interacting with others in a nonthreatening atmosphere.

6. **Social skills.** A classroom environment that fosters caring, appreciation of differences, consistent rules and boundaries, and recognition for small successes will nurture a child who has experienced family deprecation.

7. **Consistency.** Teachers can support a child's need for structure by maintaining a consistent daily schedule, by having clear expectations for performance academically, behaviorally, and affectively, and by allowing the child to provide structure in his or her own way.

A teacher's natural concern and caring for students also will promote the process of healing. Teachers have the opportunity to give an abused child the hope of a childhood, the joy of learning, the delight of play, and the sense of belonging by being cared for and valued by others.

Further, teachers can use age-appropriate discussions with children and adolescents to help them understand and avoid abuse:

- **18 months to 3 years:** Teach children the proper names for body parts.
- **3 to 5 years:** Teach children about private parts of the body and how to say "no" to sexual advances. Give straightforward, frank information about sex.
- **5 to 8 years:** Discuss safety away from home and the difference between a good touch and a bad touch. Encourage honest discussion of experiences.
- **9 to 12 years:** Stress personal safety. Discuss appropriate sexual conduct.
- **13 to 18 years:** Stress personal safety. Discuss rape, date rape, unintended pregnancy, and sexually transmitted diseases.

Treatment Plan: Prevention of Sexual Assault.

Counseling Intention: To identify and distinguish between comfortable and uncomfortable kinds of touches; to identify specific ways of saying "no" to adults and other children; to help students understand that they can tell if they encounter a difficult situation; to know what to say to a caring person.

Hitchcock & Young (1986) provided the following treatment plan for children:

You Can Say "No."

Session 1: Identifying uncomfortable feelings. For the first few minutes, the children and the counselor think of words that describe feelings. The counselor helps the children place these words into a list of comfortable feelings and another list of uncomfortable feelings. A third list may be added for confusing feelings, either comfortable or uncomfortable, depending on the maturity of the children.

Next, the counselor asks the children to describe situations in which uncomfortable feelings might occur. Children tend to focus on peer-pressure situations and threats of kidnapping by strangers. Thus, it might be necessary to explain sexual assault as an uncomfortable touch on the part of the body covered by a bathing suit. Counselors working with kindergartners sometimes explain the private area as "where you go to the bathroom." Because children focus on assault by strangers, counselors need to explain that persons whom children know might want to touch the children's private parts or want the children to touch theirs.

Session 2: Why it's hard to say "no." Often children realize that they need to say "no" but find it difficult to do so. This lesson emphasizes the reasons for that difficulty. The counselor begins by asking children why it is hard to say "no." Children typically describe bribes, threats of harm, withdrawal of affection, secrecy, and peer pressure, but counselors need to be prepared to add to these ideas. The lesson also recognizes that children often are expected to obey without question. Fears about saying "no" because of lost status with peers or punishment by an adult need to be recognized and taken seriously.

To reinforce the session, pictures are used depicting situations in which children might want to say "no." The children explain what they think is happening in the picture and are asked what they could do if something like this happened to them, emphasizing that they can say "no."

Session 3: How to say "no." When they have an understanding of uncomfortable feelings and of the difficulty in saying "no," children are
ready to learn techniques for saying "no," including these:

1. **Broken record:** *"No, I don't want to! No, I don't want to!"*
2. **Delaying:** *"Not now."*
3. **Explanation:** *"I don't feel that it would be right for me."*
4. **Leaving**
5. **Avoiding the situation:** *"No, my mom wants me home now."*
6. **Changing the subject:** *"No, I don't want to. Did you see the movie
   last night?"*
7. **Taking personal credit:** *"No, I don't want to be your friend if I
   have to do that."*

Because the last three techniques are more complicated, counselors need
to determine the appropriateness of the techniques for the children's
age level. For each technique, children practice different ways of saying "no" and are encouraged to develop their own responses. Generally, this is accomplished by having children role-play in pairs, with
the counselor and other children supplying encouragement and feedback.

Session 4: Role-playing saying "no." The fourth session is a continuation
of the previous one and may be combined easily with the third, depending on the children's maturity and time constraints. The counselor
shows children pictures of situations in which they might want to say
"no." Children then act out situations in which there is peer pressure,
and the counselor cautiously assumes the role of perpetrator in sexual
assault situations. This procedure avoids putting the children in awk-
ward situations and allows them to practice saying "no" to an adult.

Session 5: I can tell a caring person. This session helps children identify
appropriate helping persons, structures what the child should say, and
identifies appropriate times for talking. Occasionally, children will find
adults who will not believe them, so suggestions are provided on how
to find someone who will believe them.

Session 6: Telling a caring person. In this final session, three situations
are described in which a child is approached sexually, once by a stranger
and twice by a known adult. Children gain additional experience in
saying "no" and in reporting to a caring adult. Because the adult is
known, children have the opportunity to discuss their fears about "tat-
tling" on the person. Again, discussions sometimes flow more smoothly
if the counselor takes the part of the abuser and openly acknowledges
the difficulties of saying "no."

Treatment Plan: Guided Exercise for Telling the Story of Sexual Abuse.
Counseling Intention: To provide structure for a trauma-focused sexual abuse treatment group; to engage the support of peers.

De Young and Corbin (1994) provided the following treatment plan for adolescents. The young person is provided with the following guided exercise for telling his or her story.

Remember, you *are in charge of how much or how little you tell. Telling what happened to you can lift shame off your shoulders. The shame belongs to those who have sexually abused you and told you lies.*

1. *Today* I feel _____ about the possibility of telling others my story.

2. The *worst* thing that can happen while telling my story is

    ____I won't remember telling it.
    ____someone may laugh.
    ____someone may not believe me.
    ____I will feel pain.
    ____I will explode with emotion.
    ____I will be embarrassed.
    ____I may cry.
    ____someone may think I'm weird.
    ____or something else, like _____

3. I *need* the group to

    ____be understanding.
    ____not laugh or talk while I'm talking.
    ____be patient with me.
    ____ask me questions in a caring way.
    ____tell me what they think and feel about what I just said.

4. The *person* (or persons) who sexually abused me *was* (include)

    ____my mother.
    ____my father.
    ____my stepfather.
    ____my mother's boyfriend.
    ____my brother.
    ____my sister.

____my uncle.
____my grandfather.
____a family friend.
____a stranger.
____and/or another person, like _____

5. This *happened* to me

____one or two times.
____many times.
____more times than I can count.

6. The sexual abuse *felt*

____good sometimes.
____gross.
____scary.
____painful.
____weird/confusing.
____I can't remember.
____I'm too scared to remember.
____other feelings, like

7. *After* the sexual abuse happened, I thought

____I did something wrong.
____this happens to all girls (boys).
____there might be something wrong with my body.
____I might be pregnant.
____I might have AIDS or some other disease.
____that if I told, something terrible would happen.
____that I could have stopped it, but I'm not sure how.
____that people could tell I was abused by just looking at me.

8. The person or persons who sexually abused me *told me*

____never to tell.
____nothing.
____they would hurt me or someone I love if I told.
____nobody would believe me if I told.
____they were in love with me.
____confusing things about my mom.

_____that I was a slut or whore.

_____that they were doing nothing wrong.

_____that they would give me money or special favors if I kept doing it.

_____other things, like _____

9. My *mother* (or parent)

_____blamed me.

_____didn't believe me.

_____seems not to care how I feel.

_____knew it was happening and didn't protect me.

_____was helpful and supportive.

_____did something else, like _____

10. The *person* who touched me wrong

_____admitted to some of the things, but not everything.

_____admitted it, but still said it wasn't wrong.

_____told the police about the sexual abuse.

_____admitted it to me, but to no one else.

_____did or said other things, like _____

_____didn't admit to anything.

11. The *person* who sexually abused me

_____went to prison or jail.

_____had to leave our house.

_____I don't know where he or she is.

_____something else happened to that person, like _____

12. If the sexual abuse had *never happened* maybe

_____I would be able to sleep through the night.

_____I would make friends more easily.

_____I wouldn't cry all the time.

_____I wouldn't feel like hurting myself so often.

_____I wouldn't feel like people are staring at me.

_____or something else, like _____

13. In the *future,* I would like to be able to

_____tell my mom or dad how I feel.

_____be more friendly.

_____stop putting myself down.
_____walk tall and proud without shame.
_____or something else, like

14. I *wish*

    _____I could go back home.
    _____my family would believe me.
    _____I would feel safe.
    _____I could stop having bad dreams.
    _____some other wish, like

*I must always remember: I **deserve** to be treated with respect and to be safe. Nothing that I did caused these bad things to happen to me.*

Treatment Plan: Preventing Sexual Assault.
Counseling Intention: To provide adolescents with strategies to prevent date rape or acquaintance rape.

Martin (1992) provided the following exercises for preventing sexual assault (the exercises have been modified for this book).

First impressions. After meeting someone for the first time, take a few minutes to write down your thoughts about him. List some concrete questions about him:

- Where does he work?
- What is he studying?
- Where does he live?
- How does he look?

Next list your intuitive feelings:

- Do you feel safe with him?
- Does he seem sensitive to your feelings?
- Does he seem overpowering?
- Could he have an uncontrollable temper?

Listen to your inner thoughts and feelings about this individual.

Finding a safe place and an escape route. Find a place where you feel physically safe: This could be your home, the library, a museum, the school, or inside a shopping mall. Then draw an escape route on paper, the route to take you to safety if you were attacked. Try to think of as many alternatives as possible and rate them as to how successful you think they would be.

Attention to detail. Police will tell you that the most useful clues in identifying someone are characteristics that make that person stand out from the rest. Birthmarks, tattoos, unusual facial or hair features are all good characteristics to report. Pick someone you recently saw (a parent, teacher, friend). Describe what they were wearing when you saw them, special characteristics, weight, height, information about how they walk or talk. You may be surprised at how little you remember about someone you are close to. Sharpen your awareness skills and practice recalling details.

Treatment Plan: Multimodal Treatment Plan for Victimization.

Counseling Intention: To provide a comprehensive intervention for victimization.

Modality and Referral Problems	Related Interventions
Behavior Reduced work performance Diminished activity Statements of self-denigration	• Implement a "pleasant event schedules" to ensure a daily sampling of personally pleasing activities
Affect Sadness, guilt, "heavy hearted" Intermittent anxiety and anger	• Standard anxiety reduction methods (e.g., relaxation, meditation, calming self-statements) combined with assertiveness training; a repertoire of self-assertive and uninhibited responses
Sensation Less pleasure from food Easily fatigued	• A specific list of pleasant visual, auditory, tactile, olfactory, and gustatory stimuli is added to the "pleasant events schedule" to create a "sensate-focus" of enjoyable events
Imagery Visions of loneliness and failure Pictures him- or herself being rejected by important people in his life	• Recalling past successes • Picturing small but successful outcomes • Applying coping imagery, using "time projection" (i.e., client pictures him- or herself venturing step-by-step into a future characterized by positive affect and pleasurable activities)
Cognition Negative self-appraisal Exaggerates real or imagined shortcomings. *"I'm not good at anything." "Things will always be bad for me."*	• Employ Ellis's (1989) methods of cognitive disputation, challenge categorical imperatives, "should and oughts," and irrational beliefs • Identify worthwhile qualities and recite them every day

Modality and Referral Problems	Related Interventions
Interpersonal Decreased social participation	• Clients are taught to "No!" to unreasonable requests; to ask for favors by expressing positive feelings; to volunteer criticism; and to "dispute with style" • Family therapy may be recommended to teach family members how to avoid reinforcing depressive behavior and how to encourage the client to engage in pleasurable activities
Drugs/Biology Appetite unimpaired but has intermittent insomnia	• Issues pertaining to increased exercise, relaxation, appropriate sleep patterns, and overall physical fitness are addressed • Biological intervention such as antidepressants are recommended in the case of bipolar disorders

Treatment Plan: Confronting Shyness.
Counseling Intention: To assist the client in becoming more assertive.

The following guidelines should be considered when framing or defining assertive behavior:

• The best way to get what you want is to ask for it.
• The best way not to get what you don't want is to say no to it.
• The best way to get someone to stop doing something you don't want them to do is to tell them how their actions make you feel.
• Assertiveness implies a special type of self-disclosure.
• Don't avoid expressing "negative" feelings. Negative feelings are just as important as positive ones.
• Focus on first-person "I" language to signify that the statement you are making is an indication of your own feelings (Wassmer, 1978).

Treatment Plan: Cost and Benefits.
Counseling Intention: To assess missed opportunities for growth.

Has being shy cost you anything? Have you missed opportunities and passed by unique experiences because you were shy? Make an itemized cost.

Time of your life	Valued event, opportunity that was delayed or diminished	Personal consequence to you
1.		
2.		
3.		
4.		

Technique: Shyness Journal.
Counseling Intention: To evaluate dimensions of shyness.

Keep a journal of the times you feel shy. White down the time, what happened, your reaction, and the consequences for you.

Time	Situation or Setting	Physical Symptoms	Mental Notation Reactions	Consequences (+) (-)
3rd bell	U.S. Government class discussion of daily current events	Heart pounding, nervous, look down, avoid eye contact	*"I can't remember anything I read this morning. I'm going to fail this class. . . I'll have to go to summer school."*	*"I've lost another opportunity for my grade. Time is running out."* Panic

Treatment Plan: Write Yourself a Letter.
Counseling Intention: To identify and validate personal attributes that are positive.

Write yourself a letter focusing on your positive attributes or record a message about your successes, hopes, and possibilities and play it back.

Treatment Plan: First Time Talking.
Counseling Intention: To focus on critical social skills.

If you find that you have a hard time talking to "anyone," try some of these less-threatening experiences.

- Call information and ask for the telephone numbers of people you want to call. Thank the operator and note his or her reaction.
- Call a department store and check on the price of something advertised in the paper.
- Call a radio talk show, compliment the format, then ask a question.
- Call a local movie theater and ask for the discounted show times.
- Call the library and ask the reference librarian some question about the population in your town or the United States.
- Call a restaurant and make reservations for four, then call back within the hour and cancel them. Thank the person at the reservation desk and note his or her reaction.

Treatment Plan: Saying Hello.
Counseling Intention: To begin a experiential hierarchy of anxiety-provoking situation.

On the campus or in the workplace, smile and say hello to people you don't know.

Treatment Plan: Beginning a Dialogue with a Stranger.
Counseling Intention: To continue structured interpersonal experiences.

An ideal way to practice initial conversational skills is to initiate safe conversations with strangers in public places, like grocery store lines, theater lines, the post office, a doctor's waiting room, the bank, the library, or the lunch room.

Start a conversation about a common experience, such as, *"It looks like mystery meat for lunch again." "I hope this will be my lucky lotto ticket."* Or *"Who do you hope will win the Super Bowl?"*

Treatment Plan: Giving and Accepting Compliments.
Counseling Intention: To provide an opportunity to integrate social skills into interpersonal relationships.

Giving and accepting compliments is an easy way to start a conversation and make the other person feel good. Yet it is probably the most overlooked ice breaker between people. Here are some examples:

- Comment on what a person is wearing: *"That's a cool jacket."*
- Comment on how a person looks: *"I like your haircut."*
- Note a skill: *"You sure know how to catch those waves."*

- Complement a personality trait: *"I love your laugh."*
- Note a possessions: *"That car is awesome!"*

To get further into the conversations, simply ask a question: *"What an awesome car. How long have you had it?"*

Treatment Plan: Starting a Conversation.
Counseling Intention: To identify comfort levels in interacting with others.

There are a number of ways to start a conversation. Choose the one that is the most appropriate and comfortable for you.

Introduce yourself. *"Hello, my name is . . ."* (Practice this in a mirror at home.) This is a good approach at gatherings where everyone is a stranger.

Give a compliment, then follow it up with a question. *"That's a terrific suit. Where did you get it?"*

Request help. Make it obvious you need it and be sure the other person can provide it. *"Last time I came to this library, I used the card catalogue. How can I find the works of Carl Rogers with this computer terminal?"*

Try honesty and self-disclosure. When you make an obviously personal statement, it will create a positive, sympathetic response. Be honest and say, *"I'm not sure what I'm doing here. I'm really quite shy."*

Cultivate your normal social graces: *"Looks like you need a refill; let me get it for you; I'm headed that way."* Or, *"Here, let me help you with those groceries."*

Once you have initiated a conversation, there are several techniques you can use to keep it going:

- Ask a question that is either factual (*"Can you believe how bad the Redskins look this year?"*) or personal (*"How do you feel about President Clinton's health care package?"*)
- Offer one of your own personal stories or opinions.
- Read a lot about political or cultural issues and become knowledgeable about them (e.g., the national deficit or violence in society).
- Come up with a few interesting things that have happened to you recently. and turn them into brief interesting stories. For example, you could talk about registering for classes, incidents on the job, a new video game, learning to surf or skate, teachers, parents, brothers, and sisters. When you meet people, be ready with several stories to tell or

interesting comments to make. Practice ahead of time in the mirror or on a tape recorder.

- Get the other person to talk about him- or herself: interests, hobbies, work, education.
- Express interest in the other person's expertise: *"How were you able to land a job like that?" "How did you make it through Gaskin's class?"*
- Above all, share your reactions to what is taking place at that moment. Relate your thoughts or feelings about what the other person has said or done (Zimbardo, 1977, p. 180).

Treatment Plan: Becoming More Outgoing.
Counseling Intention: To increase the client's repertoire of interpersonal experiences.

Start with the easiest reaching-out exercise and progress to those that are more difficult. Record your reactions to each of these opportunities.

- Introduce yourself to a new person in one of your classes.
- Invite someone who is going your way to walk with you.
- Ask someone you don't know if you can borrow a quarter for a phone call. Arrange to pay them back.
- Find someone of the opposite sex in your class. Call him or her on the phone and ask about the latest class assignment.
- Stand in line at a grocery store. Start a conversation about the line with whomever is near you.
- Ask three people for directions.
- Go to the beach, swimming pool, or sports stadium and converse with two or three strangers you meet.
- Notice someone who needs help in school or class. Offer to help.
- Invite someone to eat with you.
- Say "Hi" to five new people during the week. Try to provoke a smile and a return "Hi" from them.

Treatment Plan: Making a Date with Someone of the Opposite Sex.
Counseling Intention: To decrease irrational fears of rejection.

Dating is a social contact that is anxiety-provoking for many. Shy daters feel more vulnerable to irrational thoughts of rejection. Here are some guidelines for overcoming fears:

- Make your date by telephone initially. Be prepared ahead of time and have two specific activities in mind.

- When you contact the person by phone, identify yourself by name and explain when you met (if applicable). *"This is Jim Thompson. I met you at the yearbook signing party."*
- Be sure you are recognized.
- Pay the person a compliment related to your last meeting, one that recognizes his or her talent, values, or position on an issue. *"You really did a great job designing the cover of the yearbook."*
- Be assertive in requesting a date: *"I was wondering if you'd like to come to a movie with me this Saturday?"* Be specific in your request, state the activity in mind, and the time it will take place.
- If "yes," decide together on the movie and the time. End the conversation smoothly, politely, and quickly.
- If "no," suggest an alternative, such as a more informal get together: *"How about meeting me at MacDonald's after school on Monday— my treat?"*
- If the answer is still "no," politely end the conversation. Refusal is not necessarily rejection. There may be previous commitments such as school, work, or family.

Treatment Plan: Speaking in Public.
Counseling Intention: To alleviate performance anxiety and stage fright.

The following strategies are useful for combating stage fright:

Rehearse. Practice listening to your voice. Use a tape recorder and a mirror to detect distracting verbal and visual mannerisms. Time your presentation. Focus on making the phraseology comfortable and conversational. Also consider enunciation (nervousness can make you slur or clip the ending of words), organization (speakers cannot rely on punctuation marks and headings), and speed (inexperienced speakers tend to rush).

Declare your anxiety. If your start speaking and you hear your voice tightening and your mouth getting dry, your anxiety will also begin to rise. The worse you sound, the more upset you will feel. To break this destructive cycle, tell your audience at the beginning how you feel. If the audience knows you are anxious, you know you will not need to hide your discomfort.

Prepare an out. Anxiety can be so acute that you feel trapped. Once your name is called, you are "it" until you finish. Rehearse a graceful exit, such as, *"I'm sorry, but I don't feel comfortable enough to present today; I'll do it another time"* (Wassmer, 1978, p. 109).

Treatment Plan: Expressing Anger.

Counseling Intention: To study styles of expressing anger in a group setting; to study effects of anger in a group setting; to identify behaviors that elicit anger in others; to explore ways of coping with anger.

For this exercise you will need felt-tipped markers, four 3" × 8" strips of paper for each participant, and masking tape.

Distribute four strips of paper, a felt-tipped marker, and strip of masking tape to each participant. Tell participants they will be given four sentences to complete, one at a time, and that they are to write down the few responses that occur to them, without censoring or modifying the response. They are to print their responses clearly on the newsprint so that others will be able to read them.

Read the following four sentences, one at a time, allowing each participant to complete his or her response. After each sentence is read and the responses have been made, ask each participant to tape the strip of paper to his or her chest.

1. I feel angry when others . . .
2. I feel my anger is . . .
3. When others express anger toward me, I feel . . .
4. I feel that the anger of others is . . .

As a variation, participants can tape their strips to a wall behind them or to the backs of their chairs.

The processing phase can be followed by a practice session on expressing anger. Dyads may be formed to role-play various situations from the groups history. Members should be urged to explore how they may cope with anger more effectively within the group session.

The same design can be used with other emotions, such as fright, tenderness, or boredom. Several rounds can be experienced.

Subgroups can be formed of participants who have similar (or highly dissimilar) responses to the four items. Participants can share critical incidents in which they have been involved in which anger was present. Alternative coping behaviors are then discussed.

Collective Community Initiatives

Young people who are isolated, who have been victimized, or who have been abused need to learn how to be assertive and how to manage anxiety and post-traumatic stress. Empowerment also is critical. Rencken (1989) outlined the sequence of empowerment as follows:

- Reinforcement of the report
- Rebonding with the nonabusing adult
- Assertiveness and self-protection
- Redefining the relationship with the abuser
- Resumption of age-appropriate roles
- Positive control and attitudes regarding violence (physical abuse) or sexuality (sexual abuse)
- The right to safety, to saying "no" to inappropriate touches, and assertiveness in reporting abuse (p. 166).

Empowerment includes the concept of positive, assertive control and mutual support during confrontation of inappropriate behavior. Being victimized, homeless, or isolated from the mainstream affects physical, psychological, social, emotional, and cognitive well-being. Collaborative efforts between various institutions and community agencies are paramount in providing essential services, resources, prevention, and intervention.

CONCLUSION

Helping professionals are active in professional growth and educational renewal in most school/community agencies and institutional/counseling settings. All helping professionals working with children and adolescents can create a heightened awareness among colleagues regarding the epidemic of child abuse and neglect in this country, and assist through referral or treatment opportunities. Helping professionals concerned with violence can help by clarifying attitudes toward rape, developing an awareness of the epidemic proportions, and creating an understanding that the legal definition of rape includes date rape.

It is imperative that counselors and mental health professionals respond to the developmental challenges that follow victimization and abuse by providing more than traditional clinical services. When issues are not addressed, children and adolescents are at significant risk for developing anxiety, depression, phobias, and post-traumatic stress disorder.

SOCIAL, EMOTIONAL, AND COGNITIVE SKILLS

Social Literacy Skills

Social literacy skills are *interpersonal skills* essential for meaningful interaction with others. Social skills are those behaviors that, within a given situation, predict important social outcomes such as peer acceptance, popularity, self-efficacy, competence, and high self-esteem. Social skills fall into categories such as being kind, cooperative, and compliant to reduce defiance, aggression, conflict, and antisocial behavior; and showing interest in people and socializing successfully to reduce behavior problems associated with withdrawal, depression, and fearfulness. Social skills include problem solving, assertiveness, thinking critically, resolving conflict, managing anger, and utilizing peer pressure refusal skills.

(*Note*: **Permission is granted to reproduce skills boxes for individual client use.**)

Problem Solving

A convenient acronym for the five steps of problem solving is SOLVE.

State your problem

Outline your response

List your alternatives

View the consequences

Evaluate your results

Source: M. McKay, M. Davis, & P. Fanning (1981). *Thoughts and feelings.* Reprinted with permission by New Harbinger Publications, Inc., Oakland, California.

Assertive Responses

Step 1. *"When . . . "* (describe the other individual's behavior)

Step 2. *"The effects are . . . "* (describe how the other person's actions have affected you)

Step 3. *"I feel . . . "* (describe your feelings)

Step 4. *"I prefer . . . "* (describe what you would like to happen)

Being Socially Responsible

Being socially responsible means analyzing and responding to the needs of others. Analyze the needs of others by considering the following:

Openness and acceptance of diversity: Our differences enhance our relationships.

Togetherness: We can do things together that can't be done alone.

Helping: Be ready to lend a hand.

Empathy: refine your sensitivity to others' needs.

Respect: Show respect for others' ideas.

Sowing good deeds: What you sow, you reap.

Source: Adapted from G. Bedley (1985). *The Big R: Responsibility* (p. 107). People-Wise Publications, 14252 East Mall, Irvine, CA 92714.

DESCA Inspirations

DESCA Inspirations are comments designed to stir appreciation of the inherent dignity of all students, appropriate personal energy, intelligent self-management, healthful community of relationships, and searching, open awareness. Their purpose is to inspire new growth in dignity, energy, self-management, community, and awareness (DESCA). Here are some "I appreciate" messages that promote DESCA:

Dignity

I really appreciate the way that you spoke up for yourself.
I recognize the confidence you are showing.
I like how you said it like you mean it.

Energy

I like the way that you are persisting at this task.
I appreciate your brain power.
I like how you go one more step rather than giving up.

Self-Management

I like how you organize your papers.
I'm impressed with your time management plan.
I like it when you can think it through on your own.

Community

I appreciate that you respect the rights of others.
I like it when you pitch in and help without being asked.
Your ability to listen to the opinions of others is highly valued.

Awareness

Thank you for being so perceptive and aware.
Thank you for noticing that someone needed help.
Thank you for ignoring the distraction outside.

Source: Adapted from M. Harmin (1994), *Inspiring Active Learning: A Handbook for Teachers,* published by the Association for Supervision and Curriculum Development (ASCD). Printed here by permission from the author.

Steps in Negotiating a Conflict of Interest

Even when people are striving for the same goals, sometimes there are conflicts of interest. Cooperators resolve conflicts as partners, not as adversaries. Below are six steps in negotiating a conflict of interests:

1. Describe what each person wants.

2. Describe how each person feels.

3. Exchange reasons for positions.

4. Understand each other's perspective.

5. Invent options for mutual benefit.

6. Reach a wise agreement.

Source: Adapted from D. W. Johnson & R. T. Johnson (1995), *Reducing School Violence Through Conflict Resolution* (p. 52). Alexandria, VA: Association for Supervision and Curriculum Development. Copyright © 1995 ASCD. Printed here by permission of publisher and authors.

Conventional Arbitration

Mediation is an extension of negotiation in which the mediator assists disputants in negotiating a constructive resolution. By contrast, in arbitration, an outside person makes a judgment. The arbitrator does not assist the disputants in improving their conflict. Disputants leave the decision to the arbitrator, who hears both sides and then makes a decision. The process goes as follows:

1. **Both persons agree to abide by the arbitrator's decision.** Agreement is based on the assumption that after disputants have presented their sides of the conflict, the arbitrator will be able to make a fair decision. The arbitrator should be familiar with the subject matter of the case and have access to all available documents and evidence.
2. **Each person defines the problem.** Both have the opportunity to tell their side of the conflict.
3. **Each person presents his or her case, with documented evidence to support it.** No interruptions are allowed.
4. **Each person has an opportunity to refute the other's contentions.** After one person has presented his or her case, the other may attempt to refute the person's contentions. Both have a turn to show the arbitrator a different perspective on the issues.
5. **The arbitrator makes a decision.** After each person has presented his or her case, refuted the other person's case, and given a closing statement, the arbitrator decides what to do. Usually, the decision is a win-lose situation. Winning or losing is secondary to having had the fair opportunity to be heard.

Source: Adapted from E. W. Johnson & R. T. Johnson (1995), *Reducing school violence through conflict resolution* (pp. 96-97). Alexandria, VA: Association for Supervision and Curriculum Development. Copyright © 1995 ASCD. Printed here by permission of publisher and authors.

Emotional Literacy Skills

Emotional literacy skills are *intrapersonal* abilities such as knowing one's emotions by recognizing a feeling as it happens and monitoring it; managing emotions (i.e., shaking off anxiety, gloom, irritability, and the consequences of failure); motivating oneself to attain goals, delay gratification, stifle impulsiveness, and maintain self-control; recognizing emotions in others with empathy and perspective taking; and handling interpersonal relationships effectively. Emotional skills fall into categories such as knowing the relationship between thoughts, feelings, and actions; establishing a sense of identity and acceptance of self; learning to value teamwork, collaboration, and cooperation; regulating one's mood; empathizing; and maintaining hope.

(*Note*: **Permission is granted to reproduce skills boxes for individual client use.**)

"I" Language Assertion

Language assertion is helpful when expressing difficult feelings. "I" language assertion can be broken down into four components:

First, objectively describe the behavior that is creating negative feelings.

Second, describe how the behavior affects you, such as costing you money, time, or effort.

Third, describe your own feelings.

Fourth, describe what you want the other person to do.

For example: *When you cancel a meeting with just a few hours' notice* (describe the behavior), *I don't have enough time to make other arrangements and I'm left with empty down time* (describe how it affects you). *I feel irritated and unproductive* (describe how you feel). *We need to make other arrangements about changing meetings at the last minute* (describe what you want the other person to do)."

Assertive Empathy

Assertive empathy can be used to express sensitivity toward a person's circumstances.

First, make a statement that expresses sensitivity to the person's circumstances, situation, or needs. Then, describe your circumstances, situation, or needs.

For example: *"I can understand you are upset with me and probably not in the mood to discuss it right now. I would very much like to talk it over when you're ready."*

Source: From *The Assertive Option: Your Rights and Responsibilities* (p. 162) by J. Jakubowski & A. J. Lange (1978). Champaign, IL: Research Press. Copyright 1978 by the authors. Adapted by permission.

Confrontive Assertion

A confrontive assertion can be used when someone has neglected to follow through on a previous agreement. It is most appropriate when someone's actions contradict their words. A confrontive assertion has three parts:

First, describe what the other person said would be done.

Second, describe what the person actually did (i.e., the discrepancy between what they said and what they did).

Third, reiterate your need and express what you want.

For example: *"I was supposed to review the article before it was sent to the typesetter, but I see the typesetter is working on it as we speak. Before he finishes it, I want to review the article and make the corrections I think are needed. In the future, I want to the opportunity to review the article before it goes to the typesetter."*

Source: From *The Assertive Option: Your Rights and Responsibilities* (p. 162) by J. Jakubowski & A. J. Lange (1978). Champaign, IL: Research Press. Copyright 1978 by the authors. Adapted by permission.

Checking Your Perception

Perception checking can help avoid actions you may later regret, actions based on false assumptions. Our impressions are often biased by our own fears, expectations, and feelings.

Before you respond to someone's feelings, it is important to make sure you know what the person actually feels. A perception check communicates the message, *"I want to understand your feeling. Is this the way you feel?"* It shows you care enough about the person to want to understand how he or she feels. Here are the steps to follow in a perception check:

Describe what you think the other person's feelings are.

Ask whether your perception is accurate.

Refrain from expressing approval or disapproval of the feelings.

For example, *"You seem confused about the roles and responsibilities. Are you?"*

Source: Adapted from D. W. Johnson & R. T. Johnson (1995), *Reducing School Violence Through Conflict Resolution* (p. 63). Alexandria, VA: Association for Supervision and Curriculum Development. Copyright © 1995 ASCD. Printed here by permission of publisher and authors.

Avoiding Conflict by Paraphrasing

Paraphrasing in conflict mediation helps you clarify a person's views of the problem and their feelings about it. It is important to listen attentively and summarize accurately using the following techniques:

Restate the facts and summarize the events. Follow these paraphrasing rules:

- Put yourself in the other person's shoes.

- State the other person's ideas and feelings in your own words.

- Use "you" to begin your statements (e.g., *"You want," "You feel,"* and *"You think"*),

- Show understanding and acceptance by nonverbal behaviors, such as tone of voice, facial expressions, gestures, eye contact, and posture.

Reflect feelings. Pay attention to the emotional element in each person's position. Use the statement, *"You feel . . .* (name the feeling) *because . . .* (explain why)."

- Offer alternatives.

- Reach a compromise.

- Agree on a solution.

Source: Adapted from D. W. Johnson & R. T. Johnson (1995), *Reducing School Violence Through Conflict Resolution* (p. 81). Alexandria, VA: Association for Supervision and Curriculum Development. Copyright © 1995 ASCD. Printed here by permission of publisher and authors.

Reframing a Conflict

Reframing means thinking of the conflict and the other person's actions from another angle. There are a number of ways to reframe perceptions:

- View the conflict as a mutual problem to be jointly solved rather than as a win-lose situation.

- Change perspectives.

- Distinguish between the intent of an action and the actual result of the action.

- Continue to differentiate between one's interest and one's reasoning. Seeking information about the other person's reasoning will result in a new "frame."

- Explore the multiple meanings of any one behavior. Ask: *"What else might that behavior mean?"*

Source: Adapted from D. W. Johnson & R. T. Johnson (1995), *Reducing School Violence Through Conflict Resolution* (p. 84). Alexandria, VA: Association for Supervision and Curriculum Development. Copyright © 1995 ASCD. Printed here by permission of publisher and authors.

PART III
CREATING POSITIVE
RELATIONSHIPS THROUGH
EMPOWERMENT OF OTHERS

Chapter 10

EMPOWERING YOUTH, FAMILIES, SCHOOLS, AND COMMUNITIES

"It takes a village to raise a child." (African proverb)

You Make a Difference. A man was strolling along a beach one day when he noticed a young man ahead of him.

The man was stooping and picking up starfish that had been cast beyond the tide's reach.

He threw them back, far out into the sea.

The first man watched the younger one for awhile and then approached him with a question.

"Why," he asked, "do you pick up those starfish and toss them back into the water?"

The second man replied, "because they will die if they are left stranded on the sand."

"But there are thousands of miles of beaches and millions of starfish. You can't possibly attend to them all. What difference can it make?" asked the first man.

The young man looked for a moment at the starfish he'd just picked up, and as he tossed it into the sea he replied, "It makes a difference to this one."

—Anonymous

SCHOOLS, NEIGHBORHOODS, AND COMMUNITIES

Collectively, schools, neighborhoods, and communities develop distinctive norms that draw youth and families toward or away from particular activities and domains of development (social, emotional, and cognitive). These norms often have profound and long-term effects on self-esteem, values, wellness, and coping skills. Personalities interact within the social system productively or unproductively, with subtle influences on achievement, motivation, employment readiness, and interpersonal relationships.

And there is no "escape to the suburbs." Many "exclusive" schools, neighborhoods, and communities manifest a superficial sophistication, in which the primary goals are finding "the right friends, the right drugs, the right clothes, and the right kind of car." The goals reflect a "depressive core in the school/community."

Without goals or traditions to unite energies, hostility is directed inward and divisions intensify across racial, class, and ethnic lines. Major cliques or gangs within these divisions also create highly stratified cultures that exaggerate differences. The "brains," the "jocks," the "hicks," the "metal heads," the "skaters and surfers," "the skinheads," the "grunge rockers," "the crips," and "the bloods" are examples of subgroups that emerge in oppressive environments.

The emphasis on community in most cities is not particularly strong, as reflected by the presence of youth subcultures and the lack of tolerance for different values, preferences and cultures manifested in hate crimes, and gang membership. Indeed, many young people come to school alienated and depersonalized and find little to help them cope with this alienation. Many schools, neighborhoods, and communities are repressive and punitive places where youth feel little power to change things. Lawton (1995) asserted that "families, schools, youth-serving organizations, healthcare agencies, and the media have fallen behind in their vital functions" and must now join together to create a mutually reinforcing system of support for children.

Perhaps the most fundamental and critical intervention for youth and families is to develop trust. Margolis and Brannigam (1986) captured this notion when they wrote this:

To build trust you need to (a) cultivate a cooperative rather than a competitive or dominating mind set; (b) make your involvement with parents understanding and concerned; (c) be open about your objectives; (d) subtly demonstrate expertise without being oppressive or signaling superiority. Building trust cannot be rushed. It is an interactive process, involving the sharing of information, ideas, and feelings. The operative word in trust building is reciprocity. It is important to share rather than conceal your feelings. Thoughts, however, should be expressed in ways parents can understand and appreciate. Estimate the parents' level of sophistication regarding each topic on the agenda so that you do not patronize or overwhelm them with information they cannot comprehend. (p. 71)

EDUCATORS AND HELPING PROFESSIONALS AS PARTNERS

Educators and helping professionals frequently reflect on how to motivate youth more effectively. And they come, again and again, to the same conclusion: *Encouragement* increases motivation among recipients and lessens feelings of inadequacy. It communicates trust, respect, competence, and ability. Dinkmeyer and Dreikurs (1963) maintained that the proper use of encouragement involves several facets:

- **Value individuals as they are**, not as their reputations indicate or as one hopes they will be. Believing individuals are good and worthwhile facilitates acting positively toward them.
- **Have faith in the abilities of others.** This enables the helper to win confidence while building the self-respect of the other person.
- **Use a group to help the person develop.** For social beings, the need to belong is basic; integrate the group so that the individual can discover his or her place and begin working positively from that point.
- **Plan for success** and assist in the development of skills that are sequentially and psychologically paced.
- **Identify and focus on strengths and assets rather than on mistakes.**
- **Give recognition for effort and for a job well done.**

Educators and helping professionals possess a unique characteristic called *sigfluence*: a positive, significant, long-term interpersonal influence over others. It requires an average of two years for youth to appreciate and understand the extent of a positive influence over their lives. The optimal influence occurs between 14 to 19 years of age. Adults with sigfluence can affect a young person's academic, social, and emotional achievement, influencing career choice and generating positive changes in self-image. Adults can nurture positive a self-concept by making all youth feel safe, accepted, wanted, appreciated, and successful. Achievement must be planned, structured, designed, implemented, and reinforced.

Vernon (1989) suggested that educators and helping professionals implement an emotional education curriculum containing a self-acceptance component. Developmentally sequenced topics could be introduced and reinforced at the appropriate grade levels. Specific topics for children could include these:

- Recognizing uniqueness
- Learning that people have many different qualities and characteristics
- Learning that people have both strengths and weaknesses
- Learning that making mistakes is natural, and doesn't make people bad or stupid
- Distinguishing between what people say about you and who you are

Topics for adolescents could include these:

- Recognizing the relationship between self-acceptance, behavior, and feelings
- Identifying the physical, intellectual, spiritual, emotional, and social aspects of self
- Learning the importance of self-acceptance despite the risk of others' disapproval
- Recognizing one's degree of personal control over events
- Differentiating criticism of *what one does* from criticism of *who one is*
- Learning to accept compliments
- Developing goal-setting techniques to overcome failure
- Using positive affirmations to increase a sense of self-worth

The task of raising competent children is becoming increasingly difficult. Dramatic changes in family structures and lifestyles and growing societal pressures for children to possess specific knowledge and skills at an early age are just two of the challenges facing contemporary parents.

SOLUTION-FOCUSED ENCOURAGEMENT

The single most important factor in motivating youth is encouragement. The feeling of inferiority that young people experience in one form or another must be overcome if they are to function well. Even small gains demonstrate growth and should be applauded. If any progress is noted, there is less chance of discouragement.

It is discouragement that educators fear. Discouraged youth tend to discourage adults. Genuine competency comes from self-sufficiency. Youth need to feel competent and autonomous. Failure and defeat will not encourage a deeply discouraged child who has lost all hope of succeeding.

Competition usually does not encourage youth. Those who see hope of winning may put forth extra effort, but the stress is on winning rather than on cooperation, contribution, or competency. Preoccupation with the obligation to succeed—to win—is intimidating, and the resulting fear and anxiety often contribute to failure. Focusing on one's contributions and cooperation promotes success.

NECESSARY COLLABORATION

Complex problems require comprehensive services. To ensure enduring interventions, a number of processes must evolve. Initially, demographics must be collected and shared with key officials and stakeholders. Agencies and institutions should be assessed regarding categorical drift (i.e., agencies, institutions, organizations working on issues in isolation rather than together with a common vision and shared goals). We must encourage information sharing, joint partnerships, and collective community initiatives; develop action plans, timelines, and outcome accountability; and be willing to commit time, energy, and long-term participation.

Barth (1996), Davies (1989), Krasnow (1990), and Ziegler (1987) listed several approaches for overcoming institutional and community obstacles, including these:

- Approach at-risk programs with the premise that no single race, religion, culture, or ethnic group holds a monopoly on at-risk youth.
- Recognize that all families have strengths. Successful programs reinforce these strengths. Focusing on deficits or failures is counterproductive.
- Start with the assumption that most parents care deeply about their children, yet may not know how to help.
- Teach parents to overcome obstacles and to learn new techniques, such

as helping with homework, teaching children to be more responsible, and developing boundaries and family rules.

- Ask parents what they are interested in doing, focusing on their agenda first.

EDUCATIONAL ALTERNATIVES

The challenges of educating today's children are unprecedented: Educators face classrooms of young people who are tired, hungry, and abused; who have no permanent homes; and who seldom have the kind of interaction with supportive adults necessary for mental, emotional, and moral development in their growing years. More and more children—from all classes, all racial and ethnic backgrounds, and all income levels—are at risk not only of failing in school but also for their personal safety and well-being. We must do all we can to increase our children's chances of success.

Currently, academic and social missions are mixed indiscriminately in our public schools. Driver's education, English as a Second Language, health services, special education programs, DARE (Drug Abuse Resistance Education), and Family Life Education are only a few of the social missions our schools are currently fulfilling. Schools in this country are being asked to take on more responsibilities with smaller staff and fewer resources. In addition, schools are asked to pick up where others have failed and to accept the blame for falling short of our collective unrealistic expectations. No institution or public entity could accommodate the burden of expectations under which the American school now labors.

As an alternative, Banner (1992) proposed a new social institution: *the parallel school*. The parallel school works in tandem with the academic school, but serves entirely separate ends. The mission of the parallel school would be to provide for the diverse and critical *nonacademic needs* of young people today (p. 486). The parallel school would be service-directed and offer largely elective programs. It would be home to extracurricular activities, athletic teams, band, chorus, recreation, and service learning projects. It also would provide tutorials and instruction in English as a second language. Early intervention and life skills instruction would be a viable part of the parallel school. Childcare, health services, extended library hours, and quiet rooms for study would be available.

More recently, Dryfoos (1996) proposed the evolution of *the full-service school*, one that provides both education and comprehensive social services under the same roof.

To better serve youth and their families, some schools have formed *partnerships with outside agencies*, including mental health, social services, health, probation, police, housing, drug, and alcohol agencies, as well as nonprofit health and service agencies. Others have integrated *family resource centers* on campus, which provide a wide range of activities along with interagency case management teams to connect families with needed services. The list below outlines some of the parameters of the full-service school.

Quality Education Provided by Schools

- Effective basic skills
- Individualized instruction
- Team teaching
- Cooperative learning
- School-based management
- Healthy school climate
- Alternatives to tracking
- Parent involvement
- Effective discipline
- Integrated curriculum
- Outcome accountability
- Technology
- Comprehensive health education
- Health promotion
- Social, emotional, and cognitive skills training
- Preparation for the world of work
- Psychoeducational groups

Quality Support Services Provided by Community Agencies

- Primary health services
- Health screening
- Immunizations
- Dental services
- Family planning
- Individual counseling
- Group counseling
- Substance abuse treatment
- Mental health services
- Nutrition/weight management
- Referral with follow-up
- Basic services: housing, food, clothes

- Recreation, sports, culture
- Mentoring
- Family welfare services
- Parent education/literacy
- Childcare
- Employment training/jobs
- Case management
- Crisis intervention
- Community policing
- Legal aid

Source: J. G. Dryfoos. "Full-service schools." *Educational Leadership, 53*(7), 18-23. Copyright © 1996 by ASCD. Reprinted by permission. All rights reserved.

Dryfoos (1996) maintained that combining prevention and intervention with school restructuring will create stronger institutions—schools as neighborhood hubs, where children's well-being is paramount and where families will want to go. Further, in full-service schools with health clinics, clients have demonstrated lower substance use, better school attendance, and lower dropout rates. Graduation rates are significantly higher, property destruction and graffiti have diminished, and neighborhood violence has decreased (Dryfoos, 1996, p. 20). Full-service schools have the potential to integrate critical services and to enhance the well-being of schools and communities, children and families.

COLLECTIVE INITIATIVES FOR AT-RISK YOUTH

An Action-Planning Paradigm

Action planning is an important part of the program implementation experience. Write a plan of action for projects in your community. At first, this task may seem tedious, but your planning time and action plan will make your projects much easier to pull together. In addition, as your team becomes familiar with the planning process, you can more easily plan other projects as opportunities develop or if barriers make it difficult to carry out your current plans.

There are four steps to the action planning process:

1. Needs assessment
2. Program design
3. Implementation
4. Evaluation

The process is ongoing. Your evaluation becomes information you can use in your next phase of needs assessment. The plan you write is important, but the continuing process of planning and developing activities is even more important.

Needs Assessment. Needs assessment is the first phase of the action-planning process. It involves three steps:

1. Gather information about your community, the extent of at-risk behavior, resources available, and potential barriers (people or things that could get in the way of completing projects).
2. Put this information in the form of a problem statement that simply states what the problem is, not how to solve it. An example of a problem statement would be this: *"Youth in Community, USA, do not have enough recreational activities."*
3. Prioritize or order the problems so that you will know which ones are realistically solvable and important to work on.

Program Design. Program design is the actual process of writing goals, objec-tives, and tasks.

Goals are the opposite of problem statements. *Goals are solution statements* that are not specific or detailed but that state the general direction of what you want to accomplish.

A goal might be: *"To increase the number of recreational activities for youth who live in Community, USA."*

Another goal might be: *"To increase community support for recreational activities."*

One to three goals should be enough for your team to work on during a school year.

Objectives are measurable activity statements. They are very specific. Each objective has four parts, so you can tell when you are finished with the objective and whether you actually did what you said you were going to do in that objective. The four parts are listed here:

*   What? (the activity)
*   Who? (target group)
*   How many? (number of people)
*   When? (completion date)

An example of an objective would be this: *"To organize a recreational club for all interested students who attend School, USA, by May 30, 19XX."*

This example answers the four questions:

- What? *A recreational club*
- Who? *Targeted youth who live in Community, USA*
- How many? *All interested youth*
- When? *May 30, 19XX*

Always start an objective with the word *to*. Try not to use the word *and*. If you use *and*, you have written two objectives. Be realistic in the number of people with whom you will work. Start small and work your way up to bigger things. You can always write more objectives. Remember, *planning is cyclical or ongoing*.

Tasks are the specific activities necessary to complete the objective. Tasks should be written in the order in which they will be accomplished. Tasks include all the logistical details you can think of. Quite often one missed detail can make it difficult to complete the objective. Some of these details might include obtaining permission, finding a meeting room, creating flyers to announce an event, and sending out mailings. Each objective may have as many as 15 different tasks.

Implementation. Implementation involves doing your project, monitoring your progress, and modifying your project as necessary. If you assess your needs, plan well, and write good, easy-to-achieve objectives, this step will be relatively easy.

Evaluation. Evaluation involves collecting information about whether or not you achieved your objectives or did what you said you were going to do. It also involves reporting this information to other individuals or organizations that were involved in planning or funding your program, and using the information to plan other programs. Your evaluation becomes information you can use in your next cycle of needs assessment. Learn from your failures and successes and work up to dealing with more difficult problems.

Remember,

- **Needs Assessment**

    Collect information
    Write problem statements

- **Program Design**

  Goals
  Objectives
  Tasks

- **Implementation**

  Do it
  Monitor it
  Change it

- **Evaluation**

  Measure it
  Report it
  Use it for more needs assessment

And the cycle continues.

Your team already may have completed the needs assessment phase of the action planning process. When you return to your community, it is up to your team to put your plans to work. (See Figures 10.1, 10.2, and 10.3 for further guidance.) Good luck!

CONCLUSION

Many of the successes and failures people experience in life are closely related to the ways they have learned to view themselves in relationship with others.

In the past, parents routinely sought the advice and counsel of relatives, friends, and extended family. Traditional sources of help and support are less available and less nurturing than at any time in history. Over the years, policy makers and educators have joined forces to battle a series of social and behavioral problems, waging war on drugs, abuse, unwanted pregnancy, AIDS, suicide, violence, and dropouts. Shriver and Weissberg, (1996) maintained that schools and communities should proactively build comprehensive programs that help children develop socially, emotionally, and cognitively as well.

Team Action Plan
TEAM NAME
Community, USA

GOAL # 1 # OF OBJECTIVES 2
Community, USA youth do not have enough recreational activities.

OBJECTIVES
Organize a recreational club.

TASKS	TIME LINE 19___ 19___									PERSON(S) RESPONSIBLE	RESOURCES BLOCKS/BARRIERS
	S	O	N	D	J	F	M	A	M	J		
Ask permission.				O								
Put up announcements.						O						
Hold a meeting.									O			
BAD EXAMPLE!												

Figure 10.1. Example of a poor team action plan.

Team Action Plan
TEAM NAME
Community, USA

GOAL # __1__ # OF OBJECTIVES __1__

To increase the number of recreational activities for youth who live in Community, USA.

OBJECTIVES To organize a recreational club for all interested students by May 30, 19--.

TASKS	TIME LINE 19__ 19__											PERSON(S) RESPONSIBLE	RESOURCES BLOCKS/BARRIERS
	S	O	N	D	J	F	M	A	M	J		
1. Obtain permission to organize a club from the *Community Services Board.*	O											Steve	The Community Services Board is very supportive.
2. Make plans to have a recreational club interest meeting.	O											All (School Team)	
3. Create flyers to announce the interest meeting.	O											All	Our sponsor will provide materials to make the flyers.
4. Put up flyers around the community.		O										All	
5. Make announcements about the meeting.		O										Joan	The secretary may forget to make the announcement.
6. Hold the meeting.		O										All	Youth may not attend because of other activities.
7. Sign-up members.		O										Bill	
8. Set date for next meeting		O										All	

GOOD EXAMPLE!

Figure 10.2. Example of a positive team action plan.

293

Team Action Plan
TEAM NAME _____

GOAL # _____ # OF OBJECTIVES _____

OBJECTIVES _____

TASKS	TIME LINE 19___ 19___										PERSON(S) RESPONSIBLE	RESOURCES BLOCKS/BARRIERS
	S	O	N	D	J	F	M	A	M	J		

Figure 10.3. Template for a team action plan.

> Comprehensive social and emotional development programs are based
> on the understanding that many different kinds of problem behav-
> iors are caused by the same risk factors, and that the best learning
> emerges from supportive and challenging relationships. Preventing
> problems such as violence, drug abuse, or dropping out is most ef-
> fective when multiyear integrated efforts develop children's social
> and emotional abilities through engaging classroom instruction; pro-
> social learning activities outside the classroom; and broad parent and
> community participation in program planning, implementation, and
> evaluation. Destructive behaviors develop in part from a complex
> web of familial, economic, and cultural circumstances. (p. 11)

Youth-serving professionals need to provide children and families with information and support. Partnerships have become increasingly critical. The content of parent programs has broadened to include significant attention to the
social context of parenthood. This shift in emphasis reflects an interest in the
interconnectedness of child, family, school, and community. Shriver and Weissberg (1996) suggested implementing a kindergarten-through-12th-grade program
for all students focusing on the promotion of social and emotional development. The impetus in such a program revolves around six basic principles:

- Social development services should simultaneously and seamlessly address students' mental, emotional, and social well-being rather than
  focusing on one categorical outcome. Ultimately, comprehensive and
  integrated programs targeting multiple social and health problem behaviors have greater potential than short-term interventions targeting
  the prevention of a single problem behavior.
- Social development services should be based on developmentally appropriate, sequential, preschool-to-high-school classroom instruction.
  Programming should start before youth are pressured to experiment with
  risky behaviors and should continue through adolescence.
- Social development services must address youths' cognitive, social, and
  emotional skills; their attitudes and values about themselves and others;
  their perceptions of social norms; and their understanding of information about targeted social and health domains. Currently, there are too
  many ineffective prevention programs that stress knowledge about specific problems and fail to concentrate on the skills and values necessary
  to help children engage in health-protective behaviors.
- Social development services should revolve around effective instruction and teaching methods that ensure active engagement, emphasize
  positive behavior, and change the ways in which children and adults
  communicate about problem situations. Innovative teaching techniques

such as cooperative learning, modeling, role-playing, performance feed-back, and positive reinforcement are critical.

- Social development services should support multilevel interventions. Children grow and develop at home and in the school and community. Combining environmental support and reinforcement from peers, family members, school personnel, helping professionals, religious leaders, and the media increases the likelihood that youth will adopt healthier lifestyles.
- System-level policies and practices to support program implementation and institutionalization must be developed. It is critical, for example, for teachers to be trained before the program is implemented and to be supported and coached for extended periods of practice.

Support and information provide buffers against stressful life experiences and precarious transitions. Our youth are in crisis; our families, schools, and communities are overwhelmed. In determining sound intervention strategies for schools and communities, policy makers, helping professionals, and parents must proceed beyond the rhetoric surrounding the maladies of American youth and begin implementing strategies that provide outcomes that can be implemented, integrated, measured, and evaluated.

EPILOGUE

Generation Next: They Are Your Kids. And Mine.

They balance precariously on skateboards, cruise the strip in mud-sprayed four-wheel drive vehicles, surf hurricane swells without the slightest trepidation, and spend hours molding locks into the latest color-moussed or cut-and-buzz craze. They spill from buses, bikes, and customized VW bugs protesting their short break from academic rigor with an occasional notebook to disclose their destination.

Who are they? They are your kids. And mine. They look like us. They share our names. They carry "our hopes" and "their dreams" on shoulders more than a boy's, less than a man's, more than a girl's, less than a woman's. They are candidates put on a waiting list for adulthood; and for some they are drafted all too quickly.

They conform to profiles of surfer, preppy, and hip-hopper hailing their styles as "baaad," wicked," "nasty," or "awesome." They can bully, and brag, and be cruel—chastising weaker peers with labels such as "geek," "dweeb," or "dork." They can cry over a rumor, laugh uncontrollably over nothing, smile to cover their hurt, and amaze us at how quickly they can move from one emotion to another.

They can find a contact lens within a radius of a thousand feet and not be able to avoid that one wet spot in an empty hallway. They can remember to get to Thursday's sale at the mall but forget their homework all too often. They are slow to settle down after a classroom interruption but can sit absolutely silent in a crowded gym when one of their peers attempts a long shot on the basketball court. They can cook, sew, run a household, publish a newspaper, put together a yearbook, handle dangerous tools, understand computer programming, make the honor roll, hold a part-time job, come to school grief-stricken, and spend time in a detention home.

They experience many "firsts" as adolescents—their first time behind the wheel, their first love, their first grief, their first loss of a peer, their first failure, their first arrest, and their first child. It also will be the last time that they will be assembled collectively with their own unique generation sharing the same interests and values among a caring community of significant adults, whom many will choose to emulate. They will spend their four years shedding a variety of impostor-selves who change constantly, from academic term to term, searching for their real selves. Some of our kids are surviving against all odds with lives filled with turmoil, stress, and clashes with adult authority.

They get tired and hurt, and they need a word of encouragement, a concerned look, or a pat on the back more often than we think. They will walk for any charity, sell everything from raffle tickets to flower bulbs in order to support their extracurricular activities, work for weeks on a homecoming float, party until they drop, and then come to physical education class with a medical excuse. They can memorize and understand the lyrics from the latest rap song but protest because of lack of understanding a parallel assignment of Shakespeare or Frost.

They can maintain their energy level on a diet of a pizza and french fries lunch, topped off by a snack cak and three cartons of chocolate milk. They revel at snowball fights on the front lawn, skateboarding down the sidewalk, and rotating soccer balls from head to toe. They never, never smoke but always hold a lit cigarette for a friend, never cut anything but study hall, or the substitute's class, are sometimes truant from school, may lie, cheat, forge notes, or misrepresent their parent on the phone, and use language fit to curl the ears of the commander of the U.S.S. Saratoga.

They play for our athletic teams in rain and snow, wallow in mud and sweat, and break bones—all in front of a very few people. They compete academically without hesitation or intimidation. They sing and play music with a talent beyond their years. They fit everything in among doctors' appointments, part-time jobs, private lessons, after school practice, volunteer work, church activities, field trips, measles, mumps, mono, family discord, family celebrations, and homework.

They are not made of steel. They have serious illnesses, spend time in the hospital, and suffer from perhaps the most devastating experience for an adolescent—a broken heart. They experience family violence and dysfunction, family illness, and death. They find comfort in a friend, support from peers, and we hope love, direction, and understanding from us.

Who are they? They are your kids. And mine. They look like us. They share our names. And they will spend most of their lives away from our direct influence. But our indirect influence, in the form of directions charted and concern given, will remain with them to strengthen and guide them for the challenges ahead. The greatest sign of a successful counselor, teacher, or parent is not what the child did while in the classroom or in the home, but what he or she does with his or her life when we are a memory or a phone call away. May that memory never be too faint or our phone too busy.

Rosemary A. Thompson, 1997

REFERENCES

Aas, H., Klepp, K. I., Laberg, J. C., Aaro, L. E. (1995). Predicting adolescents' intention to drink alcohol: Outcome expectancies and self-efficacy. *Journal of Studies on Alcohol, 56,* 293-299.

Adams, G. R., Gullotta, T., & Clancy, M. A. (1985). Homeless adolescents: A descriptive study of similarities and differences between runaways and throwaways. *Adolescence, 20*(79), 715-724.

Adams, G. R., & Munro, G. (1979). Portrait of the North American runaway: A critical review. *Journal of Youth and Adolescence, 8*(3), 359-373.

Alan Guttmacher Institute. (1989). *U.S. and cross-national trends in teenage sexual and fertility behavior.* New York: Author.

Alan Guttmacher Institute. (1991). *U.S. and cross-national trends in teenage sexual and fertility behavior.* New York: Author.

Albee, G. W. (1982). Preventing psychopathology and promoting human potential. *American Psychologist, 37,* 1043-1050.

Albee, G. W. (1986). Advocates and adversaries of prevention. In M. Kessler & S. E. Goldston (Eds.), *A decade of progress in primary prevention* (pp. 309-332). Hanover, NH: University Press of New England.

Albee, G. W., Bond, L. A., & Monsey, T. V. C. (Eds.). (1992). *Improving children's lives: Global perspectives on prevention.* Newbury Park, CA: Sage.

Albee, G. W., Gordon, S., & Leitenberg, H. (1983). *Promoting sexual responsibility and preventing sexual problems.* Hanover, NH: University Press of New England.

Albee, G. W., & Joffe, J. M. (Eds.). (1977). *The primary prevention of psychopathology: The issues.* Hanover, NH.: University Press of New England.

Albee, G. W., & Ryan-Finn, K. D. (1993). An overview of primary prevention. *Journal of Counseling and Development, 7,* 2, 115-123.

Alberti, R., & Emmons, M. (1974). *Your perfect right.* San Luis Obispo, CA.: Impact Publishers.

Alderman, M. K. (1990). Motivation for at-risk students. *Educational Leadership, 48,* 1, 27-30.

Alderman, M. K., & Cohen, M. W. (1985). *Motivational theory and practice for preservice teachers.* Washington, DC: Eric Clearinghouse on Teacher Education, Monograph #4.

Allen, P. B. (1985). Suicide adolescents: Factors in evaluation. *Adolescence, 20,* 754-762.

Alter-Reid, K. (1992). Sexual abuse of children: A review of the empirical findings. *Clinical Psychology Review, 6,* 249-266.

American Psychiatric Association. (1987). *Diagnostic and statistical manual of mental disorders—DSM-III-R* (3rd ed., revised). Washington, DC: Author.

American Psychiatric Association. (1994). *Diagnostic and statistical manual of mental disorders—DSM-IV* (4th ed.). Washington, DC: Author.

American Psychological Association. (1993). *Violence and youth: Psychology's response* (Vol. 1). Washington, DC: Author.

Amerikaner, M., & Summerlin, M. (1982). Group counseling with learning disabled children: Effects of social skills and relaxation training on self-concept and classroom behavior. *Journal of Learning Disabilities, 15*(6), 340-343.

Ames, C., & Ames, R. (1989). *Research on motivation in education goals and cognition* (Vol. 3). San Diego: Academic Press.

Ames, C., & Archer, J. (1988). Achievement goals in the classroom: Students learning strategies and motivational processes. *Journal of Educational Psychology, 80,* 260-267.

Anderson, A. E. (1985). *Overview of bulimia: Practical comprehensive treatment of anorexia and bulimia.* Baltimore: Johns Hopkins University Press.

Anderson, R. F., Kinney, J., & Gerler, E. R. (1984). The effects of divorce groups on children's classroom behavior and attitudes toward divorce. *Elementary School Guidance and Counseling, 17,* 4.

Anderson, T. H. (1980). Study strategies and adjunct aids. In R. J. Spiro, B. C. Bruce, & W. F. Brewer (Eds.), *Theoretical issues in reading comprehension.* Hillsdale, NJ: Erlbaum.

Angold, A. (1988). Childhood and adolescent depression II: Research in clinical populations. *British Journal of Psychiatry, 153,* 476-492.

Aptekar, L. (1989). The psychology of Colombian street children. *International Journal of Health Services, 19*(2), 295-310.

Armstrong, S. W., & McPherson, A. (1991). Homework as a critical component in social skills instruction. *Teaching Exceptional Children, 34*(6), 46.

Armstrong, T. (1994). *Multiple intelligences in the classroom.* Alexandria, VA: Association for Supervision and Curriculum Development.

Armsworth, M. W., & Holaday, M. (1993). The effects of psychological trauma on children and adolescents. *Journal of Counseling & Development, 72*(1), 49-56.

Arredondo, D. E., & Marzano, R. J. (1986). One district's approach to implementing a comprehensive K-12 thinking skills program. *Educational Leadership, 43*(8), 28-32.

Asbury, F. R.(1984). The empathy treatment. *Elementary School Guidance and Counseling, 18,* 181-187,

Asche, J. A. (1993). *Finish for the future: America's communities respond.* Alexandria, VA: National Association of Partners in Education.

Association for Specialists in Group Work. (1990). *Professional standards for the training of group counselors.* Alexandria, VA: Author.

Bahr, S. J., Marcos, A. C., & Maughan, S. L. (1995). Family, educational, and peer influences on the alcohol us of female and male adolescents. *Journal of Studies on Alcohol, 56,* 457-469.

Baker, C. (1990). *Development of an outreach group for children ages five through thirteen who have witnessed domestic violence.* Fort Lauderdale, FL: Nova University.

Baker, N. (1983, August). Why women stay with men who beat them. *Glamour,* 312-313, 365-367.

Bandura, A. (1976). Effecting change through participant modeling. In J. D. Krumboltz & C. E. Thorensen (Eds.), *Counseling methods.* New York: Holt, Rinehart, Winston.

Banner, J. M. (1992). The parallel school. *Phi Delta Kappan, 73*(6), 486-488.

Barnes, N. D., & Harrod, S. E. (1993). Teen pregnancy prevention: A model using school and community collaboration. *The School Counselor, 41*(2), 137-140.

Barrow, J., & Hayashi, J. (1990). Shyness clinic: A social development program for adolescents. *Personnel & Guidance Journal, 59,* 58-61.

Bartell, N. P., & Reynolds, W. (1986). Depression and self-esteem in academically gifted and nongifted children: A comparison study. *Journal of School Psychology, 24,* 55-61.

Barth, R. (1996). A personal vision of a good school. *Phi Delta Kappan, 71*(7), 512-515.

Baucom, J. O. (1989). *Help your children say no to drugs.* Grand Rapids MI: Zondervan.

Bauer, A. M. (1987). A teacher's introduction to childhood depression. *Clearing House, 61,* 81-84.

Bear, T., Schenk, S., & Buckner, L. (1993). Supporting victims of child abuse. *Educational Leadership, 50*(4), 42-47.

Beardslee, M. D., & Podorefsky, M. A. (1988). Resilient adolescents whose parents have serious affective and other psychiatric disorders: Importance of self-understanding and relationships. *American Journal of Psychiatry, 145,* 63-69.

Bedley, G. (1985). *The big R: Responsibility.* Irvine, CA: People-Wise Publications.

Bellanca, J., & Fogarty, R. (1992). *Catch them thinking: A handbook of classroom strategies.* Palatine, IL: Skylight Publishing.

Benedek, R. S., & Benedek, M. Z. (1979). Children of divorce: Can we meet their needs? *Journal of Social Issues, 35,* 155-169.

Bennett, W. E. (1993). Is our culture in decline? *Education Week, 13*(33), 56.

Bergin, J. J. (1991). *Escape from pirate island.* Doyleston, PA: MarCo Products.

Bergin, J. J. (1993). Group counseling with children and adolescents. *Counseling and Human Development, 25*(9), 1-20.

Berkowitz, A., & Persins, H. W. (1988). Personality characteristics of children of alcoholics. *Journal of Consulting and Clinical Psychology, 56,* 2.

Berman, A. L. (1986). Helping suicidal adolescents: Needs and responses. In C. A. Corr & J. N. McNeil (Eds.), *Adolescence and death* (pp. 151-166). New York: Springer.

Bernstein, G. A., Garfinkel, B. D., & Hoberman, H. M. (1989). Self-reported anxiety in adolescents. *American Journal of Psychiatry, 146,* 384-386.

Besharov, D. (1990). *Recognizing child abuse.* New York: Free Press.

Biden, J. (1993). Violence against women: The congressional response. *American Psychologist, 48,* 1059-1061.

Black, C. (1984). COA: Teaching, talking, touching. *Alcoholism, 26,* 28.

Black, C., & DeBlassè, R. (1985). Adolescent pregnancy: Contributing factors, consequences, treatment, and plausible solutions. *Adolescence, 20,* 281-289.

Blum, D. J., & Jones, L. A. (1993). Academic growth group and mentoring program for potential dropouts. *The School Counselor, 40*(3), 25-29.

Blume, E. (1990). *Secret survivors.* New York: Free Press.

Blythe, B., Gilchrist, L., & Schinke, S. (1981). Pregnancy prevention groups for adolescents. *Social Work, 26*(6), 503-504.

Bolig, R., & Weddle, K. D. (1988). Resiliency and hospitalization of children. *Children's Health Care,* 16, 255-260.

Bolton, R. (1979). *People skills: How to assert yourself, listen to others, and resolve conflicts.* New York: Simon & Schuster.

Bond, L. A., & Compas, B. E. (Eds.). (1989). *Primary prevention and promotion in the schools.* Newbury Park, CA: Sage.

Bonkowski, S. E., Bequette, S. O., & Boonhower, S. (1984). A group design to help children adjust to parental divorce. *Social Casework: Journal of Contemporary Social Work, 65,* 131-137.

Bonnington, S. B. (1993). Solution-focused brief therapy: Helpful interventions for school counselors. *The School Counselor, 41,* 126-127.

Boscolo, L., Cecchin, G., Hoffman, L., & Penn, P. (1987). *Milan systemic family therapy: Conversations in theory and practice.* New York: Basic Books.

Botvin, G. J. (1983). *Life skills training: A self-improvement approach to substance abuse prevention.* New York: Smithfield Press.

Botvin, G. J. (1985). Prevention of adolescent substance abuse through the development of personal and social competence. In T. J. Glynn, C. G. Leukefeld & J. P. Ludford (Eds.), *Prevention of adolescent drug abuse* (pp. 23-62). Rockville, MD: Department of Health, Education, and Welfare; National Institute of Drug Abuse.

Botvin, G. J. (1986). Substance abuse prevention efforts: Recent developments and future direction. *Journal of School Health, 56,* 369-374.

Botvin, G. J., & Tortu, S. (1988). Preventing adolescent substance abuse through life skills training. In R. H. Price, E. L. Cowen, R. P. Lorion, & J. Ramos-McKay (Eds.), *14 ounces of prevention: A casebook for practitioners.* Washington, DC: American Psychological Association.

Bradford, A. (1992). *Parting: A counselor's guide for children of separated parents.* Columbia: South Carolina State Department of Education.

Bradshaw, J. (1988). *Bradshaw on the family: A revolutionary way of self-discovery.* Deerfield Beach, FL: Health Communications.

Brazelton, T. B. (1992). *Heart start: The emotional foundation of school readiness.* Arlington, VA: National Center for Clinical Infant Programs.

Brazzell, J. F., & Acock, A. C. (1988). Influence of attitudes, significant others, and aspirations on how adolescents intend to resolve a premarital pregnancy. *Journal of Marriage and Family, 50*(2), 413-415.

Brendtro, L. K., Brokenleg, M., & Van Bockern, S. (1990). *Reclaiming youth at risk: Our hope for the future.* Bloomington, IN: National Education Service.

Breunlin, D. C. (1980). Multimodal behavior treatment of a child's eliminative disturbance. *Psychotherapy: Theory, Research, and Practice, 17,* 17-23.

Brewster, K., Billy, J., & Grady, W. (1993). Social context and adolescent behavior: The impact of community on the transition to sexual activity. *Social forces, 71*(3), 713-740.

Bronfenbrenner, U. (1986). Alienation and the four worlds of childhood. *Phi Delta Kappan, 42,* 6-14.

Brook, J. S., Whiteman, M., & Gordon, A. S. (1983). Stages of drug use in adolescence: Personality, peer, and family correlates. *Developmental Psychology, 19*(271), 184-199.

Brookman, R. (1993). *Making a difference in your community: A planning guide for community prevention of youth suicide and other youth problems.* Richmond: Virginia Health Council.

Brooks-Gunn, J., & Furstenberg, F. F. (1986). The children of adolescent mothers: Physical, academic and psychological outcomes. *Developmental Review, 6,* 224.

Brown, C., & Brown, J. (1982). *Counseling children for social competence: A manual for teachers and counselors.* Springfield, IL: Charles C. Thomas.

Brunell, L. F. (1990). Multimodal treatment of depression: A strategy to break through the "strenuous lethargy" of depression. *Psychotherapy in Private Practice, 8*(3), 13-23.

Buel, S. (1993). Presentation to the first meeting of the Virginia Domestic Violence Coordinating Council. Richmond, Virginia.

Bundy, M. L., & Gumaer, J. (1984). Families in transition. *Elementary School Guidance and Counseling, 19,* 4-8.

Burgess, D. M., & Streissguth, A. P. (1992). Fetal alcohol syndrome and fetal alcohol effects: Principles for educators. *Phi Delta Kappan, 74*(1), 24-30.

Burke, D., & Van de Streek, L. (1989). Children of divorce: An application of Hammond's group counseling for children. *Elementary School Guidance and Counseling, 24*(2), 112-118.

Burns, D. E., & Reis, S. M. (1991). Developing a thinking skills component in the gifted program. *Roper Review, 14*(2), 72-79.

Burrett, K., & Rusnak, T. (1993). *Integrated character education.* Bloomington, IN: Phi Delta Kappa Education Foundation.

Bushweller, K. (1994). The faces of childhood. *The American School Board Journal, 181*(12), 8-31.

Campbell, C. A. (1991). Group guidance for academically undermotivated children. *Elementary School Guidance and Counseling, 25*(1), 23-28.

Campbell, C., & Myrick, R. (1990). Motivational group counseling for low-performing students. *Journal of Specialist in Group Work, 15*(10), 43-50.

Canfield, J., & Wells, H. C. (1976). *100 ways to enhance self-concept in the classroom.* Englewood Cliffs, NJ: Pergamon Press.

Cantor, W., & Winkinson, J. (1982). *Social skills manual.* Somerset, NJ: Wiley.

Cantrell, R. (1986). Adjustment to divorce. *Elementary School Guidance and Counseling, 20*(3), 163-173.

Cantwell, D. P., & Carlson, G. A. (1983). *Affective disorders in childhood and adolescence.* New York: Spectrum.

Capuzzi, D. (1988). *Counseling and intervention strategies for adolescent suicide prevention* (Contract No. 400-86-0014). Ann Arbor, MI: ERIC Clearinghouse.

Carey, A. R. (1986). Imagery: Painting in the mind. *Elementary School Guidance and Counseling, 21,* 150-154.

Carlson, G. A. (1981). The phenomenology of adolescent depression. *Adolescent Psychiatry, 19,* 411-421.

Carlson, G. A., & Cantwell, D. P. (1980). Unmasking masked depression in children and adolescents. *American Journal of Psychiatry, 137*(4), 445-449.

Carlson, G. A., & Garber, J. (1986). Developmental issues in the classification of depression in children. In M. Rutter, C. E. Izard, & P. B. Read (Eds.), *Depression in young people* (pp. 299-343). New York: Guilford.

Carlson, J. (1990). Counseling through physical fitness and exercise. *Elementary School Guidance and Counseling, 24,* 298-302.

Carnegie Foundation (1990). *Turning points: Preparing American youth for the 21st century.* New York: Carnegie Corporation.

Carnevale, J. P. (1989). *Counseling gems: Thoughts for the practitioner.* Muncie Indiana: Accelerated Development.

Casas, M. (1990). Respondent. In D. Brown (Ed.), *Work in America: Report of the Gallup survey.* Scottsdale, AZ: National Career Development Association.

Catterall, J. S. (1987). An intensive group counseling dropout prevention intervention: Some cautions on isolating at-risk adolescents within high schools. *American Educational Research Journal, 24*(4), 521-540.

Cawelti, G. (1989). Designing high schools for the future. *Educational Leadership, 47,* 30-35.

Centers for Disease Control. (1991). Premarital sexual experience among adolescent women. *Morbidity and Mortality Weekly Report* (January), 4.

Charles Stewart Mott Foundation. (1994). *A fine line: Losing American youth to violence.* Flint, MI: Author.

Chasnoff, I. J., Burns, W. J., & Schnoll, S. H. (1985). Cocaine use in pregnancy. *The New England Journal of Medicine, 313*(11), 666-669.

Chasnoff, I. J., Burns, K. A., Burns, W. J., & Schnoll, S. H. (1986). Prenatal drug exposure: Effects on neonatal and infant growth and development. *Neurobehavioral toxicology and teratology, 8,* 357-362.

Chasnoff, I. J., Griffith, D. R., MacGregor, S., Dirkes, K., & Burns, K. A.(1989). Temporal patterns of cocaine use in pregnancy: Perinatal outcome. *Journal of the American Medical Association, 261*(12), 1741-1744.

Chasnoff, I. J., Landress, H. J., & Barrett, M. E. (1990). The prevalence of illicit-drug or alcohol use during pregnancy and discrepancies in mandatory reporting in Pinellas County, Florida. *The New England Journal of Medicine, 322*(17), 1202-1206.

Chilcoat, G. W. (1988). Developing student achievement with verbal feedback. *NASSP Bulletin, 72,* 507.

Children's Defense Fund. (1986). *Preventing adolescent pregnancy: What schools can do.* Washington, DC: Author.

Children's Defense Fund. (1988). *Model programs: Preventing adolescent pregnancy and building youth self-sufficiency.* Washington, DC: Author.

Christopher, F., & Roosa, M.(1990). An evaluation of adolescent pregnancy programs: Is "just say no" enough? *Family Relations, 39,* 68-72.

Clarizio, H. F. (1985). Cognitive-behavioral treatment of childhood depression. *Psychology in the Schools, 22,* 308-322.

Codega, S. A. (1990). Coping behaviors of adolescent mothers: An exploratory study and comparison of Mexican-Americans and Anglos. *Journal of Adolescent Research, 5,* 1.

Cohen, S. (1981). *The substance abuse program.* New York: Haworth Press.

Cohen-Sandler, R., Berman, A. L., & King, R. A. (1982). Life stress and symptomatology: Determinants of suicidal behavior in children. *Journal of the American Academy of Child Psychiatry, 21,* 178-186.

Comer, J. P. (1989). *School development program.* Annual Lela Rowland Award in prevention, National Mental Health Association, Alexandria, VA.

Conyne, R. K. (1994). Preventive counseling. *Counseling & Human Development, 27*(1), 345-346.

Cormier, W. H., & Cormier, L. S. (1985). *Interviewing strategies for helpers* (2nd ed.). Monterey, CA: Brooks/Cole.

Costa, A. (Ed.). (1991). *Developing minds: A resource book for teaching thinking.* Alexandria, VA: Association of Supervision and Curriculum.

Cox, B. J., Norton, G. R., Dorward, J., & Fergusson, P. A. (1989). The relationship between panic attacks and chemical dependency. *Addictive Behaviors: An International Journal, 14,* 1.

Crosbie-Burnett, M., & Pulvino, C. J. (1990). Pro-tech: A multimodal group intervention for children with reluctance to use computers. *Elementary School Guidance & Counseling, 24,* 272-280.

Crumley, F. E. (1990). Substance abuse and adolescent suicidal behavior. *The Journal of the American Medical Association, 263,* 222.

Daly, M., & Wilson, M. (1985). Child abuse and other risks of not living with both parents. *Ethnology and Sociobiology, 6*(4), 97-210.

Daniels, D., & Moos, R. H. (1990). Assessing life stressors and social resources among adolescents: Applications to depressed youth. *Journal of Adolescent Research, 5,* 3.

Danielson, H. A. (1984). The quieting reflex and success imagery. *Elementary School Guidance & Counseling, 19,* 152-155.

Daroff, L. H., Masks, S. J., & Friedman, A. S. (1986). Adolescent drug abuse: The parent's predicament, *Counseling and Human Development, 24*(13), 215-219

Davidson, L., Franklin, J., Mercy, J., Rosenburg, M. L., & Simmons, J. (1989). An epidemiological study of risk factors in two teenage suicide clusters. *The Journal of the American Medical Association, 262*(8), 36-42.

Davies, D.(1989). *Poor parents, teachers and the schools: Comments about practice, policy, and research.* Paper presented at the annual meeting of the American Educational Research Association. San Francisco, CA: ED308 574.

de Shazer, S. (1982). *Patterns of brief family therapy.* New York: Guilford.

de Shazer, S. (1988). *Investigating solutions in brief psychotherapy.* New York: Norton.

de Shazer, S. (1991). *Putting difference to work.* New York: Norton.

de Young, M., & Corbin, B. A. (1994). Helping early adolescents tell: A guided exercise for trauma-focused sexual abuse treatment groups. *Child Welfare League of America, 75*(2), 141-151.

Dean, D. (1979). Emotional abuse of children. *Children Today, 8,* 18-20.

DeAnda, D. (1983). Pregnancy in early and late adolescence. *Journal of Youth and Adolescence, 12,* 33-42.

Dinkmeyer, D., & Dreikurs, R. (1963). *Encouraging children to learn: The encouragement process.* Englewood Cliffs, NJ: Prentice-Hall.

Donald, K., Carlisle, J. S., & Woods, E. (1979). *Before assertiveness: A group approach for building self-confidence.* Santa Barbara: University of California.

Downing, J. (1988). Counseling interventions with depressed children. *Elementary School Guidance and Counseling, 22,* 231-240.

Downing, J., & Harrison, T. (1992). Solutions and school counseling. *The School Counselor, 39,* 5.

Dryfoos, J. G. (1990). *Adolescent at risk: Prevalence and prevention.* New York: Oxford University Press.

Dryfoos, J. G. (1996). Full-service schools. *Educational Leadership, 53,* 7, 18-23.

Dugan, T., & Coles, R. (Eds.). (1989). *The child in our times: Studies in the development of resiliency.* New York: Brunner/Mazel.

Durbin, D. M. (1982). Multimodal group sessions to enhance self-concept. *Elementary School Guidance and Counseling, 16,* 288-295.

Dweck, C. (1986). Motivational processes affecting learning. *American Psychologist, 4*(10), 1040-1048.

Dyer, W. W., & Vriend, J. (1977). *Counseling techniques that work.* New York: Funk & Wagnall.

Dysinger, B. J. (1993). Conflict resolution for intermediate children. *The School Counselor, 40*(4), 29-35.

Edelman, M. W. (1988). Preventing adolescent pregnancy: A role for social work services. *Urban Education, 22,* 496-509.

Edelman, M. W. (1994). *State of America's children yearbook 1994.* Washington, DC: Children's Defense Fund.

Edwards, P. A., & Lowe, J. L. (1988). Young adult books dealing with the crisis of teenage suicide. *The High School Journal, 72,* 1.

Edwards, S. S. (1978). Multimodal therapy with children: A case analysis of insect phobia. *Elementary School Guidance and Counseling, 13,* 23-29.

Edwards, S. S., & Klein, P. A. (1986). Multimodal consultation: A model for working with gifted adolescents. *Journal of Counseling and Development, 64*(9), 214-219.

Egan, G. (1982). *The skilled helper: A model for systematic helping.* Monterey, CA: Brooks Cole.

Eheart, B. K., & Leavitt, R. L. (1985). Supporting toddler play. *Young Children, 35*(2), 18-22.

Elias, M. J. (1989). Schools: A source of stress to children: An analysis of causal and ameliorative influences. *Journal of School Psychology, 27,* 393-407.

Elkind, D. (1988). *The hurried child: Growing up too fast too soon.* New York: Addison-Wesley.

Ellis, A. (1989). Comments on my critics. In M. E. Bernard & R. DiGiuseppe (Eds.), *Inside rational emotive therapy: A critical appraisal of the theory and therapy of Albert Ellis* (pp. 199-260). San Diego: Academic Press.

Elster, A. B., & Panzarine, S. (1983). Teenage fathers: Stresses during gestation and early parenthood. *Clinical Pediatrics, 22,* 700-703.

Englander, S. E. (1984). Some self-reported correlates of runaway behavior in adolescent females. *Journal of Consulting and Clinical Psychology, 53*(3), 484-485.

Farber, S. S., Primavera, J., & Felner, R. D. (1983). Older adolescents and parental divorce: Adjustment problems and mediators of coping. *Journal of Divorce, 7,* 59-75.

Feldman, S., Rubenstein, J., & Rubin, C. (1988). Depressive affect and restraint in early adolescence: Relationships with family process and friendship support. *Journal of Early Adolescence, 14*(1), 218-223.

Ferran, E., & Sabatini, A. (1985). Homeless youth: The New York experience. *International Journal of Family Psychiatry, 6*(2), 117-128.

Fisch, R., Weakland, J. H., & Segal, L. (1983). *The tactics of change: Doing brief therapy.* San Francisco: Jossey-Bass.

Fontana, V. (1985). *Report* to the Conference on Child Abuse and Neglect. Richmond, Virginia.

Foreman, S., & Seligman, L. (1983). Adolescent abuse. *School Counselor, 31*(1), 17-25.

Forman, S. G., & Neal, J. A. (1987). School-based substance abuse prevention programs. *Special Services in the Schools, 3,* 3-4.

Forrest, D. V. (1990). Understanding adolescent depression: Implications for practitioners. *Counseling and Human Development, 23*(1), 221-227.

Frey, D. (1984). The counselor's role in the treatment of anorexia nervosa and bulimia. *Journal of Counseling and Development, 63*(4), 248-249.

Furstenberg, F. F., Brooks-Gunn, J., & Morgan, P. (1987). *Adolescent mothers in later life.* New York: Cambridge University Press.

Gabriel, A., & McAnarney, E. R. (1983). Parenthood in two subcultures: White middle-class couples and black low-income adolescents in Rochester, New York. *Adolescence, 71,* 679-694.

Gage, N. L. (1990). Dealing with the dropout problem. *Phi Delta Kappan, 72*(4), 280-285.

Gallop International Institute. (1994). Many teenagers feel fear at school, survey shows. *Education Week, 13*(11), 6.

Gardner, H. (1983). *Frames of mind: The theory of multiple intelligences.* New York: Harper & Row.

Gardner, H. (1991). *The unschooled mind.* New York: Basic Books.

Gardner, H. (1993). *Multiple intelligence: The theory in practice.* New York: Basic Books.

Garland, A., & Zigler, E. (1993). Adolescent suicide prevention: Current research and social policy implications. *American Psychologist, 48,* 169-182.

Garland, A. F, & Zigler, E. (1993). Adolescent suicide prevention: Current research and social policy implications. *American Psychologist, 43*(2), 169-182.

Garmezy, N.(1981). Children under stress: Perspectives on anecdotes and correlates of vulnerability and resistance to psychopathology. In A. I. Rabin, A. M. Barclay, & R. A. Zucker (Eds.), *Further explorations in personality* (pp. 196-270). New York: Wiley.

Garmezy, N., Masten, A. S., & Tellegen, A. (1984). The study of stress and competence in children: A building block for developmental psychopathology. *Child Development, 55,* 97-111.

Garrison, C. Z., Schuchter, M. D., Schoenbach, V. J., & Kaplan, B. K. (1989). Epidemiology of depressive symptoms in young adolescents. *Journal of American Academy of Child and Adolescent Psychiatry, 28,* 343-351.

Gates, M. (1988, August 22). The changing fortunes of U.S. families: a University of Michigan study provides a surprising view of the dynamics of poverty, and offers insights for upcoming welfare reform. *The Ann Arbor News,* p. b-1.

Gentner, D. S. (1991). A brief model for mental health counseling. *Journal of Mental Health Counseling, 13*(1), 58-68.

Gerler, E. R. (1977). The BASIC ID in career education. *The Vocational Guidance Quarterly, 25,* 238-244.

Gerler, E. R. (1978a). The school counselor and multimodal education. *The School Counselor, 13,* 166-171.

Gerler, E. R. (1978b). Counselor-teacher collaboration in a multimodal reading program. *Elementary School Guidance and Counseling, 13,* 64-67.

Gerler, E. R. (1979). Preventing the delusion of uniqueness: Multimodal education in mainstream classrooms. *The Elementary School Journal, 14,* 35-40.

Gerler, E. R. (1980). A longitudinal study of multimodal approaches to small group psychological education. *The School Counselor, 27,* 184-190.

Gerler, E. R. (1982). *Counseling the young learner.* Englewood Cliffs, NJ: Prentice-Hall.

Gerler, E. R. (1984). The imagery in BASIC ID: A factor in education. *Journal of Humanistic Education and Development, 22,* 115-122.

Gerler, E. R., & Herndon, E. Y. (1993). Learning how to succeed academically in middle school. *Elementary School Guidance & Counseling, 27*(3), 186-197.

Gerler, E. R., & Keat, D. B. (1977). Multimodal education: Treating the BASIC ID of the elementary classroom. *The Humanist Educator, 15,* 148-154.

Gerler, E. R., Kinney, J., & Anderson, R. (1985). The effects of counseling on classroom performance. *Journal of Humanistic Education and Development, 23*(4), 155-165.

Gibbs, J. (1985). Psychological factors associated with depression in urban adolescent females: Implications of assessment. *Journal of Youth and Adolescence, 14*(1), 316-320.

Gill, S. J., & Barry, R. A. (1982). Group-focused counseling: Classifying the essential skills. *The Personnel and Guidance Journal, 60*(5), 66-71.

Gillman, R., & Whitlock, K. (1989). Sexuality: A neglected component of child sexual abuse education and training. *Child Welfare, 68*(3), 110-115.

Gill-Wigal, J. (1988). Societal trends and the world of the adolescent. In D. Capuzzi & L. Golden (Eds.), *Preventing adolescent suicide* (pp.140-152). Muncie, IN: Accelerated Development.

Girard, K., Rifkin, J., & Townley, A. (1985). *Peaceful persuasion: A guide to creating mediation dispute resolution programs on college campuses.* Amherst, MA: University of Massachusetts Mediation Project.

Goldstein, A. P. (1988). *The prepare curriculum: Teaching prosocial competencies.* Champaign, IL: Research Press.

Goldstein, A. P., & Huff, C. R. (1993). *Gangs in the United States*. Champaign, IL: Research Press.

Goldstein, A. P., Glick, B., Irwin, M. J., Pask-McCartney, C., & Rubama, I. (1989). *Reducing delinquency: Intervention in the community*. New York: Pergamon Press.

Goldstein, A. P., Sprafkin, R. P., Gershaw, N. J., & Klein, P. (1982). *Skillstreaming the adolescent: A structured learning approach to teaching prosocial skills*. Champaign, IL: Research Press.

Goleman, D. (1994a). A great idea in education: Emotional literacy. *Connections: The Newsletter of Social and Emotional Learning, 1*(1, June).

Goleman, D. (1994b). *Emotional literacy: A field report*. Kalamazoo, MI: Fetzer Institute.

Goleman, D. (1995). *Emotional intelligence*. New York: Bantam Books.

Goodman, R. W. (1987). Point of view: Adult children of alcoholics. *Journal of Counseling and Development, 66,* 162-163.

Gravitz, H. L., & Bowden, J. D. (1985). *Recovery: A guide for adult children of alcoholics*. New York: Simon & Schuster.

Green, B. J. (1978). HELPING children of divorce: A multimodal approach. *Elementary School Guidance and Counseling, 13,* 31-45.

Greenberger, E., & Steinberg, L. (1987). *The work of growing up*. New York: Basic Books.

Gresham, F. M. (1981). Validity of social skills measures for assessing the social competence in low-status children: A multivariate investigation. *Developmental Psychology, 17,* 390-398.

Gresham, F. M., & Elliot, S. N. (1984), Assessment and classifications of children's social skills: A review of methods and issues. *School Psychology Review, 13,* 292-301.

Growald, K. (1994). Meeting the challenge of at-risk students. *The American School Board Journal, 181*(12), 2-6.

Gumaer, J. (1990). Multimodal counseling of childhood encopresis: A case example. *The School Counselor, 38,* 58-64.

Gwynn, C., & Brantley, H. (1987). Effects of a divorce group intervention with elementary school children. *Psychology in the Schools, 24,* 161-164.

Hafen, B. Q., & Frandsen, K. J. (1986). *Youth suicide: Depression and loneliness.* Evergreen, CO: Cordillera Press.

Hamer, R. J. (1995). Counselor intentions: A critical review of the literature. *Journal of Counseling and Development, 73*(3), 259-270.

Hammond, J. (1981). *Group counseling for children of divorce: A guide for the elementary school.* Flint, MI: Cranbrook Publishing.

Hansen, J. C., Warner, R. W., & Smith, E. J. (1980). *Group counseling: Theory and practice* (2nd ed.). Chicago: Rand McNally.

Harmin, M. (1994). *Inspiring active learners: A handbook for teachers.* Alexandria, VA: Association for Supervision and Curriculum Development.

Hart, S. L. (1991). Childhood depression: Implications and options for school counselors. *Elementary School Guidance and Counseling, 25,* 277-289.

Hartley, R., & Goldenson, R. (1963). *The complete book of children's play.* New York: Cromwell.

Harvey, S. M., & Spigner, R. (1995). Factors associated with sexual behavior among adolescents: A multivariate analysis. *Adolescence, 30,* 253-264.

Hawkins, J. D., Lishner, D. M., & Catalano, R. F. (1985). Childhood predictors and the prevention of adolescent substance abuse. In C. L. Jones & T. L. Battjes (Eds.), *Etiology of drug abuse: Implications for Prevention.* Washington, DC: Government Printing Office, National Institute on Drug Abuse.

Hawkins, J. D., Lishner, D. M., Catalano, R. F., & Howard, M. O. (1986). Childhood predictors of adolescent substance abuse: Towards an empirically grounded theory. *Journal of Children and Contemporary Society, 8,* 11-47.

Hawks, S. (1993). Fetal alcohol syndrome: Implications for health education. *Journal of Health Education, 24,* 22-26.

Hawton, K. (1986). *Suicide and attempted suicide among children and adolescents.* Beverly Hills, CA: Sage.

Heldenbrand, L., & Hixon, J. E. (1991). Video-assisted training of study skills. *Elementary School Guidance & Counseling*, 26, 121-129.

Hendricks, L. E. (1988). Outreach with teenage fathers: A preliminary report on three ethnic groups. *Adolescence, 23*(91), 711-720.

Hendricks, L. E., & Montgomery, T. (1983). A limited population of unmarried Black adolescent fathers: A preliminary report of their views on fatherhood and the relationship with the mother of their children. *Adolescence, 18*(69), 201-210.

Hendricks, L. E., & Solomon, A. M. (1987). Reaching Black adolescent parents through nontraditional techniques. *Child and Youth Services, 9*(1) 111-124.

Hill, C. E. (1989). *Therapist techniques and client outcome: Eight cases of brief psychotherapy.* Newbury Park, CA: Sage.

Hill, C. E., Helms, J. E., Spiegel, S. B., & Tichenor, V. (1988). Development of a system for categorizing client reactions to therapist reactions. *Journal of Counseling Psychology, 35,* 27-36.

Hill, C. E., & O'Grady, K. E. (1985). List of therapist intentions illustrated in a case study with therapists of varying theoretical orientations. *Journal of Counseling Psychology, 32*(5), 3-12.

Hofferth, S. (1991). Programs for high risk adolescents: What works? *Evaluation and Program Planning, 14,* 3-16.

Hofferth, S. L., & Kahn, B. W. (1987). Premarital sexual activity among U.S. teenage women over the past three decades. *Pediatrics Journal, 83*(3), 11-17.

Huber, C. H., & Backlund, B. A. (1991).*The twenty-minute counselor.* New York: Continuum.

Huey, W. (1983). Reducing adolescent aggression through group assertiveness training. *The School Counselor, 30*(3), 193-203.

Huey, W. (1987). Counseling teenage fathers: The maximizing a life experience (MALE) group. *The School Counselor, 35*(1), 40-47.

Husain, S., & Vandiver, T. (1984). *Suicide in children and adolescents.* New York: Medical and Scientific Books.

Hussong, A. M., & Chassin, L. (1994). The stress-negative affect model of adolescents use: Disaggregating negative affect. *Journal of Studies on Alcohol, 55,* 707-718.

Institute for Mental Health Initiatives. (1995). *RETHINK.* Washington, DC: Author.

Ivey, A. E. (1988). *Intentional interviewing and counseling* (2nd ed.). Pacific Grove, CA: Brooks/Cole.

Jakubowski, P., & Lange, A. J. (1978). *The assertive option: Your rights and responsibilities.* Champaign, IL: Research Press.

Janus, M. D., Burgess, A. W., & McCormack, A. (1987). *Adolescent runaways: Causes and consequences.* Lexington, MA: Lexington Books.

Jens, K. G., & Gordon, B. N. (1991). Understanding risk: Implications for tracking high-risk infants and making early service decisions. *International Journal of Disability, 38,* 211-224.

Jensen-Scott, R. L., & DeLucia-Waack, J. L. (1993). Developmental guidance programming in junior and senior high schools: Eating disorders and weight management units. *The School Counselor, 41*(3), 109-119,

Jessor, R., & Jessor, S. L. (1978). Theory testing in longitudinal research. In D. Kandel (Ed.), *Longitudinal research in drug use.* Washington, DC: Hemisphere Publishing.

Johnson, D. W. (1990). *Reaching out: Interpersonal effectiveness and self-actualization* (4th ed.). Englewood Cliffs, NJ: Prentice-Hall.

Johnson, D. W., & Johnson, F. P. (1991). *Joining together: Group theory and group skills.* Englewood Cliffs, NJ: Prentice-Hall.

Johnson, D. W., & Johnson, R. T. (1995). *Reducing school violence through conflict resolution.* Alexandria, VA: Association for Supervision and Curriculum Development.

Johnson, L., Bachman, J. G., & O'Malley, C. T. (1982a). *Highlights from drugs and the American high school student, 1975-1983.* Rockville, MD: U.S. Institute on Drug Abuse.

Johnson, L., Bachman, J. G., & O'Malley, C. T. (1982b). *Student drug use, attitudes, and beliefs: National trends 1975-1982.* Washington, DC: Government Printing Office.

Johnson, W. Y., & Wilborn, B. (1991). Group counseling as an intervention in anger expression and depression in older adults. *The Journal of Specialists in Group Work, 16,* 3.

Jones, L. P. (1988). A typology of adolescent runaways. *Child and Adolescent Social Work Journal, 5*(1), 16-29.

Jones, P. (1996). Adding care to the curriculum. *Education Update, 38,* 7.

Judah, R. D. (1978). Multimodal parent training. *Elementary School Guidance and Counseling, 13,* 46-54.

Kain, C. J., Downs, J. C., & Black, D. D. (1988). Social skills in the school curriculum: A systematic approach. *NASSP Bulletin, 41*(2), 107-110.

Kamerman, S. B., & Kahn, A. J. (1980). *Social service in international perspective.* Washington, DC: U.S. Department of Health, Education, & Welfare.

Kammer, P., & Schmidt, D. (1987). Counseling runaway adolescents. *The School Counselor, 35*(2), 149-154.

Kaplan, A. S., & Woodside, D. B. (1987). Biological aspects of anorexia nervosa and bulimia nervosa. *Journal of Consulting and Clinical Psychology, 55,* 645-653.

Kashani, J. H., & Simonds, J. F. (1979). The incidence of depression in children. *American Journal of Psychiatry, 136,* 1203-1205.

Kazdin, A. E., French, N. H., Unis, A. S., Esveldt-Dawson, K., & Sherick, R. B. (1983). Hopelessness, depression and suicidal intent among psychiatrically disturbed inpatient children. *Journal of Consulting and Clinical Psychology, 51,* 504-510.

Keat, D. B. (1976a). Multimodal counseling with children: Treating the BASIC ID. *Pennsylvania Personnel and Guidance Journal, 4,* 21-25.

Keat, D. B. (1976b). Multimodal therapy with children: Two case histories, In A. A. Lazarus (Ed.), *Multimodal behavior therapy* (pp. 22-39). New York: Springer.

Keat, D. B. (1979). *Multimodal therapy with children.* New York: Pergamon Press.

Keat, D. B. (1985). Child-adolescent multimodal therapy: Bud the boss. *Journal of Humanistic Education and Development, 23,* 183-192.

Keat, D. B. (1990). Change in child multimodal counseling. *Elementary School Guidance and Counseling, 24,* 4.

Keat, D. B., Metzgar, K. L., Raykovitz, D., & McDonald, J. (1985). Multimodal counseling: Motivating children to attend school through friendship groups. *Journal of Humanistic Education and Development, 23,* 166-175.

Kehayan, V. A. (1990). *SAGE: Self-awareness growth experiences.* Rolling Hills Estates, CA: Jalmar Press.

Kelly, J., Murphy, D., Sikkema, K., & Kalichman, S. (1993). Psychological interventions to prevent HIV infection are urgently needed: New priorities for behavioral research in the second decade of AIDS. *American Psychologist, 48,* 1023-1034.

Kelly, J. B. (1983). Mediation and psychotherapy: Distinguishing the differences. In J. A. Lemmon (Ed.), *Dimensions and practice of divorce mediation* (pp. 33-44). San Francisco: Jossey-Bass.

Kelly, J. B., & Wallerstein, J. S. (1976). The effects of parental divorce: Experiences of the child in early latency. *American Journal of Orthopsychiatry, 46,* 20-31.

Kiselica, M., Stroud, J., Stroud, J., & Rotzien, A. (1992). Counseling the forgotten client: The teen father. *Journal of Mental Health Counseling, 14*(3), 338-351.

Kiselica, M. S., & Sturmer, P. (1993). Is society giving teenage fathers a mixed message? *Youth & Society, 24,* 4.

Kivlighan, D. M. (1989). Changes in the counselor intentions and response modes and in client reactions and session evaluations after training. *Journal of Counseling Psychology, 36,* 471-76.

Kivlighan, D. M. (1990). Relation between counselors' use of intentions and clients' perception of working alliance. *Journal of Counseling Psychology, 37,* 27-32.

Kivlighan, D. M., & Angelone, E. O. (1991). Helpee introversion, novice counselor intention use, and helpee-rated session impact. *Journal of Counseling Psychology*, 38, 25-29.

Kogan, L. (1980). A family systems perspective on status offenders. *Juvenile and Family Court Journal*, *31*(2), 49-53.

Koss, M. P., Gidycz, C. J., & Wisniewski, N. (1987). The scope of rape: Incidence and prevalence of sexual aggression and victimization in a national sample of higher education students. *Journal of Consulting & Clinical Psychology*, *55*, 162-170.

Koss, M. P., & Oros, C. J. (1982). The sexual experiences survey: A research instrument investigating sexual aggression and victimization. *Journal of Consulting & Clinical Psychology*, *50*, 455-457.

Kozicki, Z. A. (1986). Why do adolescents use substances: Drugs/alcohol. *Journal of Alcohol and Drug Education*, *32*(1), 34-42.

Krasnow, J. (1990). *Building parent teacher partnerships: Prospects from the perspective of the schools reaching out project*. Boston, MA: Institute for Responsive Education, ED 318 817.

Kreidler, W. J. (1984). *Creative conflict resolution*. Glenview, IL: Scott Foresman.

Kufeldt, K., & Nimmo, M. (1987). Youth on the street: Abuse and neglect in the 1980's. *Journal of Child Abuse and Neglect*, *11*(4), 531-543.

L'Abate, L., & Milan, M. A. (Eds.). (1985). *Handbook of social skills training research*. New York: Wiley.

LaFountain, R. M., Garner, N. E., & Eliason, G. T. (1996). Solution-focused counseling groups: A key for school counselors. *The School Counselor*, *43*(4), 256-266.

Lamar, J. V. (1988, May). Kids who sell crack. *Time*, *9*, 20-33.

Landau-Stanton, J., & Stanton, M. D. (1985). Treating suicidal adolescents and their families. In M. P. Mirkin & S. L. Koman (Eds.), *Handbook of adolescent and family therapy* (pp. 309-328). New York: Gardner.

Lane, P. S., & McWhirter, J. J. (1992). A peer mediation model: Conflict resolution for elementary and middle school children. *Elementary School Guidance and Counseling, 27*(1), 24-36.

Larson, D. (1984). *Teaching psychological skills: Models for giving psychology away*. Monterey, CA: Brooks/Cole.

Lawton, M. (1994, November 9). Violence prevention curricula: What works best. *Education Week, 14*, 10.

Lawton, M. (1995, October 4). Drop in pregnancy, birthrates may not add up to trend. *Education Week, 15*, 5.

Lawton, M. (1995, October 18). Broad attack urged to meet adolescents' basic needs. *Education Week, 15*, 7.

Lazarus, A. A. (1977). *In the mind's eye: The power of imagery for personal enrichment*. New York: Rawson.

Lazarus, A. A. (1981). *The practice of multimodal therapy*. New York: McGraw-Hill.

Lazarus, A. A. (1992). The multimodal approach to the treatment of minor depression. *American Journal of Psychotherapy, 86*(1), 50-56.

Lazarus, A. A. (1993). *The practice of multimodal therapy*. Baltimore, MD: Johns Hopkins University Press.

Levine, R. S., Metzendorf, D., & VanBoskirk, K. (1986). Runaway and throwaway youth: A case for early intervention with truants. *Social Work in Education, 8*(2), 93-106.

Levinson, H. (1992). *Specific and vague criticism. Feedback to subordinates*. Waltham, MA: Levinson Institute.

Lewinsohn, P. M., Hops, H., Roberts, R., Seeley, J. R., & Andrew, J. (1993). Adolescent psychopathology: I. Prevalence and incidence of depression and other DSM-III-R disorders of high school students. *Journal of Abnormal Psychology, 102*(4), 183-204.

Lewis, K. D., Bennett, B., & Schmeder, N. H. (1989). The care of infants menaced by cocaine abuse. *American Journal of Maternal Child Nursing, 14*, 324-329.

Loeb, R. C., Burke, T. A., & Boglarsky, C. (1986). A large-scale comparison of perspectives on parenting between teenage runaways and nonrunaways. *Adolescence, 21,* 84, 921-930.

Lokken, M. (1981). *Weight: Helping kids keep it off.* Washington, DC: U.S. Department of Education.

Lumsden, L. S. (1990). *Meeting the needs of drug-affected children.* Ann Arbor, MI: ERIC Clearinghouse on Educational Management, Eric Digest Series EA 53.

Luna, C. C. (1987). Welcome to my nightmare: The graffiti of homeless youth. *Society, 24,* 73-78.

McCann, I. L., Sakheim, D. K., & Abrahamson, D. J. (1988). Trauma and victimization: A model of psychological adaptation. *Counseling Psychologist, 16,* 531-594.

McConville, B. J., & Bruce, R. T. (1985). Depressive illnesses in children and adolescents: A review of current concepts. *Canadian Journal of Psychiatry, 30,* 119-129

McCormack, A., Burgess, A. W., & Hartman, C. (1988). Familial abuse & post-traumatic stress disorder. *Journal of Traumatic Stress, 1*(2), 231-242.

McKay, M., Davis, M., & Fanning, P. (1981). *Thoughts and feelings.* Oakland, CA: New Harbinger Publications.

McKay, M., & Fanning, P. (1987). *Self-esteem: A proven program of cognitive techniques for assessing, improving, and maintaining your self-esteem.* Oakland, CA: New Harbinger Publications.

McKinlay, B., & Bloch, D. P. (1989). *Career information motivates at risk youth. Oregon School Study Council, 31*(5).

McLean, P. D. (1976). Depression as a specific response to stress. In C. D. Spielberger & I. Sarason (Eds.), *Stress and anxiety in modern life* (Vol. 3). New York: Wiley.

McMullin, R. (1986). *Handbook of cognitive therapy techniques.* New York: Norton.

McWhirter, J. J., McWhirter, B. T., McWhirter, A. M., & McWhirter, E. H. (1993). *At-risk youth: A comprehensive response*. Pacific Grove, CA: Brooks/Cole.

McWhirter, J. J., McWhirter, B. T., McWhirter, A. M., & McWhirter, E. H. (1994) High- and low-risk characteristics of youth: The five Cs of competency. *Elementary School Guidance and Counseling, 28*(3), 188-196.

Madanes, C. (1981). *Strategic family therapy*. San Francisco: Jossey-Bass.

Maeroff, G. I. (1996, March 6). Apathy and anonymity: Combating the twin scourges of modern post-adolescence. *Education Week, 15*, 24.

Magid, K., & McKelvey, C. A. (1987). *High risk: Children without a conscience*. New York: Bantam Books.

Malett, S. D. (1983). Description and subject evaluation of an objectively successful study improvement program. *The Personnel and Guidance Journal, 61*(16), 341-345.

Maracek, J. (1987). Counseling adolescents with problem pregnancies. *American Psychologist, 42*(1), 89-93.

Margolis, H., & Brannigan, G. G. (1986). Building trust with parents. *Academic Therapy, 22,* 7174.

Martin, L. C. (1992). *A life without fear: A guide to preventing sexual assault*. Nashville, TN: Rutledge Hill.

Martin, M., Martin, D., & Porter, J. (1983). Bibliotherapy: Children of divorce. *The School Counselor, 30,* 312-314.

Martin, S. H. (1988). *Healing for adult children of alcoholics.* , Nashville, TN: Broadman Press.

Martin-Causey, T., & Hinkle, J. S., (1995). Multimodal therapy with an aggressive adolescent: A demonstration of effectiveness and accountability. *Journal of Counseling & Development, 73*(3), 305-310.

Marton, P., Golombek, H., Stein, B., & Korenblum, M. (1988). The relation of personality functions and adaptive skills to self-esteem in early adolescence. *Journal of Youth and Adolescence, 17,* 393-401.

Matthews, D. B. (1986). *A comparison of relaxation strategies.* Orangeburg, SC: South Carolina State College (ERIC Document Reproduction Service No. ED 283 095).

Maultsby, M. C. (1975). *Help yourself to happiness.* New York: Institute for Rational Living.

Maynard, R. A. (Ed.). (1996). *Kids having kids. A Robin Hood Foundation special report on the cost of adolescent childbearing.* New York: Robin Hood Foundation.

Mehan, P. J., Lamb, J. A., Saltzman, L. E., & O'Carroll, P. W. (1992). Attempted suicide among young adults: Progress toward a meaningful estimate of prevalence. *American Journal of Psychiatry, 149*(1), 41-44.

Meichenbaum, D., & Cameron, R. (1973). Training schizophrenics to talk to themselves: A means of developing attentional controls. *Behavior Therapy, 4,* 515-534.

Meichenbaum, D., & Cameron, R. (1974). The clinical potential of modifying what clients say about themselves. In M. J. Mahoney & C. E. Thompson (Eds.), *Self-control: Power to the person.* Monterey, CA: Brooks/Cole.

Merritt, R., & Walley, F. (1977). *The group leader's handbook: Resources, techniques, and survival skills.* Champaign, IL: Research Press.

Messing, J. K. (1993). Mediation: An intervention strategy for counselors. *Journal of Counseling & Development,* 72(1), 67-72.

Miller, S. A. (1981). *Identifying characteristics of truant students.* Doctoral dissertation, Lehigh University, Bethlehem, PA.

Miller, S., Nunnally, E. W., & Wackman, D. B. (1975). *Alive and aware: Improving communication in relationships.* Minneapolis: Interpersonal Communication Programs.

Millman, R. B., & Botvin, G. J. (1983). Substance use, abuse and dependence. In M. D. Levin, W. B. Carey, A. C. Crocker, & R. T. Gross (Eds.), *Developmental behavioral pediatrics* (pp. 683-708). Philadelphia: W. B. Saunders.

Mitchell, J. E. (1986). Anorexia nervosa: Medical and physiological aspects. In K. D. Brownell & J. P. Foreyt (Eds.), *Handbook of eating disorders* (pp. 180-197). New York: Basic Books.

Mitchell, J. E., & Eckert, E. D. (1987). Scope and significance of eating disorders. *Journal of Consulting and Clinical Psychology, 55,* 628-634.

Monitoring the Future. (1993). *The challenge: Safe, disciplined, and drug free schools. Monitoring the Future, 5*(4), U.S. Department of Education.

Morgan, O. J. (1982). Runaways: Jurisdiction, dynamics, and treatment. *Journal of Marital and Family Therapy, 8*(1), 121-127.

Morganett, R. (1990). *Skills for living: Group counseling activities for young adolescents.* Champaign, IL: Research Press.

Morrison, J. A., Olivos, K., Dominguez, G., Gomez, D., & Lena, D. (1993). The application of family systems approaches to school behavior problems on a school-level discipline board: An outcome study. *Elementary School Guidance & Counseling, 27,* 258-272.

Morse, L. A. (1987). Working with young procrastinators: Elementary school students who do not complete school assignments. *Elementary School Guidance & Counseling, 21,* 221-228.

Murphy, J. J. (1992). Brief strategic family intervention for school-related problems. *Family Therapy, 7,* 59-71.

Murphy, J. J. (1994). Working with what works: A solution-focused approach to school behavior problems. *The School Counselor, 42*(1), 59-65.

Myrick, R. (1987). *Developmental guidance and counseling: A practical approach.* Minneapolis: Educational Media Corporation,

National Center for Educational Statistics. (1995). *Two years later: Cognitive gains and school transitions of NELS: 88 Eighth graders.* Washington, DC: Author.

National Education Association, Educational Policies Commission. (1938). *The purpose of education in American democracy.* Washington, DC: Author.

National Education Association, Educational Policies Commission. (1952). *Education for all American youth: A further look.* Washington, DC: Author.

National Institute on Alcohol Abuse and Alcoholism. (1990). *Eighth special report to the U.S. Congress on alcohol and health.* Washington, DC: Government Printing Office.

National School Safety Center. (1988). *Gangs in school: Breaking up is hard to do.* Malibu, CA: Pepperdine University.

Natriello, G., Pallas, A. M., & McDill, E. L. (1986). Taking stock: Renewing our research agenda on the causes and consequences of dropping out. *Teachers College Record, 87*(3), 430-440.

Nattiv, A., Render, G., Lemire, D., & Render, K. (1990). Conflict resolution and interpersonal skill building through the use of cooperative learning. In E. Gerler, C. Hogan, & K. O'Rourke (Eds.), *The challenge of counseling in the middle school.* Ann Arbor, MI: ERIC.

Newcomb, M. D., & Bentler, P. M. (1989). *Substance use and abuse among children and teenagers.* Washington, DC: American Psychological Association.

Newcomb, M. D., & Bentler, P. M. (1990). Consequences of adolescent drug use: Impact on the lives of young adults. *Journal of Substance Abuse Treatment, 7*(2), 134-135.

Newcomb, M. D., Bentler, P. M., & Collins, C. (1986). Alcohol use and dissatisfaction with self and life: A longitudinal analysis of young adults. *The Journal of Drug Issues, 16,* 4.

Nielsen, A., & Gerber, D. (1979). Psychological aspects of truancy in early adolescence. *Adolescence, 14*(54), 313-326.

Novaco, R. W. (1975). *Anger control: The development and evaluation of an experimental treatment.* Lexington, MA: Lexington Books.

Novaco, R. W. (1979). The cognitive regulation of anger and stress. in P. C. Kendall & S. D. Hollon (Eds.), *Cognitive-behavior interventions: Theory, research, and procedures* (pp. 312-343). New York: Academic Press.

O'Hanlon, W. H., & Weiner-Davis, M. (1989). *In search of solutions: A new direction in psychotherapy.* New York: Guilford.

Ohlsen, M. M. (1977). *Group counseling.* New York: Holt, Rinehart, Winston.

O'Keefe, E. J., & Castaldo, C. (1980). A multimodal approach to treatment in a child care agency. *Psychological Reports, 4,* 250.

Olson, L. (1989, February 22). Governors say investment in children can curb long-term costs for states. *Education Week, 10,* 130.

Omizo, M. M. (1981). Relaxation training and biofeedback with hyperactive elementary school children. *Elementary School Guidance & Counseling, 15,* 329-332.

Omizo, M. M., & Omizo, S. A. (1987a). The effects of group counseling on classroom behavior and self-concept among elementary school learning disabled children. *Exceptional Child, 34*(1), 57-64.

Omizo, M. M., & Omizo, S. A. (1987b). Group counseling with children of divorce: New findings. *Elementary School Guidance & Counseling, 22,* 46-52.

Omizo, M. M., & Omizo, S. A. (1988). The effects of participation in group counseling sessions on self-esteem an locus of control among adolescents from divorced families. *The School Counselor, 36*(1), 54-58.

O'Neil, J. (1991, January). Civic education. *ASCD Curriculum Update, 21,* 18-24.

Orr, M. T. (1987). *Keeping kids in school: A guide to effective dropout prevention programs and services.* San Francisco: Jossey-Bass.

Papagno, N.(1983). *A single model counseling group across all special needs children.* Paper presented at the American Psychological Association Annual Meeting, Anaheim, CA.

Papolos, D., & Papolos, J. (1987). *Overcoming depression.* New York: Harper & Row.

Pedro-Carroll, J. (1991). *Children of divorce intervention program.* Annual Lela Rowland Award in Prevention, National Mental Health Association, Alexandria, VA.

Perkins, D. N. (1986). *Knowledge by design.* Hillsdale, NJ: Erlbaum.

Perlstein, R., & Thrall, G. (1996). *Ready-to-use conflict resolution activities for secondary students.* West Nyack, NY: Center for Applied Research in Education.

Perrone, P. A. (1987). Counselor response to adolescent suicide. *The School Counselor, 35*(1), 12-16.

Peters, D., & Peters, S. (1984). *Why knock rock?* Minneapolis, MI: Bethany House Publishers.

Peterson, S., & Straub, R. (1992). *School crisis survival guide.* West Nyack, NY: Center for Applied Research in Education.

Pfeiffer, C. R. (1982). Interventions for suicidal children and their parents. *Suicide and Life Threatening Behavior, 12,* 240-248.

Pfeiffer, C. R. (1986). *The suicidal child.* New York: Guilford.

Pirog-Good, M. A. (1995). The family background and attitudes of teen fathers. *Youth and Society, 26,* 351-376.

Portner, J. (1995, September 20). Report on juvenile crime brings calls for new policies. *Education Week, 15,* 3.

Powell, A. G., Farrar, E., & Cohen, D. K. (1985). *The shopping mall high school.* Boston: Houghton-Mifflin.

Powell, L., & Faherty, S. (1990). Treating sexually abused latency aged girls. *The Arts in Psychotherapy, 17,* 35-47.

Presseisen, B. Z. (Ed.). (1988). *At-risk students and thinking: Perspectives from research.* Washington, DC: National Education Association; and Philadelphia, PA: Research for Better Schools.

Pressley, M., & Levin, J. (1987). Elaborating learning strategies for the inefficient learner. In S. J. Ceci (Ed.), *Handbook of cognitive, social and neuropsychological aspects of learning disabilities* (pp. 36-52). Hillsdale, NJ: Erlbaum.

Prevention Update. (1997, April). *Prevention update: A newsletter of child abuse prevention services for St. Mary's Infant Home, Norfolk, VA, 1*(1).

Prothrow-Stith, D. (1991). *Deadly consequences.* New York: HarperCollins.

Prothrow-Stith, D. (1993). *Violence prevention: A curriculum for adolescents.* Newton, MA: Education Development Center.

Pulkinnen, L., & Pitkanen, T. (1994). A prospective study of the precursors to problem drinking in young adults. *Journal of Studies on Alcohol, 55,* 578-587.

Pyle, R. L., Neuman, P. A., Halvorson, P. A., & Mitchell, J. E. (1991). An ongoing cross-sectional study of the prevalence of eating disorders in freshman college students. *International Journal of Eating Disorders, 10,* 667-677.

Pynoos, R., & Eth, S. (1985). Children traumatized by witnessing acts of personal violence: Homicide, rape, or suicide behavior. In S. Eth & R. Pynoos (Eds.), *Post-traumatic stress disorder in children* (pp. 17-43). Washington, DC: American Psychiatric Press.

Pynoos, R., & Nader, K. (1988). Psychological first aid and treatment approaches to children exposed to community violence: Research implications. *Journal of Traumatic Stress, 1,* 445-473.

Rak, C. F., & Patterson, L. E. (1996). Promoting resilience in at-risk children. *Journal of Counseling & Development, 74*(4), 368-373.

Raspberry, W. (1994, February 19). Editorial. *The Virginian-Pilot & Ledger-Star,* C24.

Rathvon, N. W. (1990). The effects of encouragement on off-task behaviors and academic productivity. *Elementary School Guidance & Counseling,* 24, 189-199.

Redican, K. J., Redican, B. L., & Baffi, C. R. (1988). Drug use, misuse, and abuse as presented in movies. *Health Education, 19,* 6.

Reiss, A., & Roth, J. (Eds.). (1993). *Understanding and preventing violence.* Washington, DC: National Academy Press.

Rencken, R. H. (1989). *Intervention strategies for sexual abuse.* Alexandria, Va: American Association for Counseling and Development.

Resnick, L. B. (1984). Cognitive sciences as educational research: Why we need it now. *Improving Education: Perspectives on educational research, 10*(1), Pittsburgh, PA: University of Pittsburgh Learning Research and Development Center.

Roberts, A. R. (1982). Stress and coping patterns among adolescent runaways. *Journal of Social Service Research, 5,* 1-2.

Robinson, B. E. (1988). *Teenage fathers.* Lexington, MA: Lexington Books.

Rodning, C. L., Beckwith, J., & Howard, J. (1989). Prenatal exposure to drugs: Behavioral distortions reflecting CNS impairment? *Neurotoxicology, 10,* 629–634.

Rogala, J., Lambert, R., & Verhage, K. (1991). *Developmental guidance classroom activities for use with the national career development guidelines.* Madison: University of Wisconsin, Vocational Studies Center.

Rogers, C. R. (1980). *A way of being.* Boston: Houghton-Mifflin.

Rose, S. (1987). Social skills training in middle school. *Journal for Specialists in Group Work, 12*(4), 144-149.

Ross, R. R., & Ross, B. (1989). Delinquency prevention through cognitive training. *Educational Horizons, 15,* 2.

Roth, S., & Lebowitz, L. (1988). The experience of sexual trauma. *Journal of Traumatic Stress, 1,* 79-107.

Russell, D. E. H. (1984). *Sexual exploitation: Rape, child sexual abuse, and workplace harassment.* Beverly Hills, CA: Sage.

Rutter, M. (1983). Stress, coping, and development. Some issues and some questions. In N. Garmezy & M. Rutter (Eds.), *Stress, coping, and development in children* (pp. 1-42). New York: McGraw-Hill.

Rutter, M. (1985). Resilience in the face of adversity: Protective factors and resistance to psychiatric disorders. *British Journal of Psychiatry, 147,* 598-611.

Ryan, L. S., Ehrlich, S., & Finnegan, L. (1987). Cocaine abuse in pregnancy: Effects on the fetus and newborn. *Neurotoxicology and Teratology, 9,* 296-299.

Salovey, P., & Mayer, J. D. (1990). Emotional intelligence. *Imagination, Cognition, and Personality, 9,* 185-211.

Sandler, R., & Ramsay, S. (1980). *Stressors in children and adolescents.* Champaign, IL.: Research Press.

Sandoval, J., Davis, J. M., & Wilson, M. P. (1987). An overview of the school-based prevention of adolescent suicide. *Special Services to the Schools, 3*(3), 103-120.

Sarvela, P. D., Newcomb, P. R., & Littlefield, E. R. (1988). Sources of drug and alcohol information among rural youth. *Health Education, 19*(3), 27-31.

Sautter, R. C. (1995). Standing up to violence: Kappan Special Report. *Phi Delta Kappan, 13,* K1-K12.

Schaefer, C. E., Briesmeister, J. M., & Fitton, M. E. (1984). *Family therapy techniques for problem behavior of children and teenagers.* San Francisco: Jossey-Bass.

Schinke, S. P., & Gilchrist, L. D. (1977). Adolescent pregnancy: And interpersonal skill training approach to prevention. *Social Work in Health Care, 3*(2), 159-167.

Schloss, P. J. (1983). Classroom-based interventions for students exhibiting depressive reactions. *Behavioral Disorders, 8,* 231-236.

Schmitz, C., & Hipp, E. (1987). *A teacher's guide to fighting invisible tigers: A 12-part course in lifeskills development.* Minneapolis: Free Spirit Publishing.

Schneider, R., & Googins, B. (1989). Alcoholism day treatment: Rationale, research, and resistance. *Journal of Drug Issues, 19*(4), 437-449.

Schrut, A. (1984). System theory and parenting. *International Journal of Family Psychiatry, 5*(3), 249-257.

Seligman, L. (1981). Multimodal behavior therapy: Case study of a high school student. *The School Counselor, 58,* 249-256.

Shaffer, D., Garland, A., Gould, M., Fisher, P., & Trautman, P. (1988). Preventing teenage suicide: A critical review. *Journal of the American Academy of Child and Adolescent Psychiatry, 27*(6), 675-687.

Sherouse, D. (1985). *Adolescent drug and alcohol abuse handbook.* Springfield, IL: Charles C. Thomas.

Shriver, T. P., & Weissberg, R. P. (1996, September 4). No new wars! Prevention should be a comprehensive strategy, not a fad. *Education Week, 15*(34).

Slavin, R. (1987). Cooperative learning: Can students help students learn? *Instructor, 3*(1), 74-78.

Slovacek, S. P. (1993). *Project support evaluation* (Report No. 1). Los Angeles: Los Angeles Unified School District.

Smith, K. (1986). *Youth suicide, depression, and loneliness.* New York: The Menninger Project.

Smith, R. L., & Southern, S. (1980). Multimodal career counseling: An application of the BASIC ID. *Vocational Guidance Quarterly, 29,* 56-64.

Smollar, J., & Ooms, T. (1987). *Young unwed fathers: Research review, policy dilemmas, and options.* Washington, DC: U.S. Department of Health and Human Services.

Snyder, C. R. (1989). Reality negotiation: From excuses to hope and beyond. *Journal of Social and Clinical Psychology, 8,* 130-157.

Snyder, C. R. (1994). *The psychology of hope: You can get there from here.* New York: Free Press.

Snyder, C. R. (1995). Conceptualizing, measuring, and nurturing hope. *Journal of Counseling & Development, 73*(3), 355-360.

Snyder, K. (1985). An intervention program for children of separated or divorced parents. *Techniques: A Journal for Remedial Education and Counseling, 1*(14), 286-296.

Snyder, S. H. (1986). *Teenage depression and suicide.* New York: Chelsea House.

Soderberg, L. J. (1988). Educators' knowledge of the characteristics of high school dropouts. *The High School Journal, 77,* 108-115

Sonenstein, F. L. (1986). Risking paternity: Sex and contraception among adolescent males. In A. B. Elster & M. Lamb (Eds.), *Adolescent fatherhood.* Hillsdale, NJ: Erlbaum.

Spergel, I. A. (1989). *Youth gangs: Problem and response. A review of the literature.* Chicago: University of Chicago School of Social Service Administration.

Starr, J., & Raykovitz, J. (1982). A multimodal approach to interviewing children. *Elementary School Guidance & Counseling, 16,* 267-277.

Steketee, G., & Foa, E. B. (1987). Rape victims: Post-traumatic stress responses and their treatment. *Journal of Anxiety Disorders, 1,* 69-86.

Stellas, E. (1992). No more victims, no more victimizers violence prevention education: Social skills for risk reduction. In Robert C. Morris (Ed.), *Solving the problems of youth at risk: Involving Parents and Community Resources.* Lancaster, PA: Technomic Publishing.

Stickel, S. A. (1990). Using multimodal social-skills groups with kindergarten children. *Elementary School Guidance & Counseling, 24,* 281-288.

Stiffman, A. R. (1989). Physical and sexual abuse in runaway youths. *Child Abuse and Neglect, 13,* 417.

Storti, E. (1988). *Crisis intervention: Acting against addiction.* New York: Crown Publishers.

Strober, M., McCracken, J., & Hanna, G. (1989). Affective disorders. In L. K. G. Hsu & M. Hersen (Eds.), *Handbook of child psychiatric diagnosis* (pp. 299-316). New York: Wiley.

Strother, J., & Jacobs, E. (1986). Parent consultation. *The School Counselor, 33,* 24-26.

Sullivan, M. (1988). *What about the boys? Teenage pregnancy prevention strategies.* Washington, DC: Children's Defense Fund.

Super, D. E. (1980). A life-span, life-space approach to career development. *Journal of Vocational Behavior, 16,* 282-298.

Sylwester, R. (1995). *A celebration of neurons: An educator's guide to the human brain.* Alexandria, VA: Association for Supervision and Curriculum Development.

Tesser, D. (1982). A group counseling program for gifted and talented students. *The Pointer, 26*(3), 43-46.

Thompson, E. C., III. (1987). The "yagottawanna" group: Improving students self-perceptions through motivational teaching of study skills. *The School Counselor, 35*(2), 134-142.

Thompson, K. L., Bundy, K. A., & Broncheau, C. (1995). Social skills training for young adults: Symbolic and behavioral components. *Adolescence, 30,* 723-734.

Thompson, K. S. (1980). A comparison of black and white adolescents' beliefs about having children. *Journal of Marriage and the Family, 3*(35), 112-117.

Thompson, R. A. (1986). The unwed adolescent mother. In D. Capuzzi & L. B. Golden (Eds.), *Helping families help children: Family interventions with school-related problems* (pp.109-121). New York: Charles C. Thomas.

Thompson, R. A. (1989). Teenage pregnancy. In D. Capuzzi & D. R. Gross (Eds.), *Youth at risk: A resource for counselors, teachers, and parents* (pp. 195-230). Alexandria, VA: American Association for Counseling and Development.

Thompson, R. A. (1990). Post-traumatic loss debriefing: Providing immediate support for survivors of suicide or sudden loss. *Highlights: An ERIC/CAPS Digest.* Ann Arbor, MI: Counseling and Personnel Services Clearinghouse.

Thompson, R. A. (1992). *School counseling renewal: Strategies for the twenty-first century.* Muncie, IN: Accelerated Development.

Thompson, R. A. (1993). Post-traumatic stress and post-traumatic loss debriefing: Brief strategic intervention for survivors of sudden loss. *The School Counselor, 36*(1), 22-27.

Thompson, R. A. (1996). *Counseling techniques.* Bristol, PA: Taylor & Francis.

Timmerman, L., Martin, D., & Martin, M. (1990). Augmenting the helping relationship: The use of bibliotherapy. *The School Counselor,* 36, 293-297.

Tomlinson-Keasey, C., & Keasey, C. B. (1988). Signatures of suicide. In D. Capuzzi & L. Golden (Eds.), *Preventing adolescent suicide* (pp. 213-240). Muncie, IN: Accelerated Development.

Turner, S., Norman, E., & Zunz, S. (1995). Enhancing resiliency in girls and boys: A case for gender-specific adolescent prevention programming. *Journal of Primary Prevention, 16,* 25-38,

Tweed, S. H., & Ryff, C. D. (1991). Adult children of alcoholics: Profiles of wellness amidst distress. *Journal of Studies on Alcohol, 52,* 2.

U.S. Congress (1986). *Teen pregnancy: What is being done? A report of the select committee on children, youth, and families.* Washington, DC: Government Printing Office.

U.S. Department of Education (1983). High school dropouts: Descriptive information from high school and beyond. *National Center for Educational Statistics Bulletin, 22,* 1-9.

U.S. Department of Education. (1991). *America 2000: An education strategy.* Washington, DC: Author.

Verderber, K. S., & Verderber, R. E. (1986). *Interact: Using interpersonal communication skills.* Belmont, CA: Wadsworth.

Vernon, A. (1989). *Thinking, feeling, behaving: An emotional education curriculum for children.* Champaign, IL: Research Press.

Vernon, A. (1990). *Thinking, feeling, behaving: An emotional education curriculum for adolescents, grades 7-12.* Champaign, IL: Research Press.

Viadero, D. (1993). Teaching right from wrong. *Teacher Magazine, 36*(2), 12-17.

Vygotsky, L. (1978). *Society of mind.* Cambridge, MA: Harvard University Press.

Waldo, M. (1985). A curative factor framework for conceptualizing group counseling. *Journal of Counseling and Development, 64*(1), p. 58.

Walen, S. R., DiGiuseppe, R., & Wessler, R. L. (1980). *A practitioner's guide to rational emotive therapy.* New York: Oxford University Press.

Wallack, L., & Corbett, K. (1990). *Illicit drug, tobacco, and alcohol use among youth: Trends and promising approaches in prevention.* Office of Substance Abuse Prevention: Monograph 6. Washington, DC: U.S. Department of Health, Human Services, and Public Health Service.

Waller, R. (1992). Cocaine-affected children. *Educational Leadership, 43*(2), 4-8.

Wassmer, A. (1978). *Making contact. A guide to overcoming shyness, making new relationships and keeping those you have.* New York: Dial Press.

Weed, R. O., & Hernandez, A. M. (1990). Multimodal rehabilitation counseling. *Journal of Applied Rehabilitation Counseling, 1*(4), 27-30.

Weeks, G. R., & L'Abate, L. (1982). *Paradoxical psychotherapy: Theory and practice with individuals, couples, and families.* New York: Brunner/Mazel.

Weikel, W. J. (1989). A multimodal approach in dealing with chronic Epstein-Barr viral syndrome. *Journal of Counseling and Development, 67,* 522-524.

Weikel, W. J. (1990). A multimodal approach in dealing with older clients. *Journal of Mental Health Counseling, 12,* 314-320.

Weinstein, C. E., & Mayer, R. F. (1986). The teaching of learning strategies. In M. Wittrock (Ed.), *Handbook of research on teaching* (pp. 120-142). Alexandria, VA: ASCD.

Werner, E. E. (1982). Resilient children. *Young Children, 40,* 68-72.

Werner, E. E. (1986). The concept of risk from a developmental perspective. *Advances in Special Education, 5,* 1-23.

Werner, E. E. (1992). *Vulnerable but invincible: A longitudinal study of resilient children and youth.* New York: McGraw-Hill.

Werner, E. E., Bierman, J. M., & French, F. E. (1971). *The children of Kauai: A longitudinal study from the prenatal period to age ten.* Honolulu: University of Hawaii Press.

Werner, E. E., & Smith, R. S. (1977). *Kauai's children come of age.* Honolulu: University of Hawaii Press.

Werner, E. E., & Smith, R. S. (1982). *Vulnerable but invincible: A longitudinal study of resilient children and youth.* New York: McGraw-Hill.

Werner, E. E., & Smith, R. S. (1992). *Overcoming the odds: High-risk children from birth to adulthood.* Ithaca, NY: Cornell University Press.

White, C., & White, M. (1991). The Adolescent Family Life Act: Content, findings, and policy recommendations for pregnancy prevention programs. *Journal of Clinical Child Psychology, 20*(1), 58-70.

Whitfield, C. L. (1987). *Healing the child within. A discovery and recovery for adults of dysfunctional families.* Dearfield, Beach, FL: Health Communications.

Wilkinson, G. S., & Bleck, R. T. (1977). Children's divorce groups. *Elementary School Guidance and Counseling, 11,* 205-213.

Wilson, J., & Blocher, L. (1990). Personality characteristics of adult children of alcoholics. *Journal of Humanistic Education and Development, 26,* 166-175.

Winbush, R. A. (1988). Growing pains: Explaining adolescent violence with developmental theory. In R. Hayes & R. Aubrey (Eds.), *Counseling and human development.* Denver, Co: Love Publishing.

Woody, R. H., Hansen, J. C., & Rossberg, R. H. (1989). *Counseling psychology strategies and services.* Pacific Grove, CA: Brooks/Cole.

Worchel, F., Nolan, B., & Wilson, V. (1987). New perspectives on child and adolescent depression. *Journal of School Psychology, 25,* 411-414.

Worrell, J., & Stilwell, W. E. (1981). *Psychology for teachers and students.* New York: McGraw-Hill.

Wright, E. E. (1989). *Good morning class—I love you!* Rolling Hill Estates, CA: Jalmar Press.

Yalom, I. (1975). *The theory and practice of group psychotherapy.* New York: Basic Books.

Yalom, I. (1985). *The theory and practice of group psychotherapy.* New York: Wiley.

Yazigi, R. A., Odem, R. R., & Polakoski, K. L. (1991). Demonstration of specific binding of cocaine to human spermatozoa. *Journal of the American Medical Association, 266*(15), 1956-1959.

Ziegler, S. (1987). *The effects of parent involvement on children's achievement: The significance of home/school links.* Ontario: Toronto Board of Education, ED 304-234.

Zieman, G. L., & Benson, G. P. (1980). School perceptions of truant adolescent boys. *Behavior Disorders, Programs, Trends, and Concerns of Children with Behavioral Problems, 5*(4), 212-222.

Zimbardo, P. G. (1977). *Shyness: What it is and what to do about it.* Menlo Park, CA: Addison Wesley.

Zimstrad, S. W. (1989). Brief systemic therapy for families of the close head injured: Therapy with two hands. *Cognitive Rehabilitation, 7*(3), 26-28.

Zitzow, D. (1992). Assessing student stress: School adjustment rating by self-report. *The School Counselor, 40*(1), 20-23.

INDEX

ABOUT THE AUTHOR

Rosemary A. Thompson, Ed.D., N.C.C., L.P.C., is administrator for Gifted and Talented Education for Chesapeake Public Schools, Chesapeake, Virginia, and Adjunct Professor, Department of Educational Leadership and Counseling, Old Dominion University, Norfolk, Virginia. During her 25 years in the public school sector, she has been a teacher, school counselor, guidance director, and school administrator. She has published widely in national counseling and educational journals on issues critical to counselors, educators, and practitioners.

Dr. Thompson is a National Board Certified Counselor and a Licensed Professional Counselor and maintains a private practice in educational consultation. She currently resides in Virginia Beach, Virginia, with her husband, Charles, and their children, Ryan and Jessica.